MARVEL'S THE AVENGERS: BLACK WIDOW STRIKES. Contains material originally published in magazine form as MARVEL'S THE AVENGERS: BLACK WIDOW STRIKES #1-3. First printing 2012. ISBN# 978-0-7851-6568-2. Published by MARVEL WORLDWIDE, INC., a subsidiary of MARVEL ENTERTAINMENT, LLC. OFFICE OF PUBLICATION: 135 West 50th Street, New York, NY 10020. Copyright © 2012 Marvel Characters, Inc. All rights reserved. $12.99 per copy in the U.S. and $13.99 in Canada (GST #R127032852); Canadian Agreement #40668537. All characters featured in this issue and the distinctive names and likenesses thereof, and all related indicia are trademarks of Marvel Characters, Inc. No similarity between any of the names, characters, persons, and/or institutions in this magazine with those of any living or dead person or institution is intended, and any such similarity which may exist is purely coincidental. **Printed in the U.S.A.** ALAN FINE, EVP - Office of the President, Marvel Worldwide, Inc. and EVP & CMO Marvel Characters B.V.; DAN BUCKLEY, Publisher & President - Print, Animation & Digital Divisions; JOE QUESADA, Chief Creative Officer; TOM BREVOORT, SVP of Publishing; DAVID BOGART, SVP of Operations & Procurement, Publishing; RUWAN JAYATILLEKE, SVP & Associate Publisher, Publishing; C.B. CEBULSKI, SVP of Creator & Content Development; DAVID GABRIEL, SVP of Publishing Sales & Circulation; MICHAEL PASCIULLO, SVP of Brand Planning & Communications; JIM O'KEEFE, VP of Operations & Logistics; DAN CARR, Executive Director of Publishing Technology; SUSAN CRESPI, Editorial Operations Manager; ALEX MORALES, Publishing Operations Manager; STAN LEE, Chairman Emeritus. For information regarding advertising in Marvel Comics or on Marvel.com, please contact Niza Disla, Director of Marvel Partnerships, at ndisla@marvel.com. For Marvel subscription inquiries, please call 800-217-9158. **Manufactured between 7/12/2012 and 8/14/2012 by QUAD/GRAPHICS, DUBUQUE, IA, USA.**

10 9 8 7 6 5 4 3 2 1

WRITER FRED VAN LENTE CHAPTER ONE PENCILER NEIL EDWARDS CHAPTER ONE INKER RICK MAGYAR CHAPTER ONE COLORIST NICK FILARDI

CHAPTER TWO PENCILER STEVE KURTH CHAPTER TWO INKER ANDREW HENNESSY CHAPTER TWO COLORIST FELIX SERRANO CHAPTER THREE PENCILER RON LIM

CHAPTER THREE COLORIST CHRIS SOTOMAYOR CHAPTER FOUR PENCILER AGUSTIN PADILLA CHAPTER FOUR INKER JAIME MENDOZA CHAPTER FOUR COLORIST VERONICA GANDINI

CHAPTER FIVE PENCILER WELLINTON ALVES CHAPTER FIVE INKER NELSON PEREIRA CHAPTER FIVE COLORIST BRUNO HANG

CHAPTER SIX ARTIST RENATO ARLEM CHAPTER SIX COLORIST JAY DAVID RAMOS LETTERER VC'S CLAYTON COWLES COVER ART, #2 ADI GRANOV

EDITOR BILL ROSEMANN ASSISTANT EDITOR JON MOISAN

BLACK WIDOW STRIKES

Natasha Romanoff, a.k.a. the Black Widow, is one of S.H.I.E.L.D.'s most experienced, effective and skilled secret agents. With the help of her fellow agent, Phil Coulson, Natasha does the work behind the scenes that the rest of the world will never know about. Her new mission to recover missing bootleg Starktech seems simple enough, but danger lurks everywhere when you are the Black Widow…

Note: This story takes place between the events of *Iron Man 2* and *Marvel's The Avengers*.

MARVEL STUDIOS

CREATIVE MANAGER WILL CORONA PILGRIM DIRECTOR OF DEVELOPMENT BRAD WINDERBAUM CREATIVE EXECUTIVE JONATHAN SCHWARTZ

SVP PRODUCTION & DEVELOPMENT JEREMY LATCHAM PRESIDENT KEVIN FEIGE

COLLECTION EDITOR JENNIFER GRÜNWALD ASSISTANT EDITORS ALEX STARBUCK & NELSON RIBEIRO EDITOR, SPECIAL PROJECTS MARK D. BEAZLEY SENIOR EDITOR, SPECIAL PROJECTS JEFF YOUNGQUIST

SENIOR VICE PRESIDENT OF SALES DAVID GABRIEL SVP OF BRAND PLANNING & COMMUNICATIONS MICHAEL PASCIULLO EDITOR IN CHIEF AXEL ALONSO CHIEF CREATIVE OFFICER JOE QUESADA PUBLISHER DAN BUCKLEY EXECUTIVE PRODUCER ALAN FINE

ONE

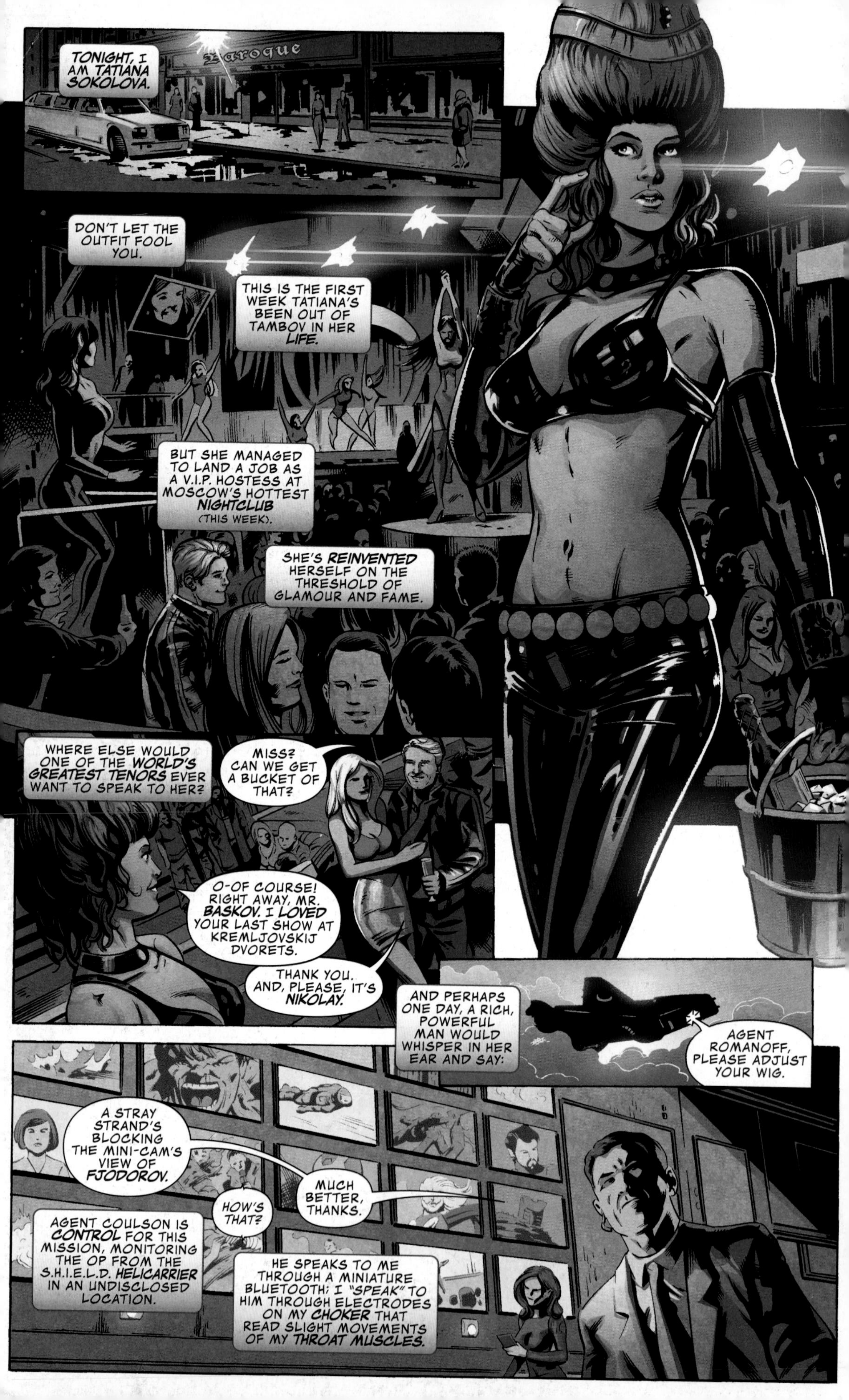
Baroque
TONIGHT, I AM TATIANA SOKOLOVA.
DON'T LET THE OUTFIT FOOL YOU.
THIS IS THE FIRST WEEK TATIANA'S BEEN OUT OF TAMBOV IN HER LIFE.
BUT SHE MANAGED TO LAND A JOB AS A V.I.P. HOSTESS AT MOSCOW'S HOTTEST NIGHTCLUB (THIS WEEK).
SHE'S REINVENTED HERSELF ON THE THRESHOLD OF GLAMOUR AND FAME.
WHERE ELSE WOULD ONE OF THE WORLD'S GREATEST TENORS EVER WANT TO SPEAK TO HER?
MISS? CAN WE GET A BUCKET OF THAT?
O-OF COURSE! RIGHT AWAY, MR. BASKOV. I LOVED YOUR LAST SHOW AT KREMLJOVSKIJ DVORETS.
THANK YOU. AND, PLEASE, IT'S NIKOLAY.
AND PERHAPS ONE DAY, A RICH, POWERFUL MAN WOULD WHISPER IN HER EAR AND SAY:
AGENT ROMANOFF, PLEASE ADJUST YOUR WIG.
A STRAY STRAND'S BLOCKING THE MINI-CAM'S VIEW OF FJODOROV.
HOW'S THAT?
MUCH BETTER, THANKS.
AGENT COULSON IS CONTROL FOR THIS MISSION, MONITORING THE OP FROM THE S.H.I.E.L.D. HELICARRIER IN AN UNDISCLOSED LOCATION.
HE SPEAKS TO ME THROUGH A MINIATURE BLUETOOTH; I "SPEAK" TO HIM THROUGH ELECTRODES ON MY CHOKER THAT READ SLIGHT MOVEMENTS OF MY THROAT MUSCLES.

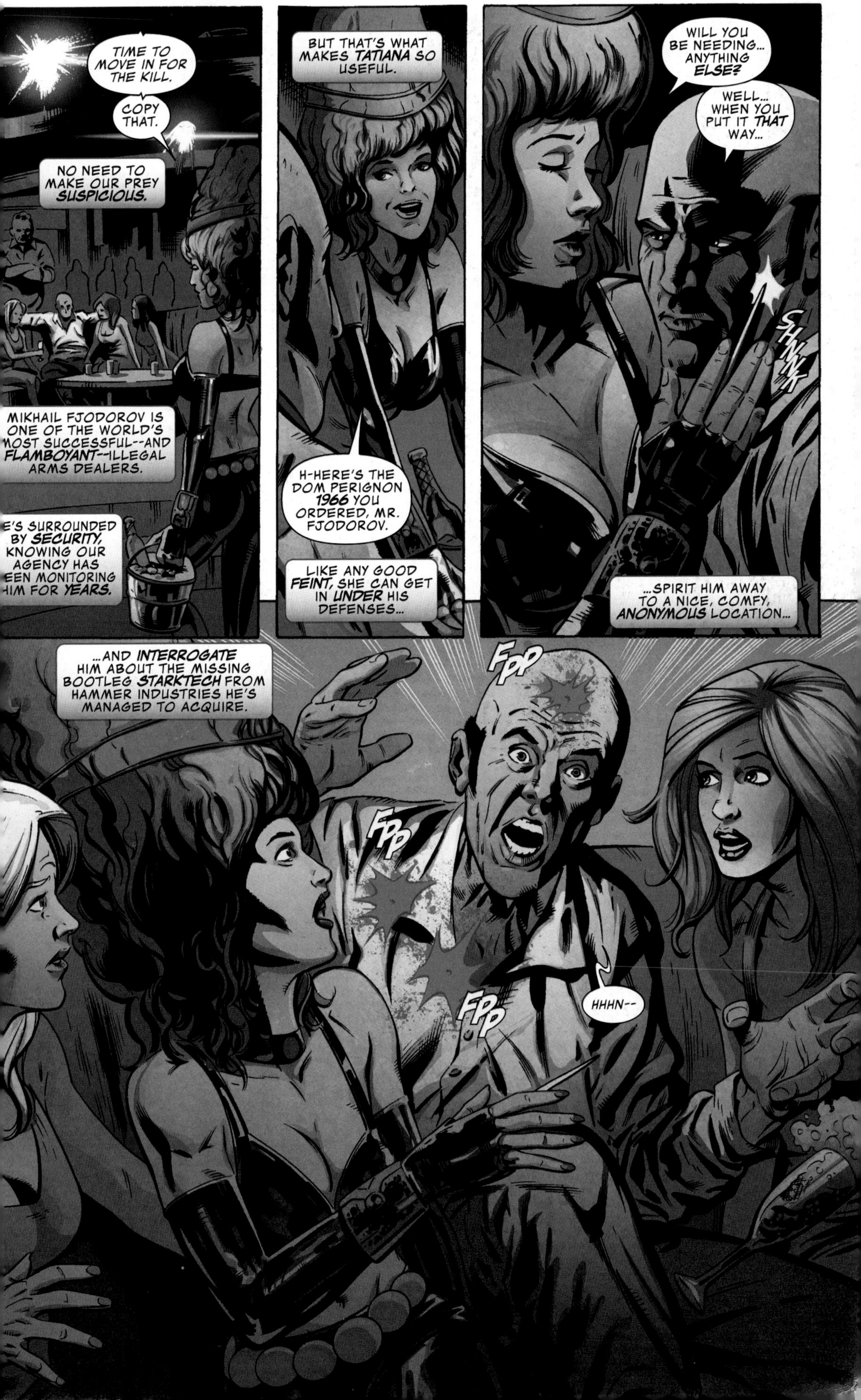
TIME TO MOVE IN FOR THE KILL.
COPY THAT.
NO NEED TO MAKE OUR PREY SUSPICIOUS.
MIKHAIL FJODOROV IS ONE OF THE WORLD'S MOST SUCCESSFUL--AND FLAMBOYANT--ILLEGAL ARMS DEALERS.
E'S SURROUNDED BY SECURITY, KNOWING OUR AGENCY HAS EEN MONITORING HIM FOR YEARS.
BUT THAT'S WHAT MAKES TATIANA SO USEFUL.
H-HERE'S THE DOM PERIGNON 1966 YOU ORDERED, MR. FJODOROV.
LIKE ANY GOOD FEINT, SHE CAN GET IN UNDER HIS DEFENSES...
WILL YOU BE NEEDING... ANYTHING ELSE?
WELL... WHEN YOU PUT IT THAT WAY...
SHNNK
...SPIRIT HIM AWAY TO A NICE, COMFY, ANONYMOUS LOCATION...
...AND INTERROGATE HIM ABOUT THE MISSING BOOTLEG STARKTECH FROM HAMMER INDUSTRIES HE'S MANAGED TO ACQUIRE.
FPP
FPP
FPP
HHHN--

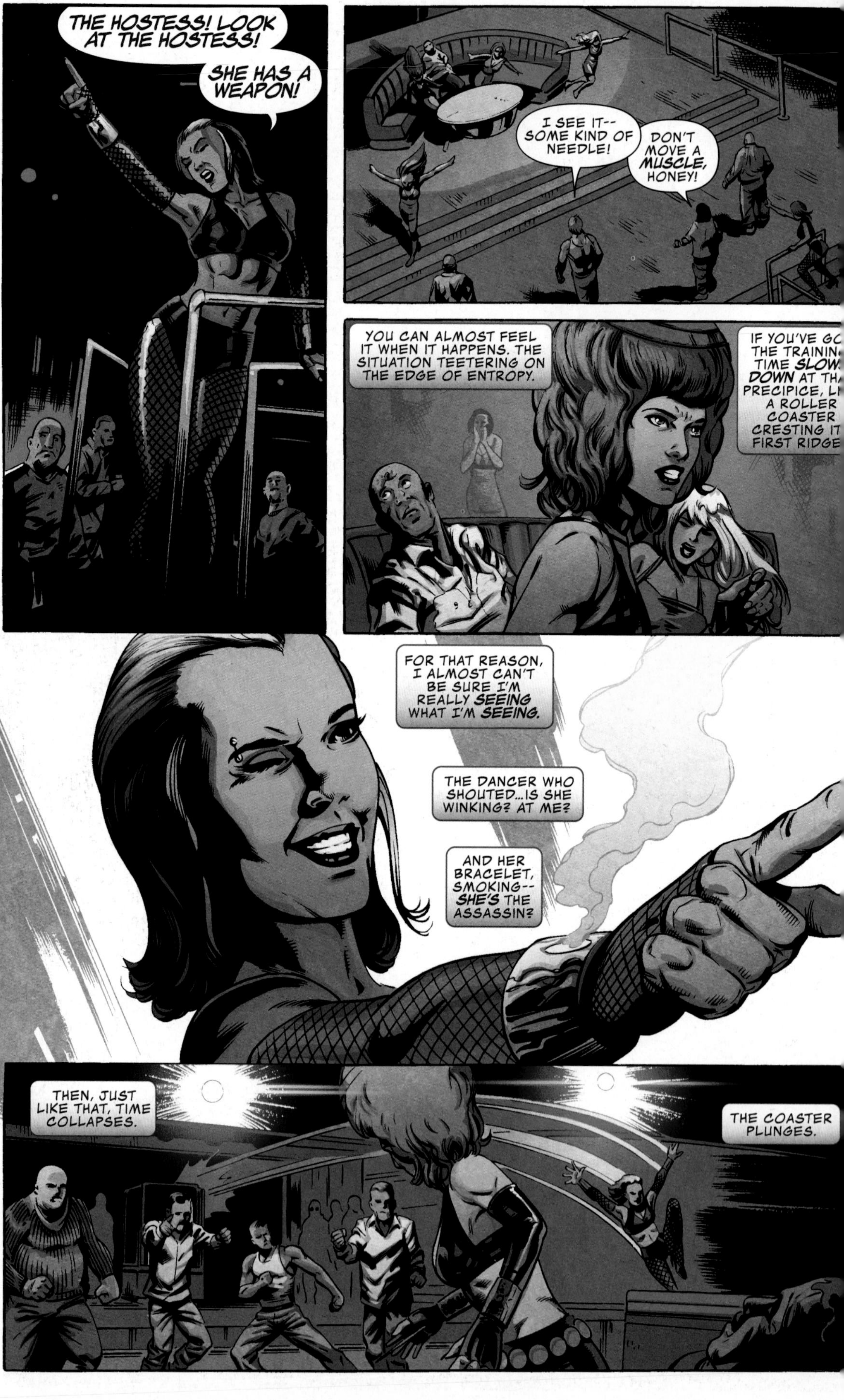
THE HOSTESS! LOOK AT THE HOSTESS!
SHE HAS A WEAPON!
I SEE IT-- SOME KIND OF NEEDLE!
DON'T MOVE A MUSCLE, HONEY!
YOU CAN ALMOST FEEL IT WHEN IT HAPPENS. THE SITUATION TEETERING ON THE EDGE OF ENTROPY.
IF YOU'VE GO THE TRAININ TIME SLOW DOWN AT TH PRECIPICE, LI A ROLLER COASTER CRESTING IT FIRST RIDGE
FOR THAT REASON, I ALMOST CAN'T BE SURE I'M REALLY SEEING WHAT I'M SEEING.
THE DANCER WHO SHOUTED...IS SHE WINKING? AT ME?
AND HER BRACELET, SMOKING-- SHE'S THE ASSASSIN?
THEN, JUST LIKE THAT, TIME COLLAPSES.
THE COASTER PLUNGES.

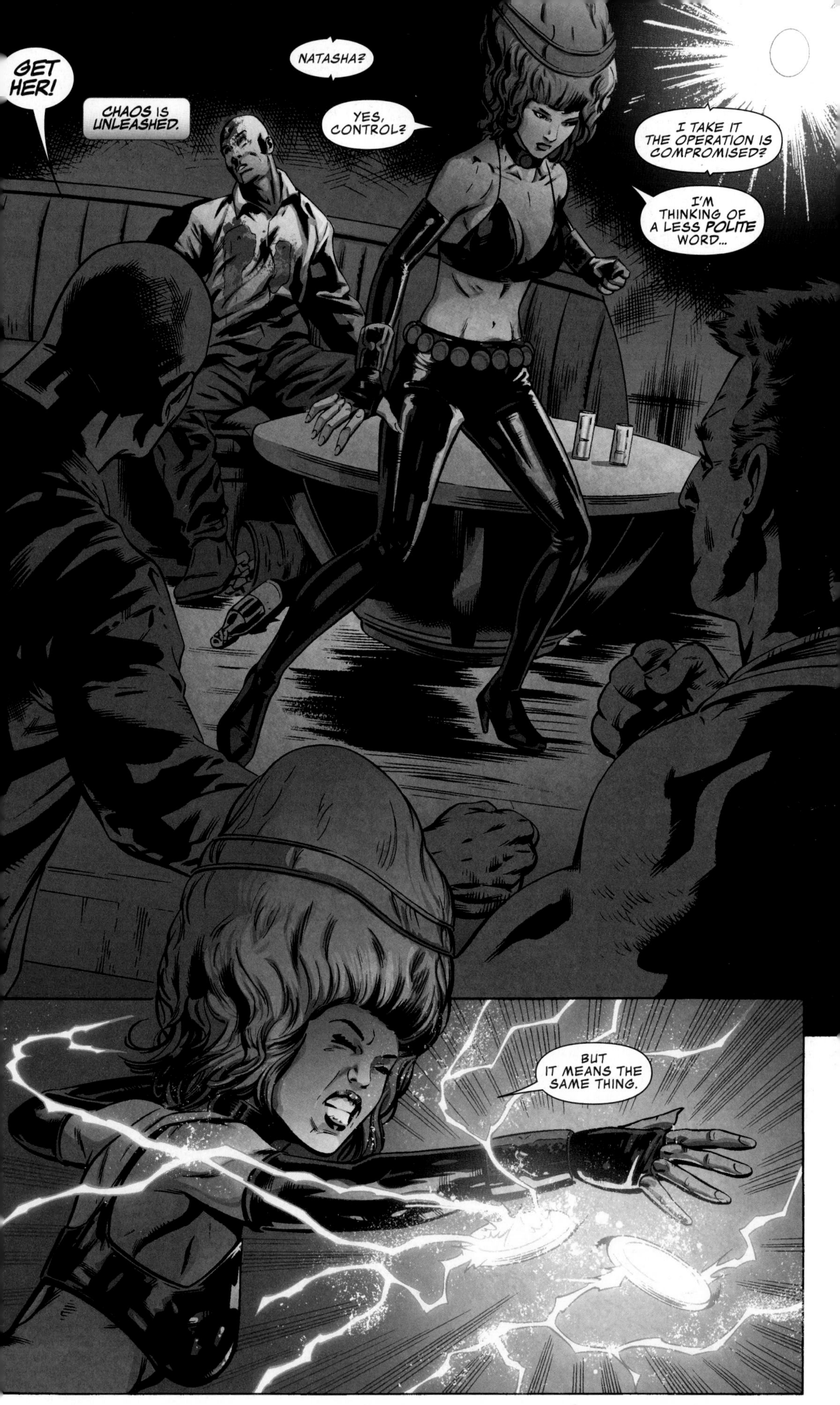
GET HER!
CHAOS IS UNLEASHED.
NATASHA?
YES, CONTROL?
I TAKE IT THE OPERATION IS COMPROMISED?
I'M THINKING OF A LESS POLITE WORD...
BUT IT MEANS THE SAME THING.

AAAGGHHHH!

TALK TO ME, COULSON.

SSKKRRZZZZTKK

I NEED AN *EXIT STRATEGY.*

NGGH!

AVOID THE FRONT. MOSCOW PD DISPATCH HAS IT LIT UP.

OFFICERS ARE ALREADY CORDONING OFF THE ENTIRE BLOCK--SIDE EXITS, TOO.

BEST HEAD TO THE ROOF.

ONE OF OUR STRINGERS LEFT A *SUPPLY DROP* FOR YOU UP THERE IN CASE OF AN EMERGENCY.

I'D SAY THIS QUALIFIES.

THER... SHE I... *STOP...*

PREPARE TO LOSE VISUAL, CONTROL.

WHY? WHAT'S WRONG WITH THE WIG?

NOTHING.

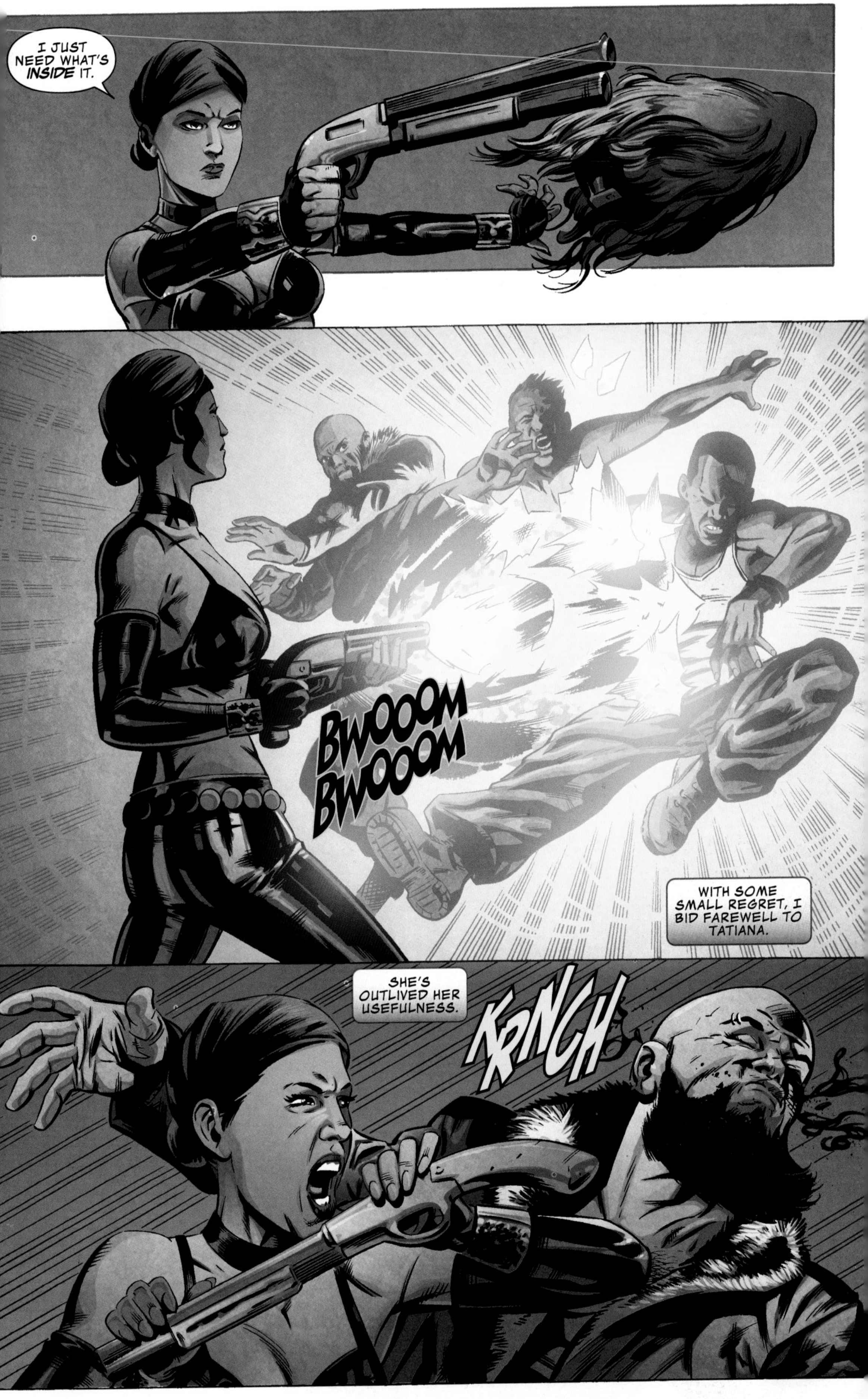
I JUST NEED WHAT'S *INSIDE* IT.
BWOOOM BWOOOM
WITH SOME SMALL REGRET, I BID FAREWELL TO TATIANA.
SHE'S OUTLIVED HER USEFULNESS.
KRNCH

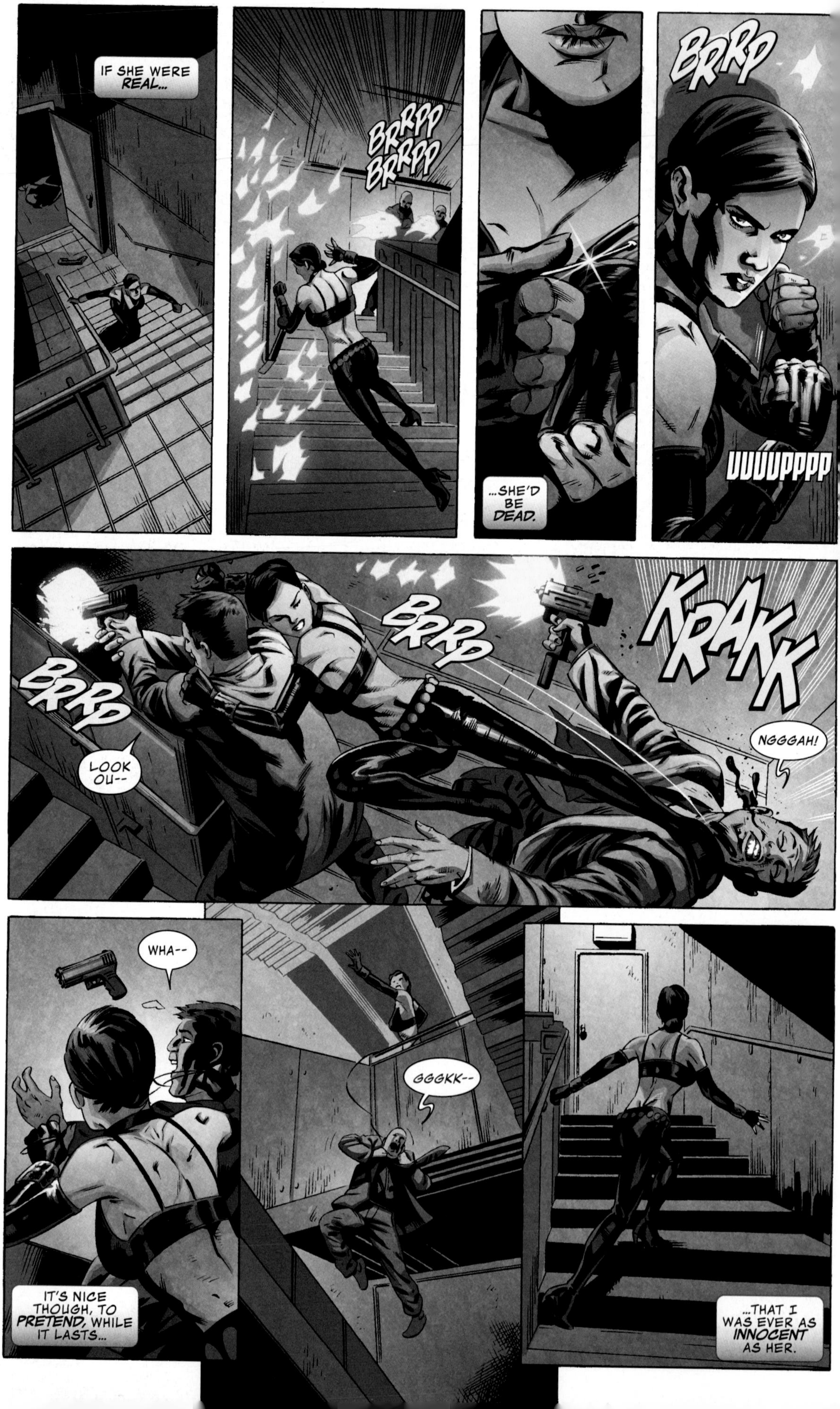
IF SHE WERE REAL...
BRRPP BRRPP
...SHE'D BE DEAD.
BRRP
UUUUPPPP
BRRP
LOOK OU--
BRRP
KRAKK
NGGGAH!
WHA--
GGGKK--
IT'S NICE THOUGH, TO PRETEND, WHILE IT LASTS...
...THAT I WAS EVER AS INNOCENT AS HER.

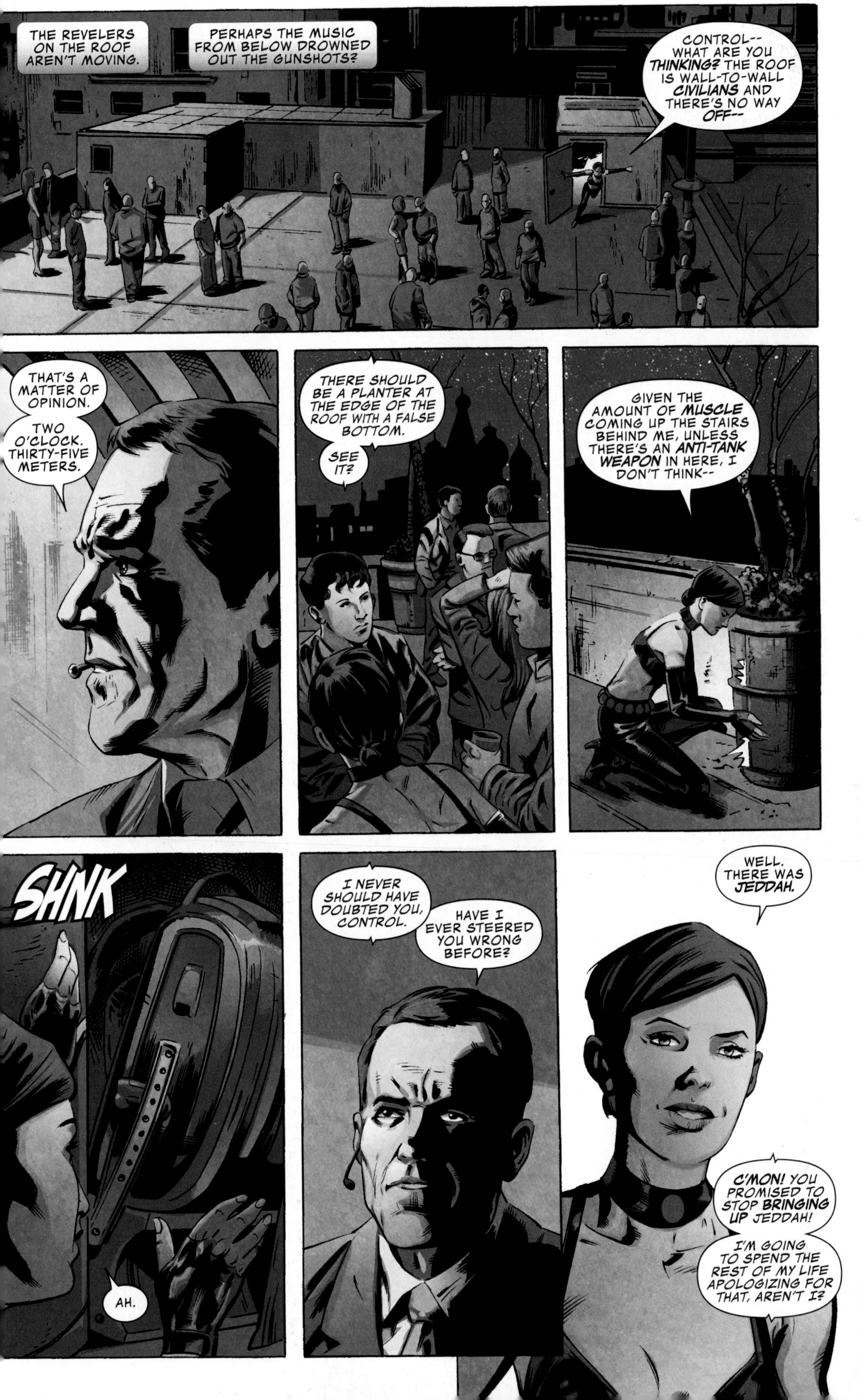
THE REVELERS ON THE ROOF AREN'T MOVING.
PERHAPS THE MUSIC FROM BELOW DROWNED OUT THE GUNSHOTS?
CONTROL-- WHAT ARE YOU THINKING? THE ROOF IS WALL-TO-WALL CIVILIANS AND THERE'S NO WAY OFF--
THAT'S A MATTER OF OPINION.
TWO O'CLOCK. THIRTY-FIVE METERS.
THERE SHOULD BE A PLANTER AT THE EDGE OF THE ROOF WITH A FALSE BOTTOM.
SEE IT?
GIVEN THE AMOUNT OF MUSCLE COMING UP THE STAIRS BEHIND ME, UNLESS THERE'S AN ANTI-TANK WEAPON IN HERE, I DON'T THINK--
SHNK
AH.
I NEVER SHOULD HAVE DOUBTED YOU, CONTROL.
HAVE I EVER STEERED YOU WRONG BEFORE?
WELL. THERE WAS JEDDAH.
C'MON! YOU PROMISED TO STOP BRINGING UP JEDDAH!
I'M GOING TO SPEND THE REST OF MY LIFE APOLOGIZING FOR THAT, AREN'T I?

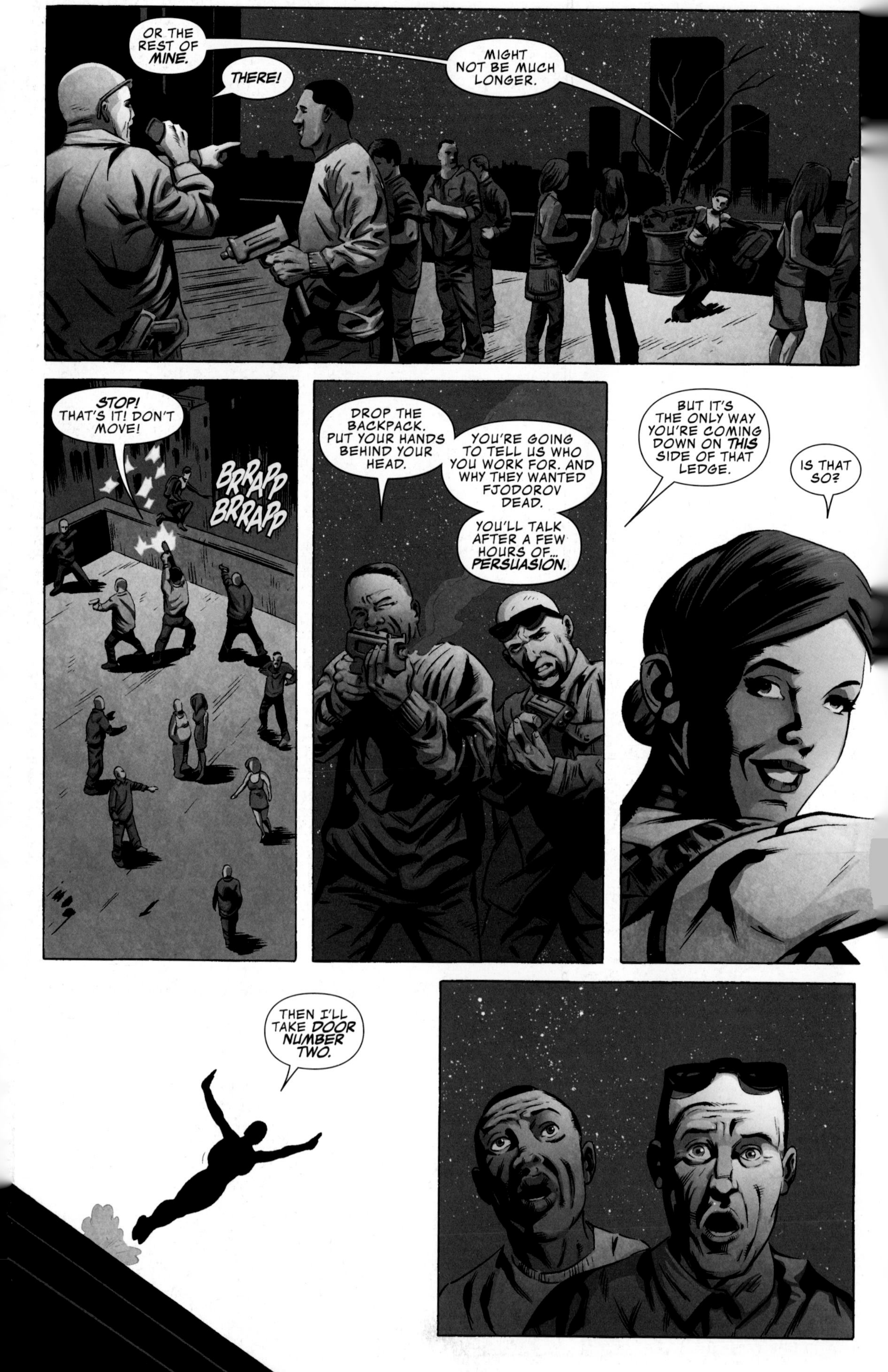

OR THE REST OF MINE.
MIGHT NOT BE MUCH LONGER.
THERE!
STOP! THAT'S IT! DON'T MOVE!
BRRAPP BRRAPP
DROP THE BACKPACK. PUT YOUR HANDS BEHIND YOUR HEAD.
YOU'RE GOING TO TELL US WHO YOU WORK FOR. AND WHY THEY WANTED FJODOROV DEAD.
YOU'LL TALK AFTER A FEW HOURS OF... PERSUASION.
BUT IT'S THE ONLY WAY YOU'RE COMING DOWN ON THIS SIDE OF THAT LEDGE.
IS THAT SO?
THEN I'LL TAKE DOOR NUMBER TWO.

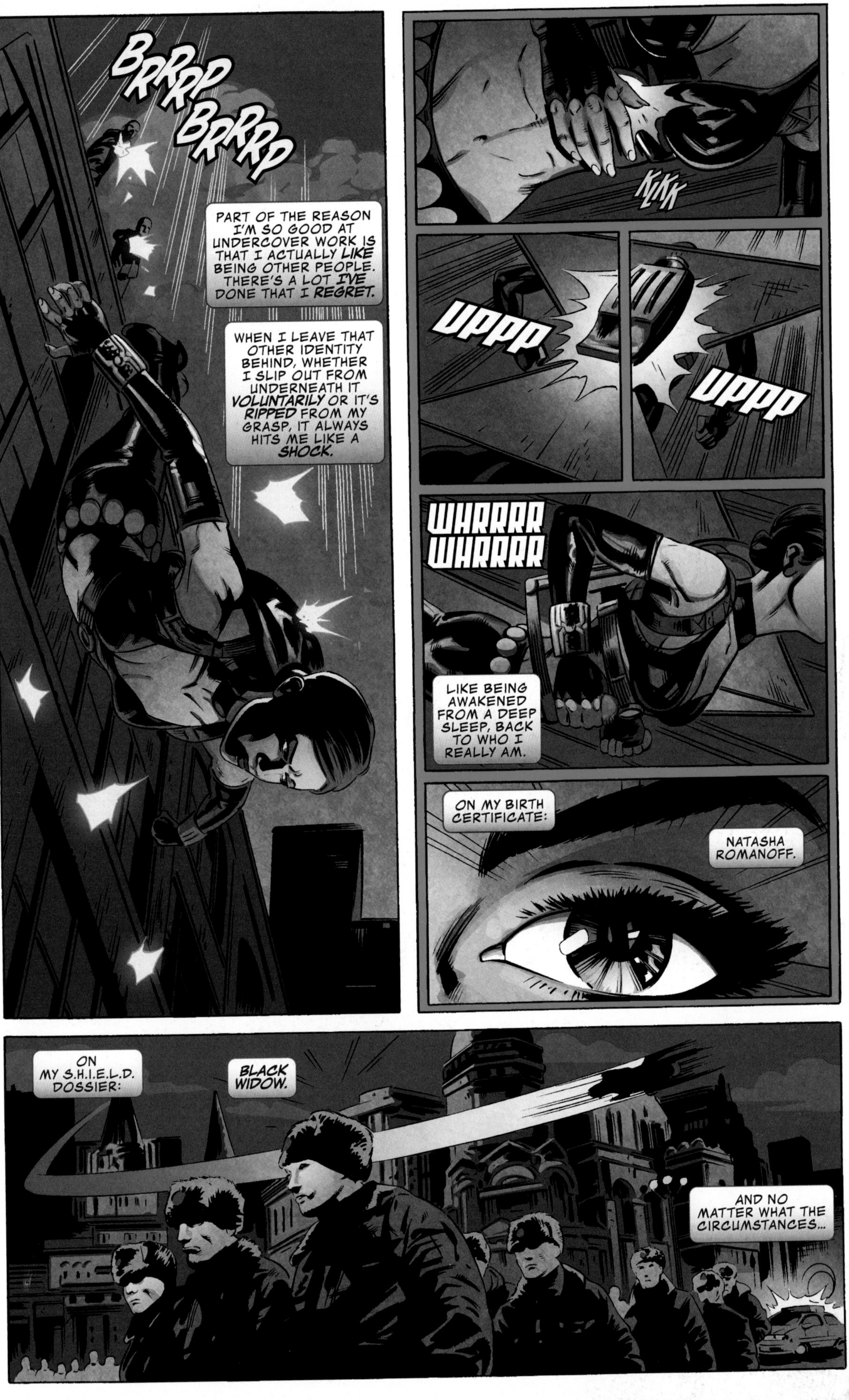
BRRRP BRRRP
PART OF THE REASON I'M SO GOOD AT UNDERCOVER WORK IS THAT I ACTUALLY LIKE BEING OTHER PEOPLE. THERE'S A LOT I'VE DONE THAT I REGRET.
WHEN I LEAVE THAT OTHER IDENTITY BEHIND, WHETHER I SLIP OUT FROM UNDERNEATH IT VOLUNTARILY OR IT'S RIPPED FROM MY GRASP, IT ALWAYS HITS ME LIKE A SHOCK.
KLIKK
UPPP
UPPP
WHRRRR WHRRRR
LIKE BEING AWAKENED FROM A DEEP SLEEP, BACK TO WHO I REALLY AM.
ON MY BIRTH CERTIFICATE:
NATASHA ROMANOFF.
ON MY S.H.I.E.L.D. DOSSIER:
BLACK WIDOW.
AND NO MATTER WHAT THE CIRCUMSTANCES...

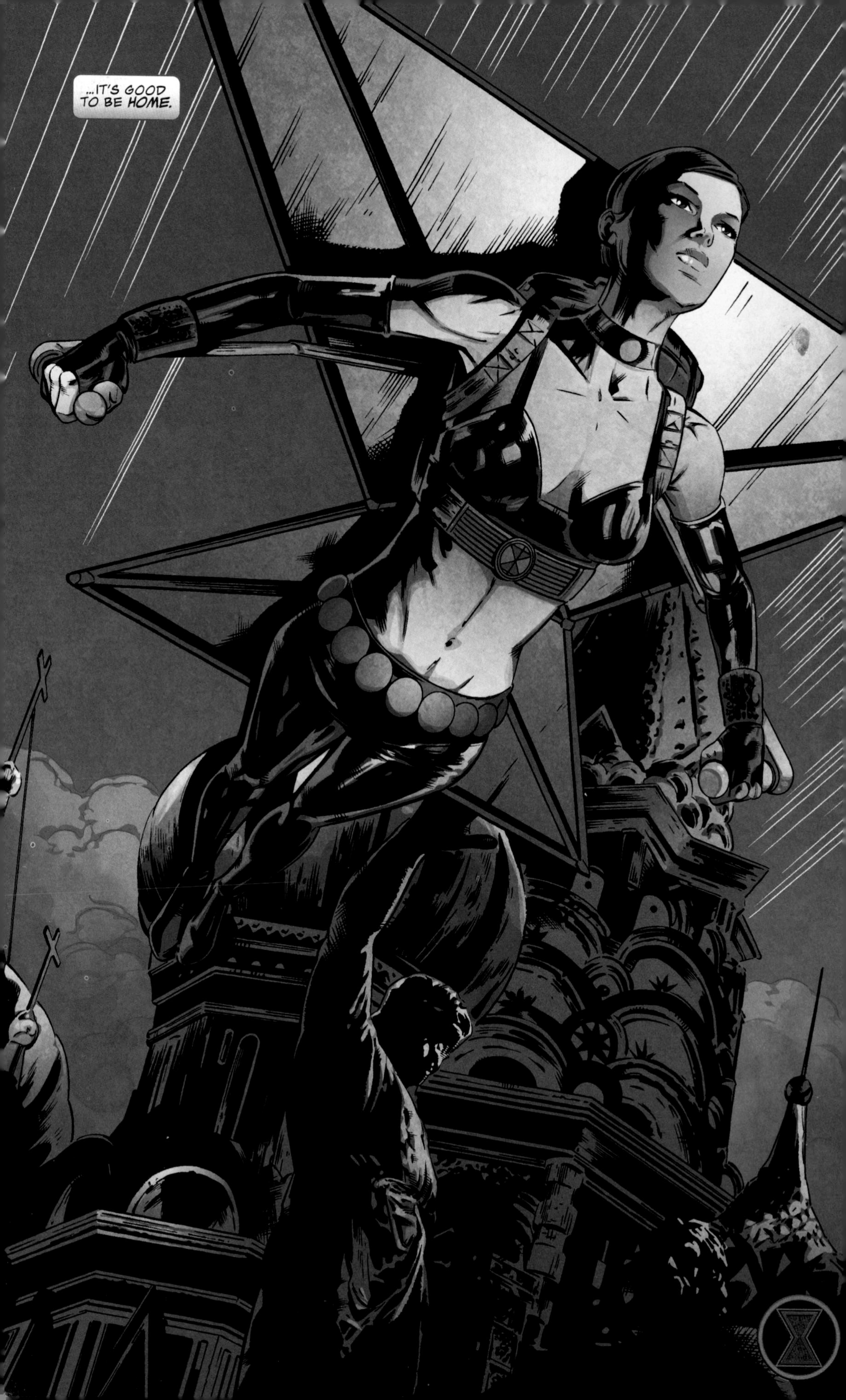
...IT'S GOOD TO BE HOME.

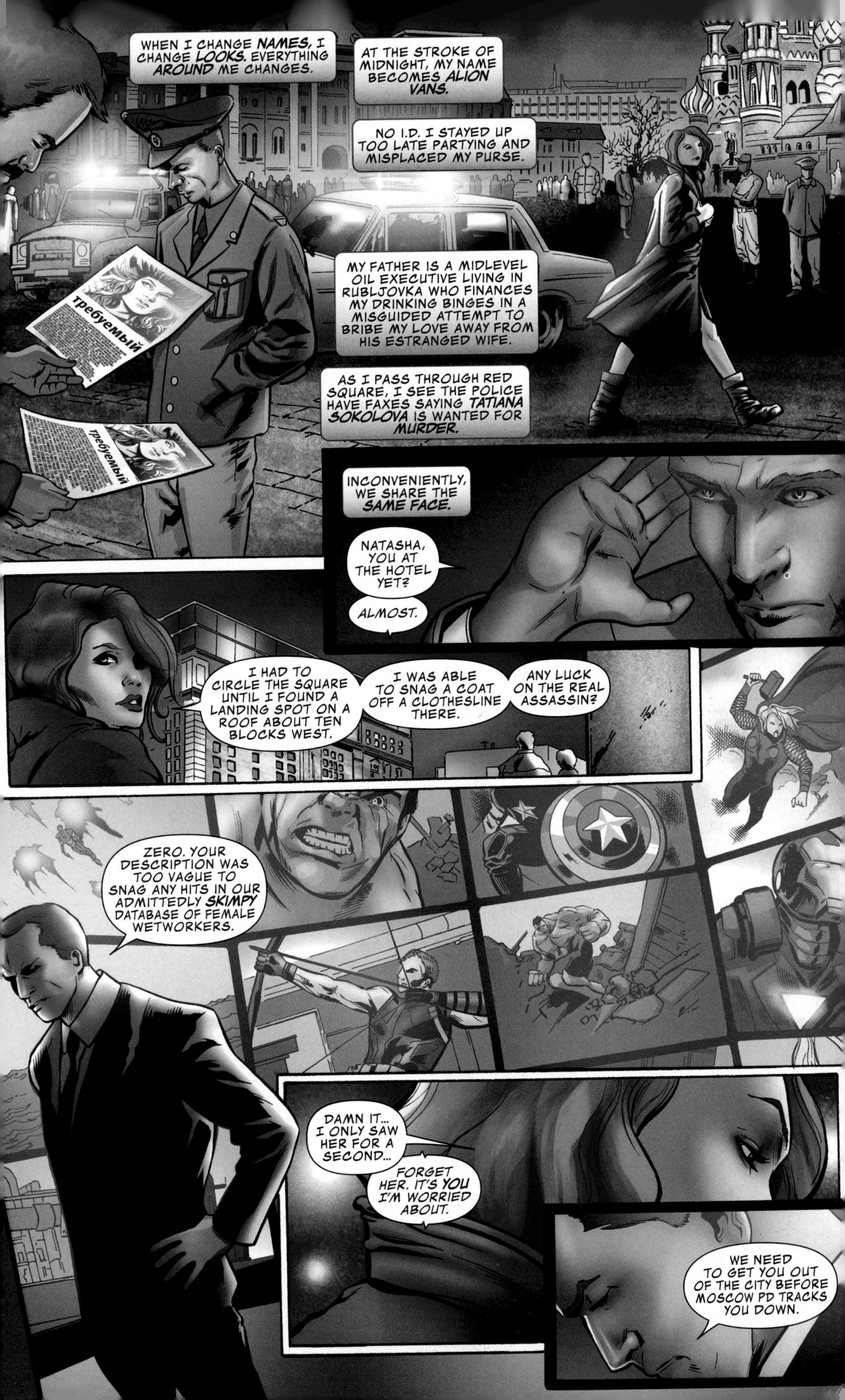

WHEN I CHANGE NAMES, I CHANGE LOOKS. EVERYTHING AROUND ME CHANGES.
AT THE STROKE OF MIDNIGHT, MY NAME BECOMES ALION VANS.
NO I.D. I STAYED UP TOO LATE PARTYING AND MISPLACED MY PURSE.
MY FATHER IS A MIDLEVEL OIL EXECUTIVE LIVING IN RUBLJOVKA WHO FINANCES MY DRINKING BINGES IN A MISGUIDED ATTEMPT TO BRIBE MY LOVE AWAY FROM HIS ESTRANGED WIFE.
AS I PASS THROUGH RED SQUARE, I SEE THE POLICE HAVE FAXES SAYING TATIANA SOKOLOVA IS WANTED FOR MURDER.
требуемый
требуемый
INCONVENIENTLY, WE SHARE THE SAME FACE.
NATASHA, YOU AT THE HOTEL YET?
ALMOST.
I HAD TO CIRCLE THE SQUARE UNTIL I FOUND A LANDING SPOT ON A ROOF ABOUT TEN BLOCKS WEST.
I WAS ABLE TO SNAG A COAT OFF A CLOTHESLINE THERE.
ANY LUCK ON THE REAL ASSASSIN?
ZERO. YOUR DESCRIPTION WAS TOO VAGUE TO SNAG ANY HITS IN OUR ADMITTEDLY SKIMPY DATABASE OF FEMALE WETWORKERS.
DAMN IT... I ONLY SAW HER FOR A SECOND...
FORGET HER. IT'S YOU I'M WORRIED ABOUT.
WE NEED TO GET YOU OUT OF THE CITY BEFORE MOSCOW PD TRACKS YOU DOWN.

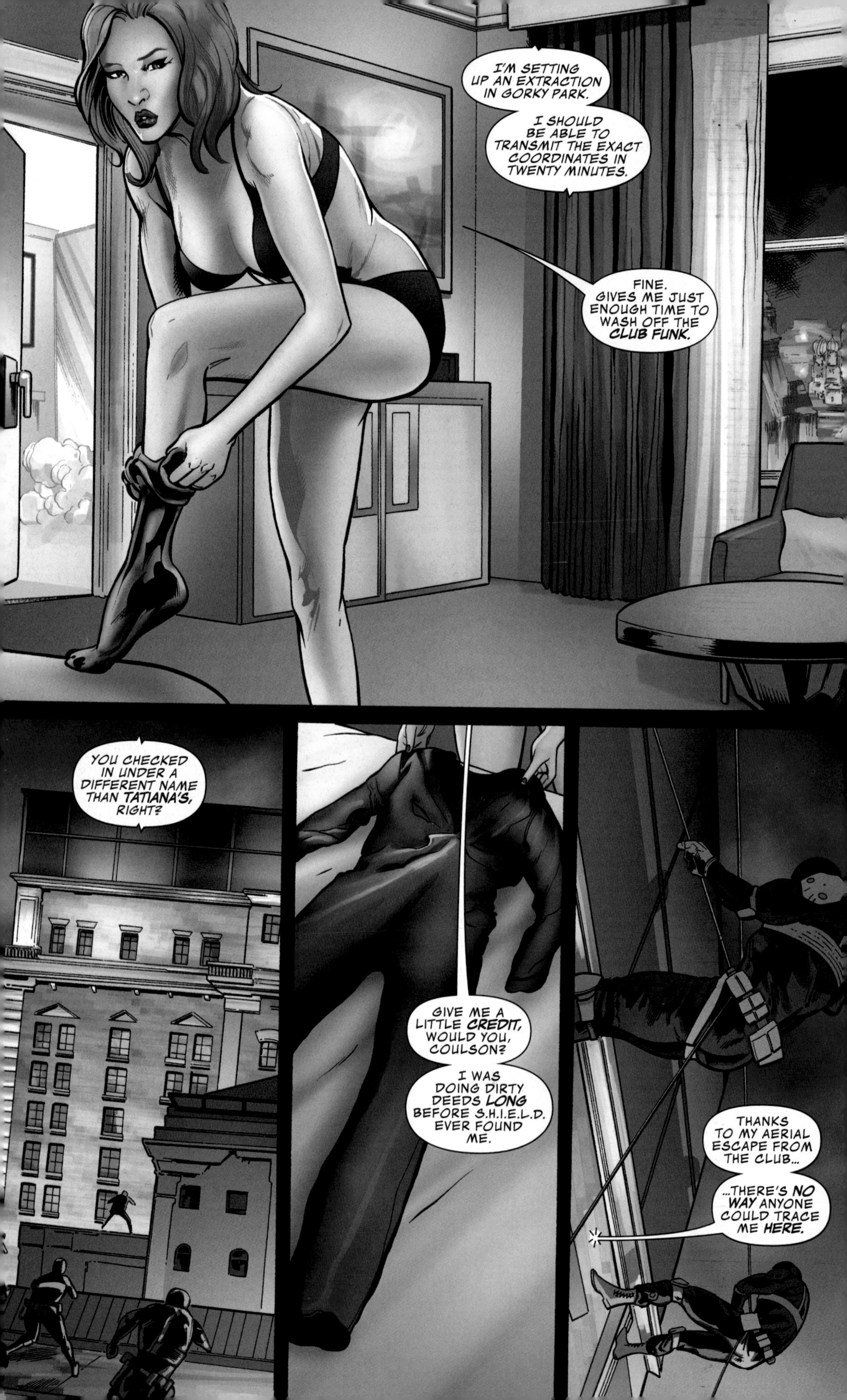

I'M SETTING UP AN EXTRACTION IN GORKY PARK.
I SHOULD BE ABLE TO TRANSMIT THE EXACT COORDINATES IN TWENTY MINUTES.
FINE. GIVES ME JUST ENOUGH TIME TO WASH OFF THE **CLUB FUNK.**
YOU CHECKED IN UNDER A DIFFERENT NAME THAN **TATIANA'S,** RIGHT?
GIVE ME A LITTLE **CREDIT,** WOULD YOU, COULSON?
I WAS DOING DIRTY DEEDS **LONG** BEFORE S.H.I.E.L.D. EVER FOUND ME.
THANKS TO MY AERIAL ESCAPE FROM THE CLUB...
...THERE'S **NO WAY** ANYONE COULD TRACE ME **HERE.**

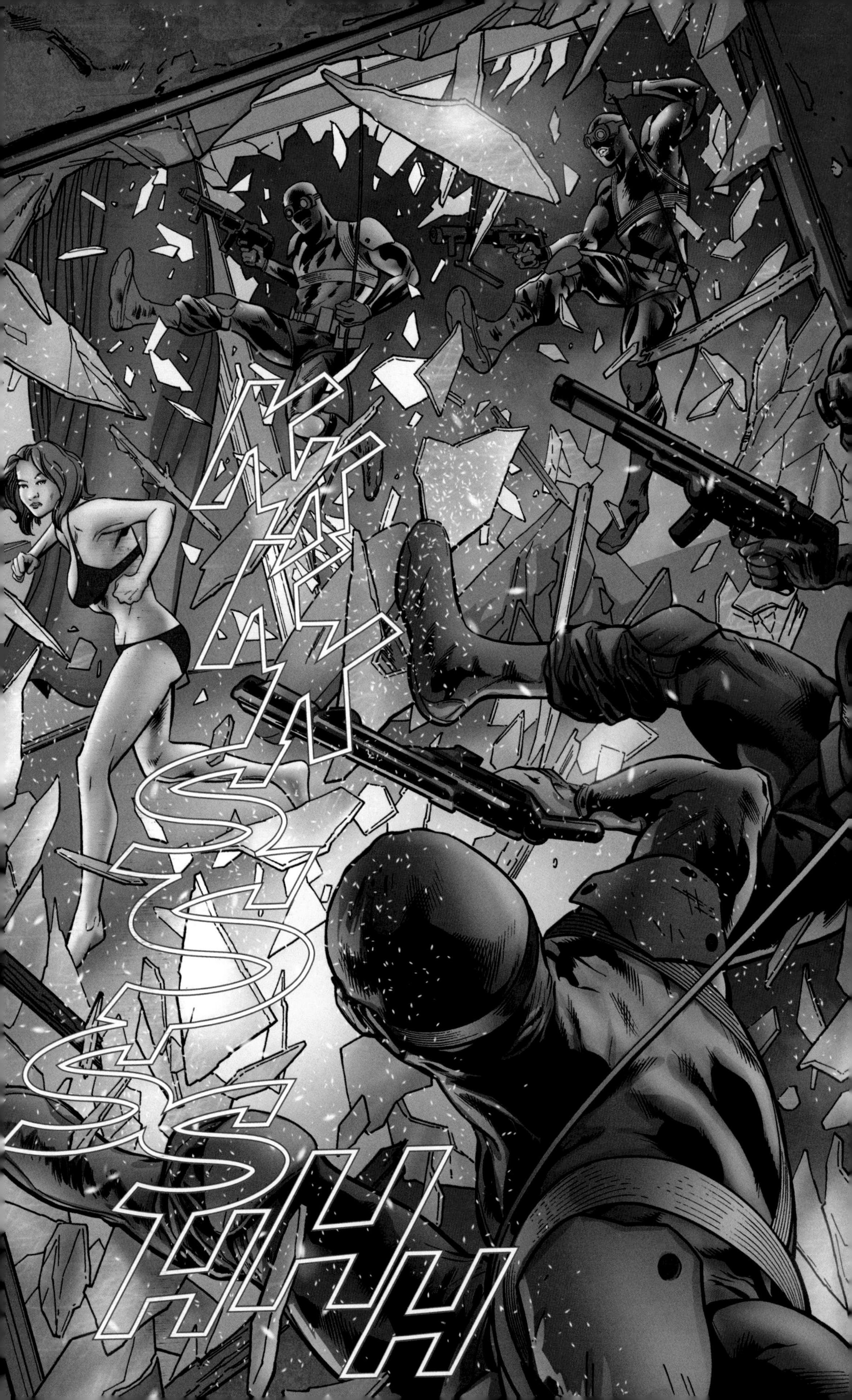

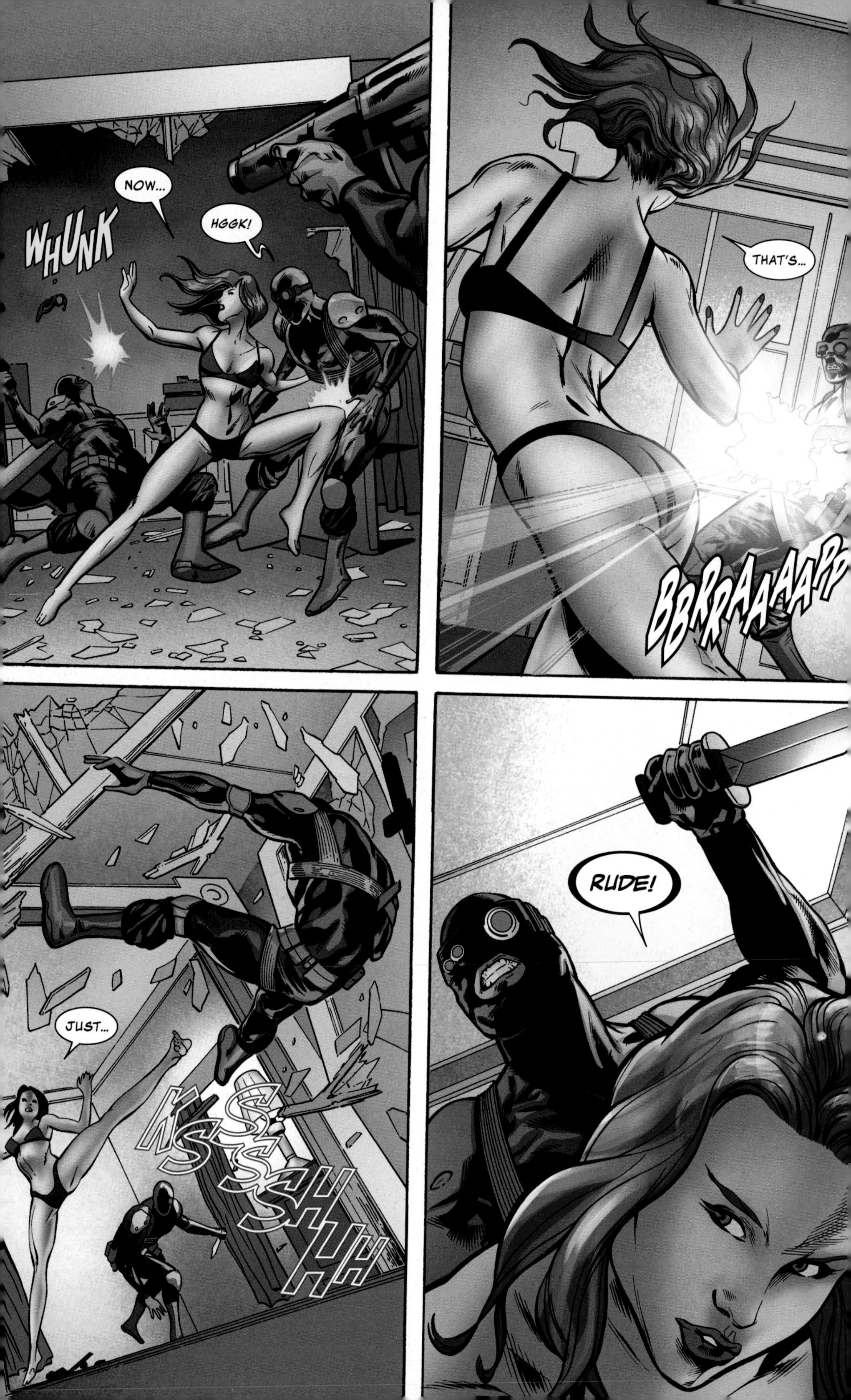
NOW...
WHUNK
HGGK!
THAT'S...
BBRRAAAAPP
JUST...
KSSSSHHH
RUDE!

GAAHH!

HFF--

AAA!

KA-SH

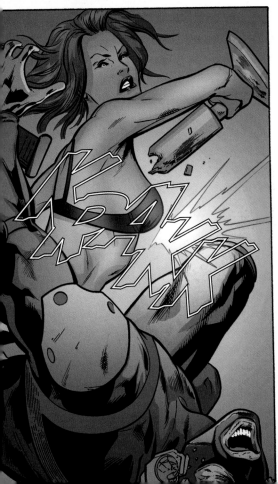

C'MERE!

HKKKK--

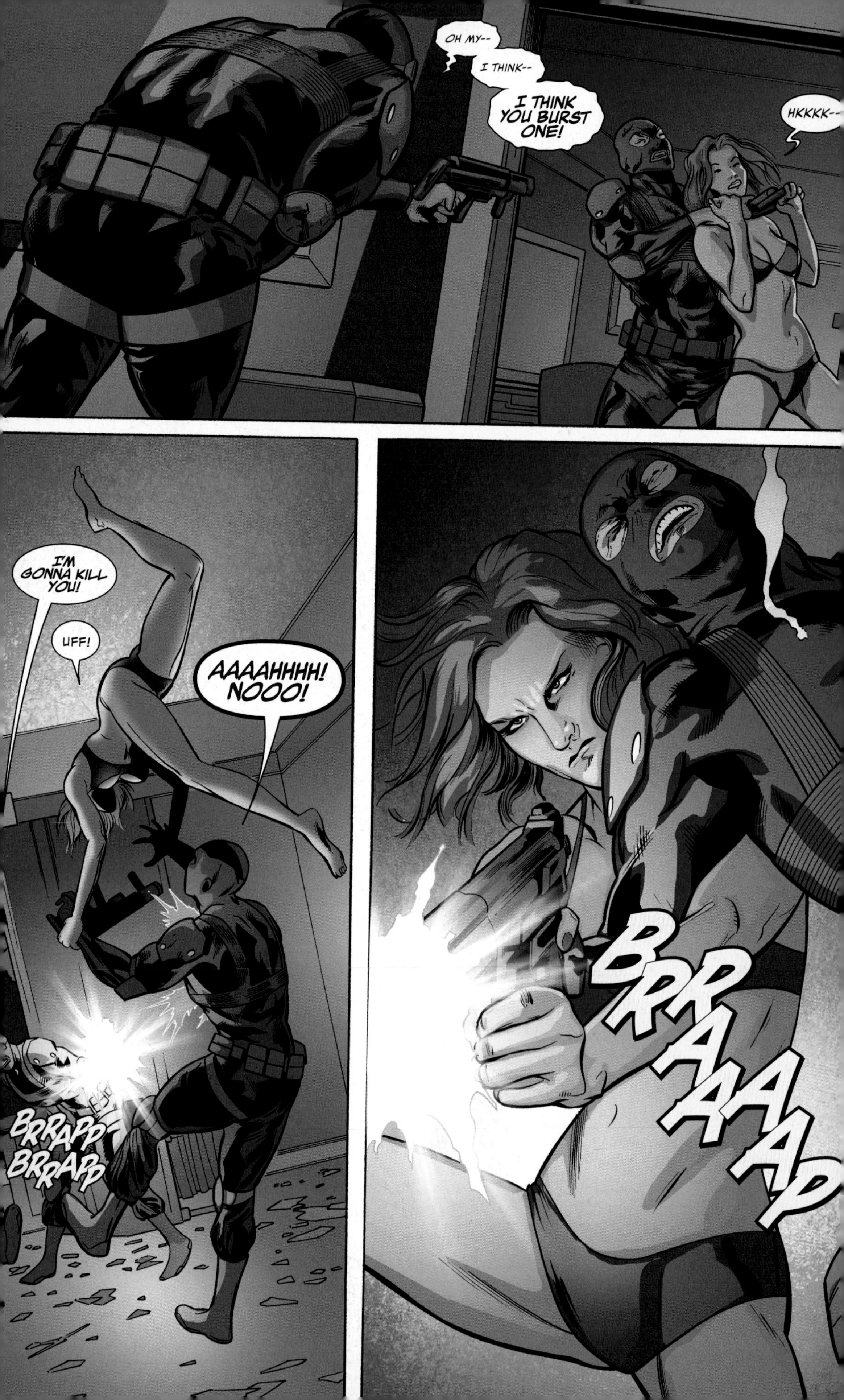
OH MY--
I THINK--
I THINK YOU BURST ONE!
HKKKK--
I'M GONNA KILL YOU!
UFF!
AAAAHHHH! NOOO!
BRRAPP BRRAPP
BRRAAAAP

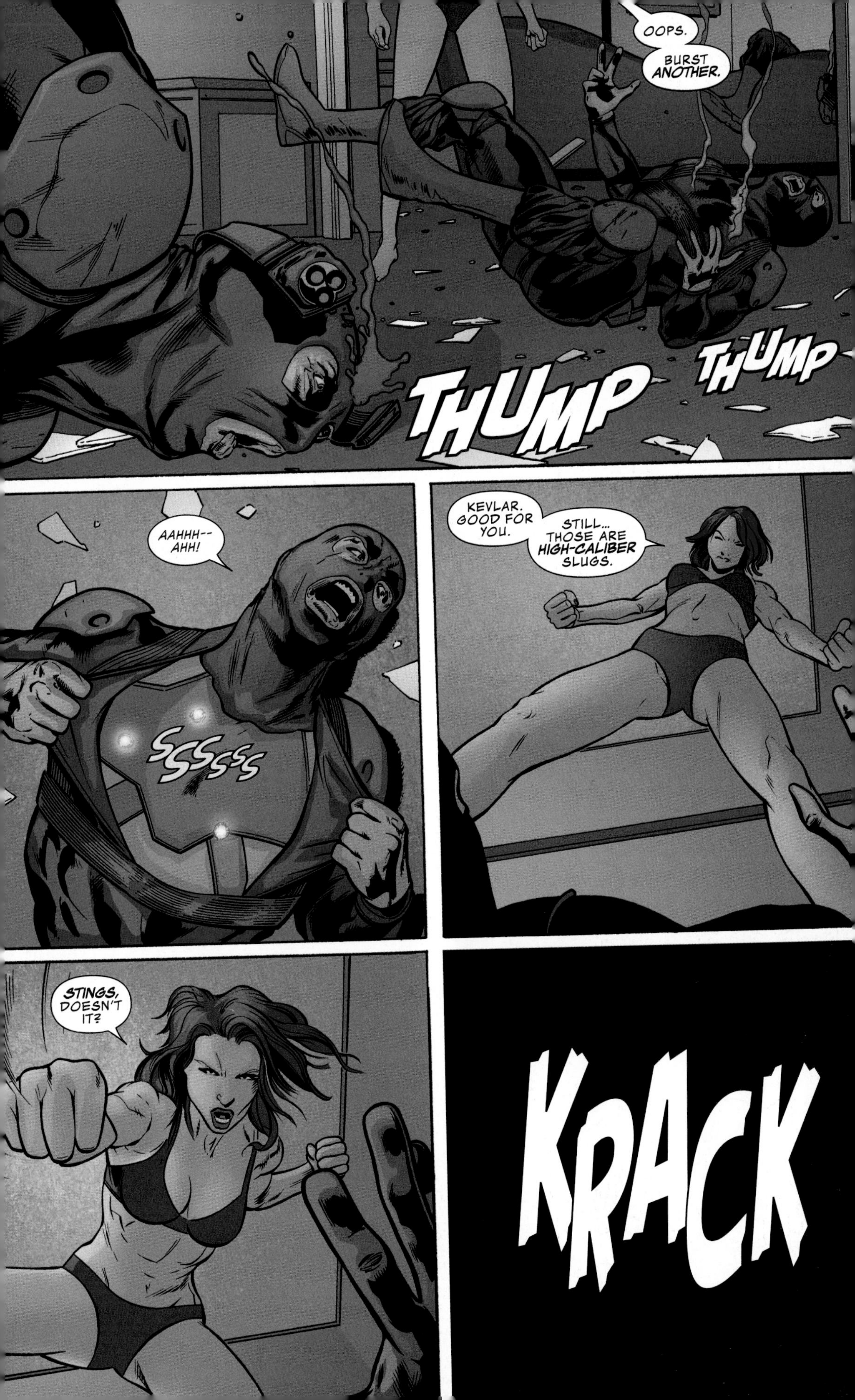
OOPS.
BURST ANOTHER.
THUMP
THUMP
AAHHH-- AHH!
SSSSSS
KEVLAR. GOOD FOR YOU.
STILL... THOSE ARE HIGH-CALIBER SLUGS.
STINGS, DOESN'T IT?
KRACK

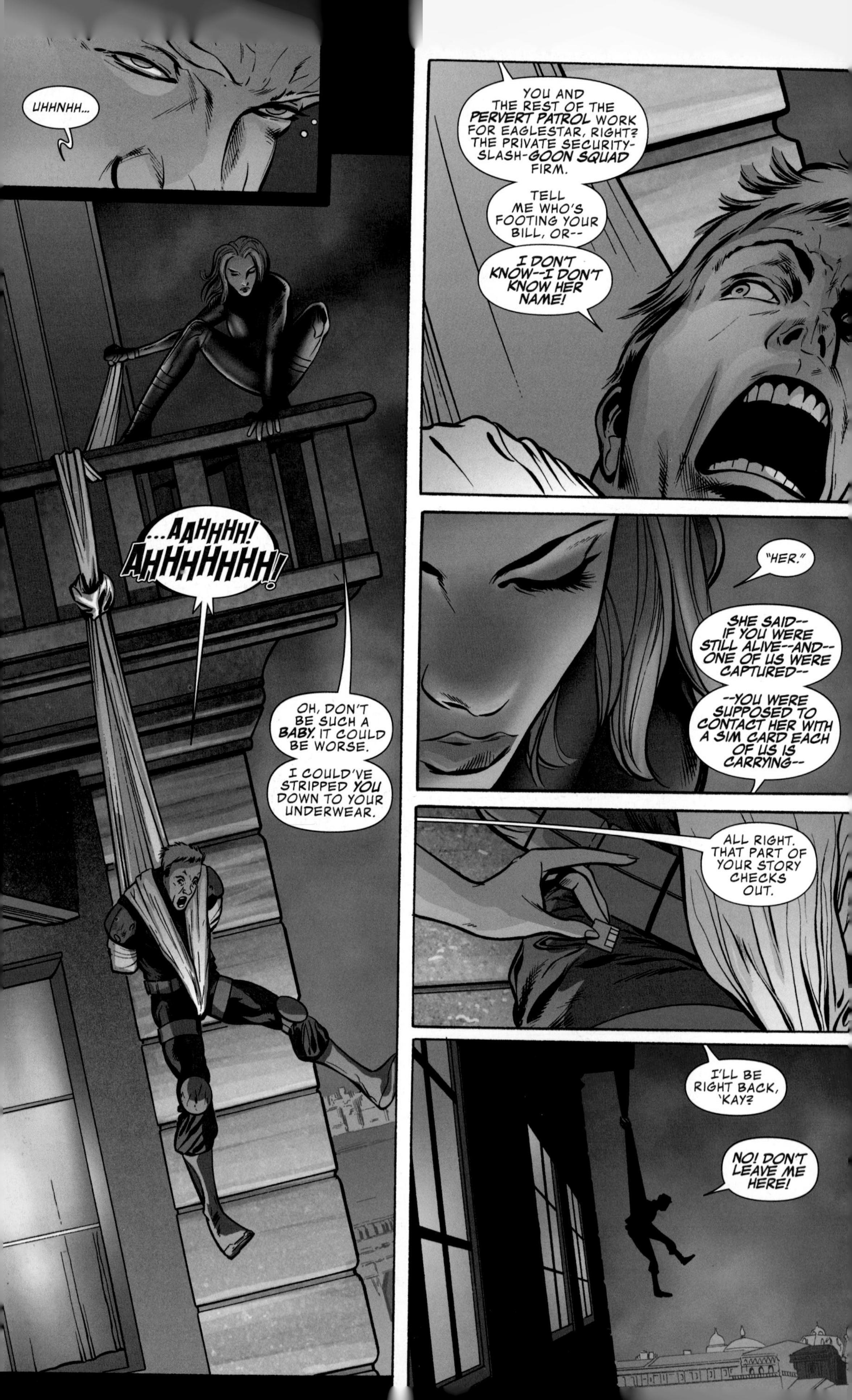
UHHNHH...
...AAHHHH! AHHHHHHH!
OH, DON'T BE SUCH A BABY. IT COULD BE WORSE.
I COULD'VE STRIPPED YOU DOWN TO YOUR UNDERWEAR.
YOU AND THE REST OF THE PERVERT PATROL WORK FOR EAGLESTAR, RIGHT? THE PRIVATE SECURITY-SLASH-GOON SQUAD FIRM.
TELL ME WHO'S FOOTING YOUR BILL, OR--
I DON'T KNOW--I DON'T KNOW HER NAME!
"HER."
SHE SAID-- IF YOU WERE STILL ALIVE--AND-- ONE OF US WERE CAPTURED--
--YOU WERE SUPPOSED TO CONTACT HER WITH A SIM CARD EACH OF US IS CARRYING--
ALL RIGHT. THAT PART OF YOUR STORY CHECKS OUT.
I'LL BE RIGHT BACK, 'KAY?
NO! DON'T LEAVE ME HERE!

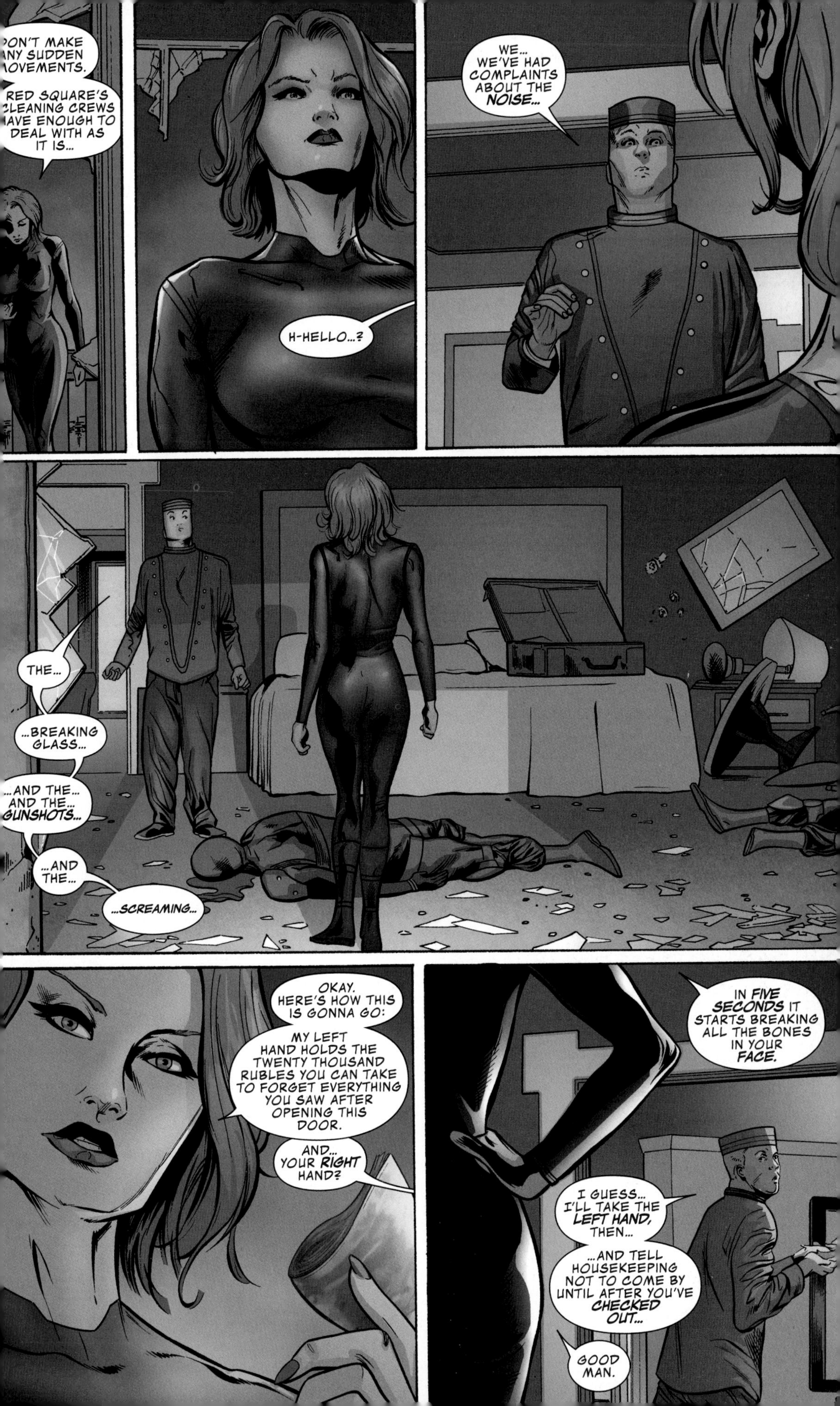

ON'T MAKE ANY SUDDEN OVEMENTS.
RED SQUARE'S CLEANING CREWS AVE ENOUGH TO DEAL WITH AS IT IS...
H-HELLO...?
WE... WE'VE HAD COMPLAINTS ABOUT THE NOISE...
THE...
...BREAKING GLASS...
...AND THE... AND THE... GUNSHOTS...
...AND THE...
...SCREAMING...
OKAY. HERE'S HOW THIS IS GONNA GO:
MY LEFT HAND HOLDS THE TWENTY THOUSAND RUBLES YOU CAN TAKE TO FORGET EVERYTHING YOU SAW AFTER OPENING THIS DOOR.
AND... YOUR RIGHT HAND?
IN FIVE SECONDS IT STARTS BREAKING ALL THE BONES IN YOUR FACE.
I GUESS... I'LL TAKE THE LEFT HAND, THEN...
...AND TELL HOUSEKEEPING NOT TO COME BY UNTIL AFTER YOU'VE CHECKED OUT...
GOOD MAN.

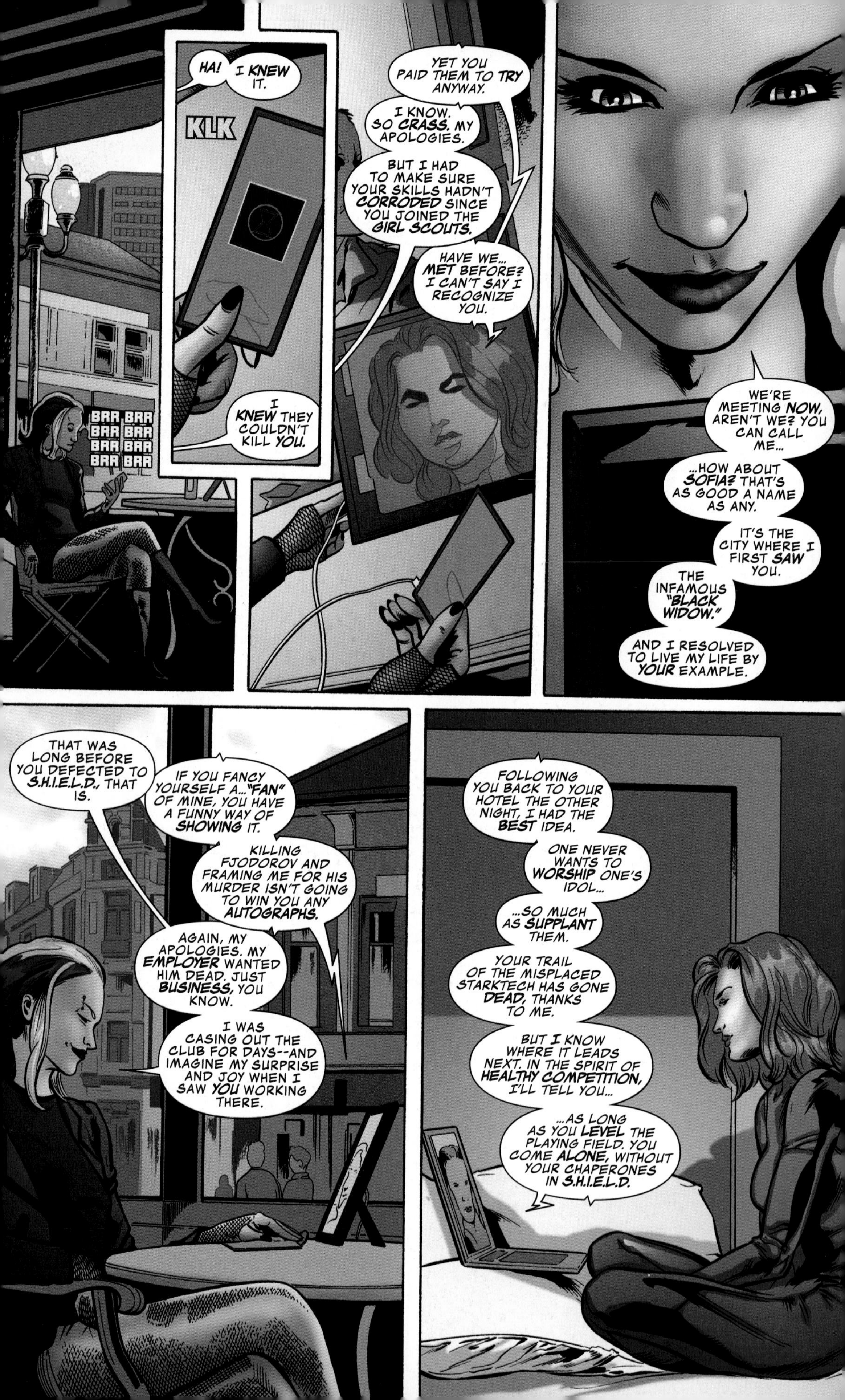
HA!
I KNEW IT.
KLK
I KNEW THEY COULDN'T KILL YOU.
BRR BRR BRR BRR BRR BRR BRR BRR
YET YOU PAID THEM TO TRY ANYWAY.
I KNOW. SO CRASS. MY APOLOGIES.
BUT I HAD TO MAKE SURE YOUR SKILLS HADN'T CORRODED SINCE YOU JOINED THE GIRL SCOUTS.
HAVE WE... MET BEFORE? I CAN'T SAY I RECOGNIZE YOU.
WE'RE MEETING NOW, AREN'T WE? YOU CAN CALL ME...
...HOW ABOUT SOFIA? THAT'S AS GOOD A NAME AS ANY.
IT'S THE CITY WHERE I FIRST SAW YOU.
THE INFAMOUS "BLACK WIDOW."
AND I RESOLVED TO LIVE MY LIFE BY YOUR EXAMPLE.
THAT WAS LONG BEFORE YOU DEFECTED TO S.H.I.E.L.D., THAT IS.
IF YOU FANCY YOURSELF A..."FAN" OF MINE, YOU HAVE A FUNNY WAY OF SHOWING IT.
KILLING FJODOROV AND FRAMING ME FOR HIS MURDER ISN'T GOING TO WIN YOU ANY AUTOGRAPHS.
AGAIN, MY APOLOGIES. MY EMPLOYER WANTED HIM DEAD. JUST BUSINESS, YOU KNOW.
I WAS CASING OUT THE CLUB FOR DAYS--AND IMAGINE MY SURPRISE AND JOY WHEN I SAW YOU WORKING THERE.
FOLLOWING YOU BACK TO YOUR HOTEL THE OTHER NIGHT, I HAD THE BEST IDEA.
ONE NEVER WANTS TO WORSHIP ONE'S IDOL...
...SO MUCH AS SUPPLANT THEM.
YOUR TRAIL OF THE MISPLACED STARKTECH HAS GONE DEAD, THANKS TO ME.
BUT I KNOW WHERE IT LEADS NEXT. IN THE SPIRIT OF HEALTHY COMPETITION, I'LL TELL YOU...
...AS LONG AS YOU LEVEL THE PLAYING FIELD. YOU COME ALONE, WITHOUT YOUR CHAPERONES IN S.H.I.E.L.D.

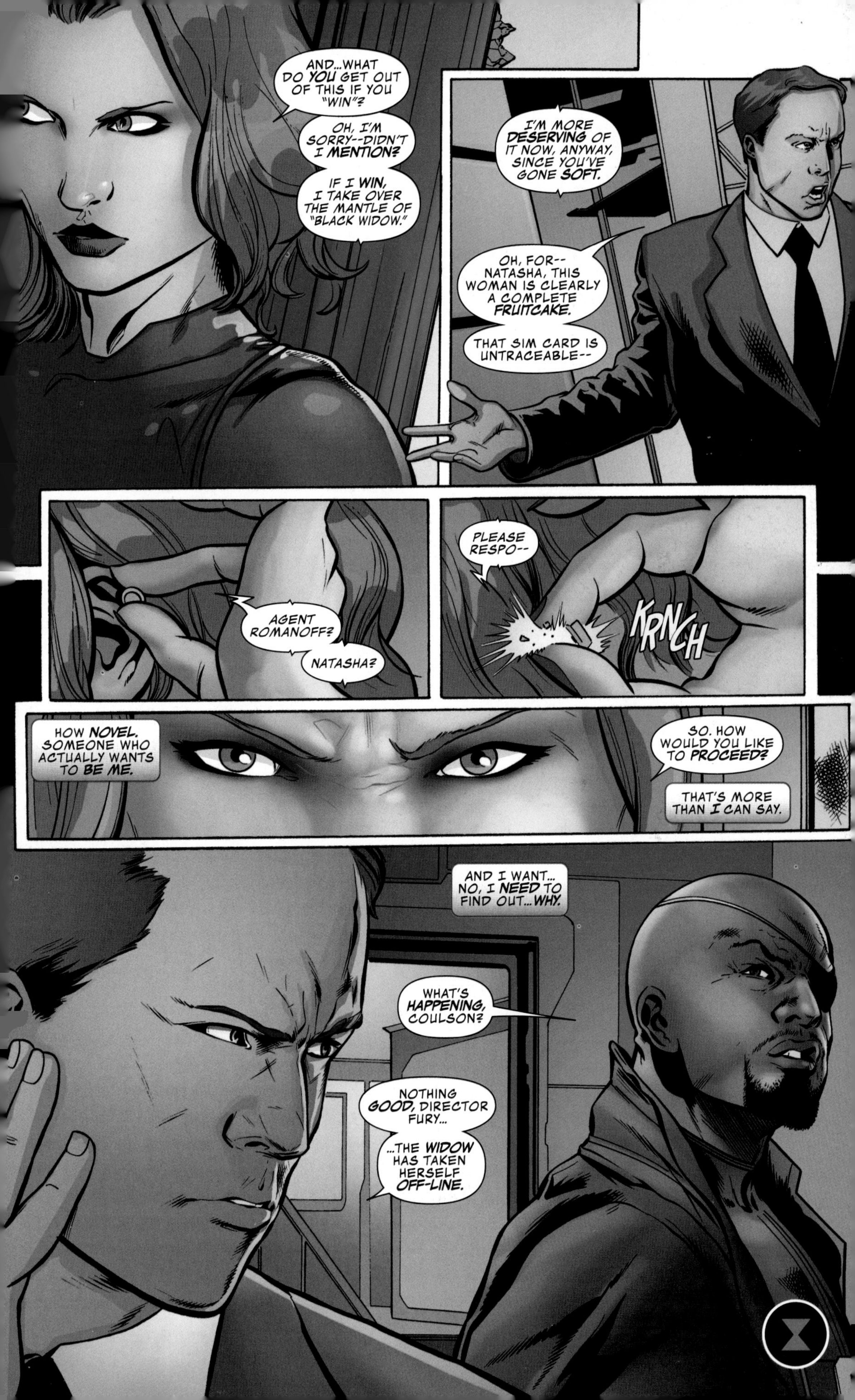

AND...WHAT DO YOU GET OUT OF THIS IF YOU "WIN"?
OH, I'M SORRY--DIDN'T I MENTION?
IF I WIN, I TAKE OVER THE MANTLE OF "BLACK WIDOW."
I'M MORE DESERVING OF IT NOW, ANYWAY, SINCE YOU'VE GONE SOFT.
OH, FOR-- NATASHA, THIS WOMAN IS CLEARLY A COMPLETE FRUITCAKE.
THAT SIM CARD IS UNTRACEABLE--
AGENT ROMANOFF?
NATASHA?
PLEASE RESPO--
KRNCH
HOW NOVEL. SOMEONE WHO ACTUALLY WANTS TO BE ME.
SO. HOW WOULD YOU LIKE TO PROCEED?
THAT'S MORE THAN I CAN SAY.
AND I WANT... NO, I NEED TO FIND OUT...WHY.
WHAT'S HAPPENING, COULSON?
NOTHING GOOD, DIRECTOR FURY...
...THE WIDOW HAS TAKEN HERSELF OFF-LINE.

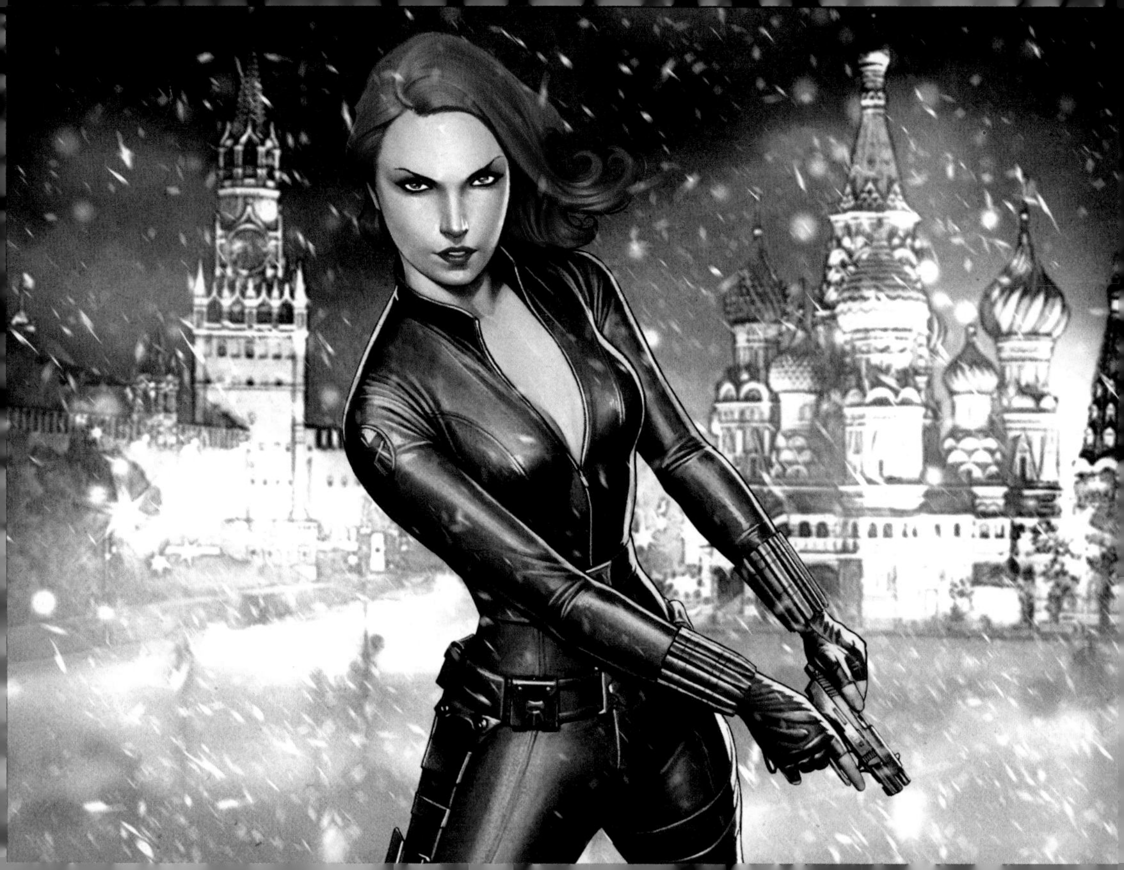

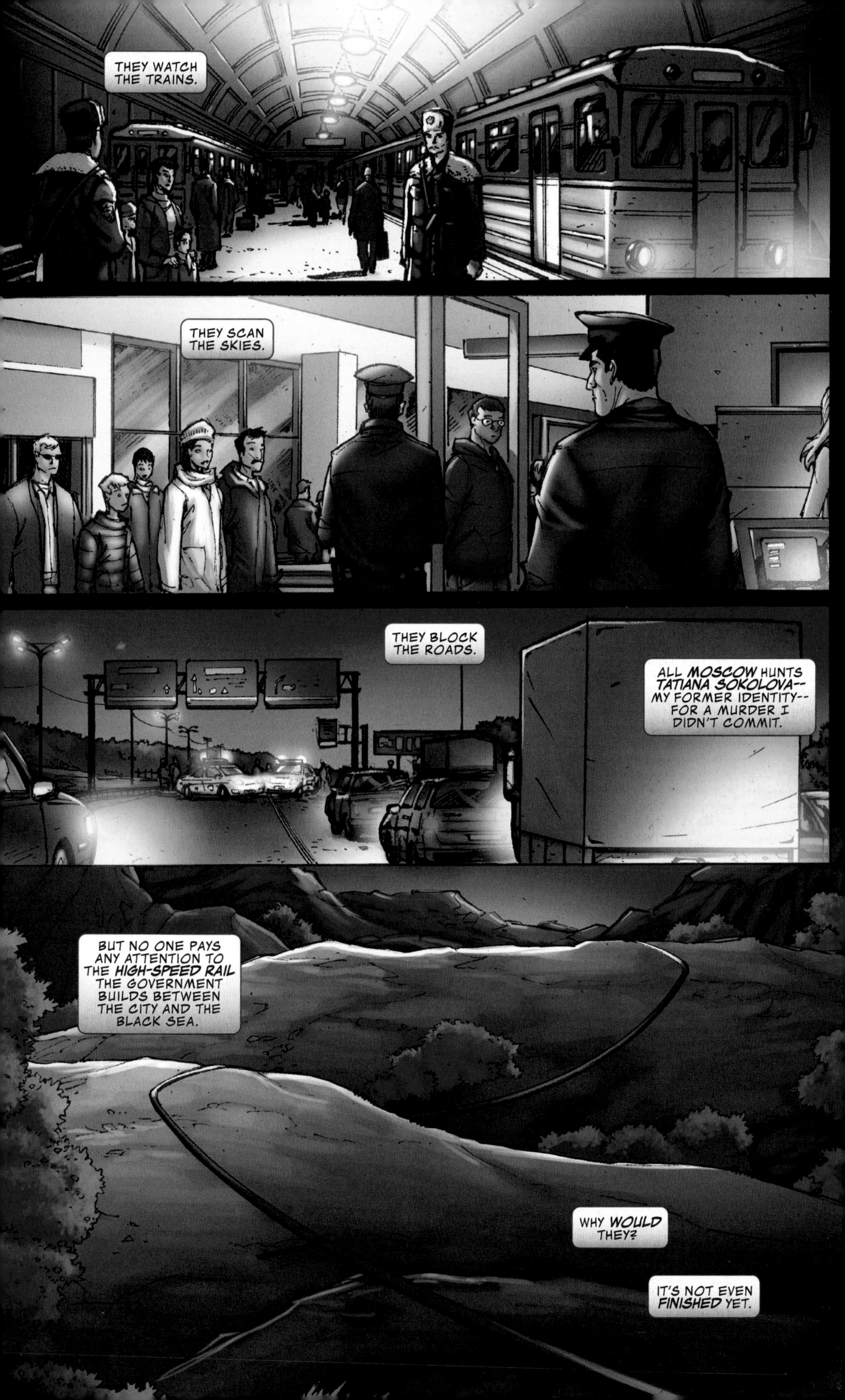
THEY WATCH THE TRAINS.
THEY SCAN THE SKIES.
THEY BLOCK THE ROADS.
ALL MOSCOW HUNTS TATIANA SOKOLOVA-- MY FORMER IDENTITY-- FOR A MURDER I DIDN'T COMMIT.
BUT NO ONE PAYS ANY ATTENTION TO THE HIGH-SPEED RAIL THE GOVERNMENT BUILDS BETWEEN THE CITY AND THE BLACK SEA.
WHY WOULD THEY?
IT'S NOT EVEN FINISHED YET.

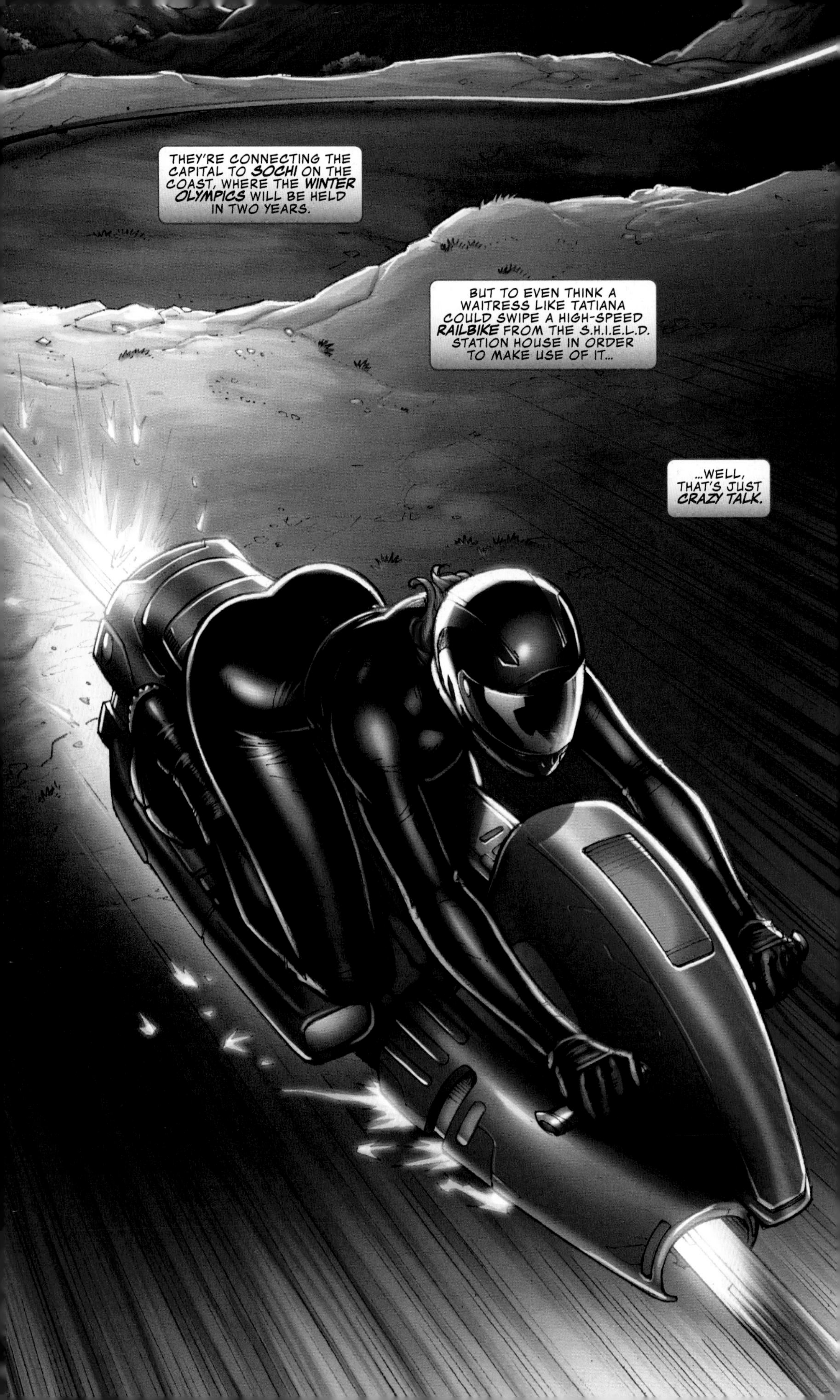

THEY'RE CONNECTING THE CAPITAL TO SOCHI ON THE COAST, WHERE THE WINTER OLYMPICS WILL BE HELD IN TWO YEARS.
BUT TO EVEN THINK A WAITRESS LIKE TATIANA COULD SWIPE A HIGH-SPEED RAILBIKE FROM THE S.H.I.E.L.D. STATION HOUSE IN ORDER TO MAKE USE OF IT...
...WELL, THAT'S JUST CRAZY TALK.

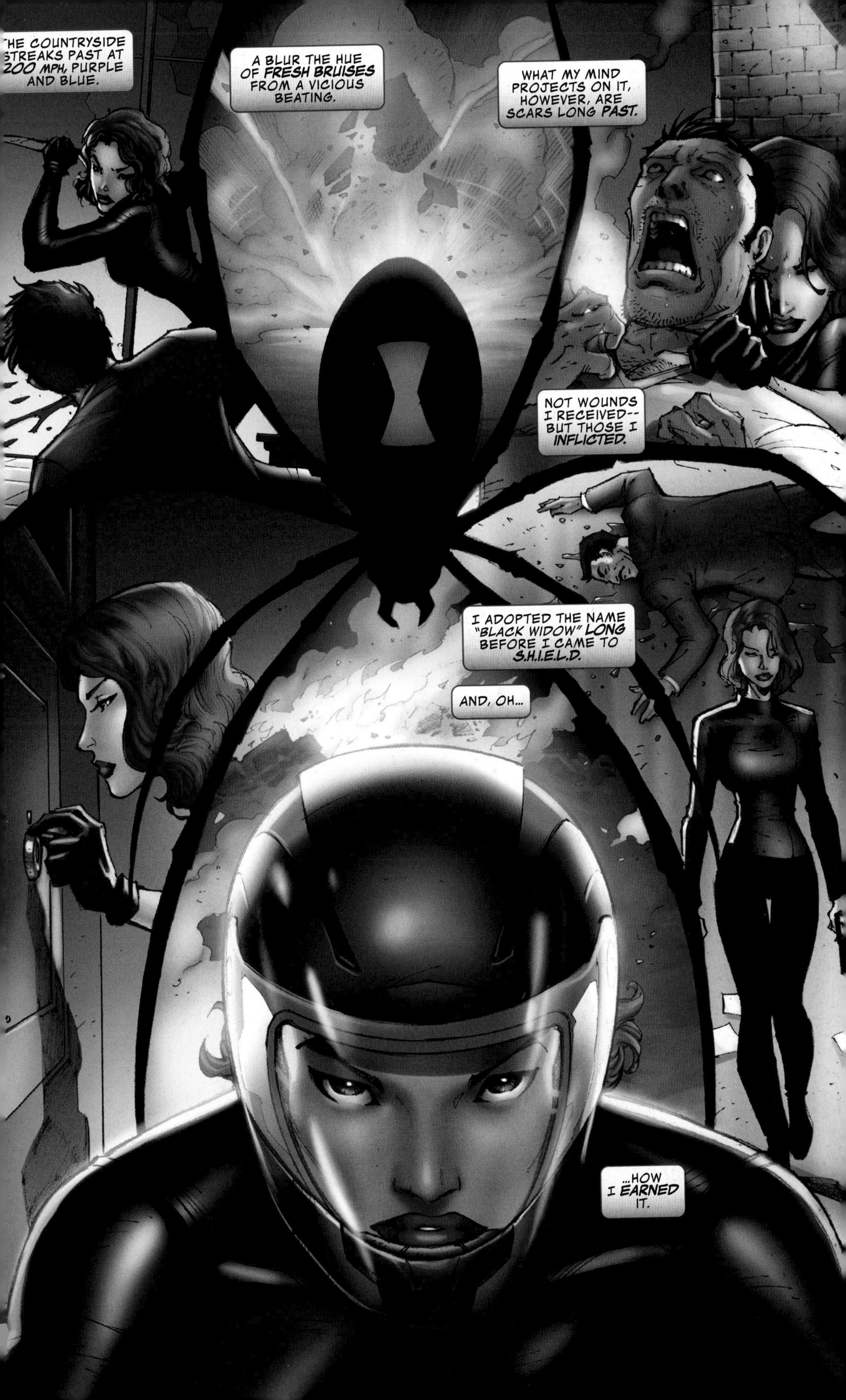
THE COUNTRYSIDE STREAKS PAST AT 200 MPH, PURPLE AND BLUE.
A BLUR THE HUE OF FRESH BRUISES FROM A VICIOUS BEATING.
WHAT MY MIND PROJECTS ON IT, HOWEVER, ARE SCARS LONG PAST.
NOT WOUNDS I RECEIVED-- BUT THOSE I INFLICTED.
I ADOPTED THE NAME "BLACK WIDOW" LONG BEFORE I CAME TO S.H.I.E.L.D.
AND, OH...
...HOW I EARNED IT.

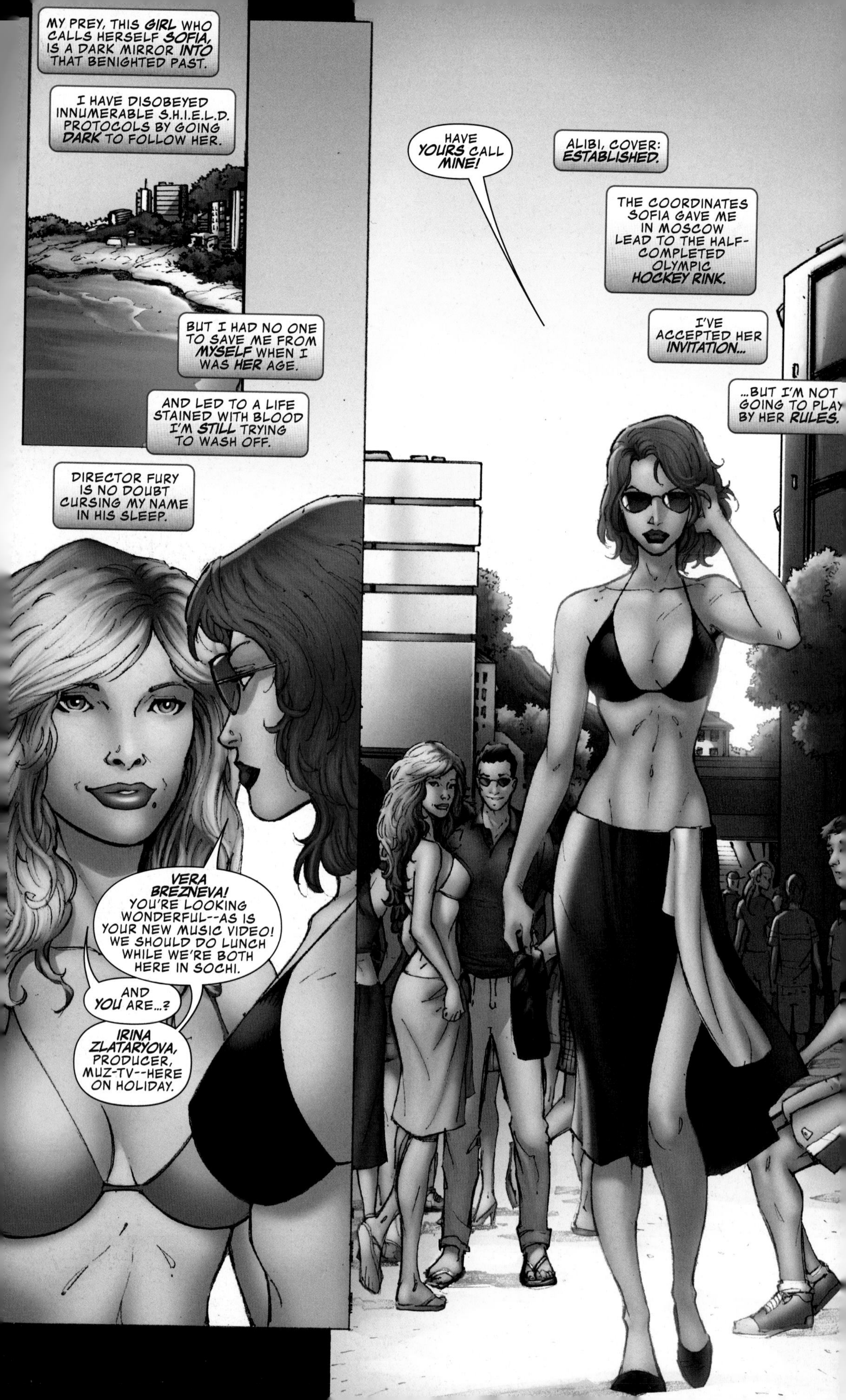
MY PREY, THIS GIRL WHO CALLS HERSELF SOFIA, IS A DARK MIRROR INTO THAT BENIGHTED PAST.
I HAVE DISOBEYED INNUMERABLE S.H.I.E.L.D. PROTOCOLS BY GOING DARK TO FOLLOW HER.
BUT I HAD NO ONE TO SAVE ME FROM MYSELF WHEN I WAS HER AGE.
AND LED TO A LIFE STAINED WITH BLOOD I'M STILL TRYING TO WASH OFF.
DIRECTOR FURY IS NO DOUBT CURSING MY NAME IN HIS SLEEP.
VERA BREZNEVA! YOU'RE LOOKING WONDERFUL--AS IS YOUR NEW MUSIC VIDEO! WE SHOULD DO LUNCH WHILE WE'RE BOTH HERE IN SOCHI.
AND YOU ARE...?
IRINA ZLATARYOVA, PRODUCER, MUZ-TV--HERE ON HOLIDAY.
HAVE YOURS CALL MINE!
ALIBI, COVER: ESTABLISHED.
THE COORDINATES SOFIA GAVE ME IN MOSCOW LEAD TO THE HALF-COMPLETED OLYMPIC HOCKEY RINK.
I'VE ACCEPTED HER INVITATION...
...BUT I'M NOT GOING TO PLAY BY HER RULES.

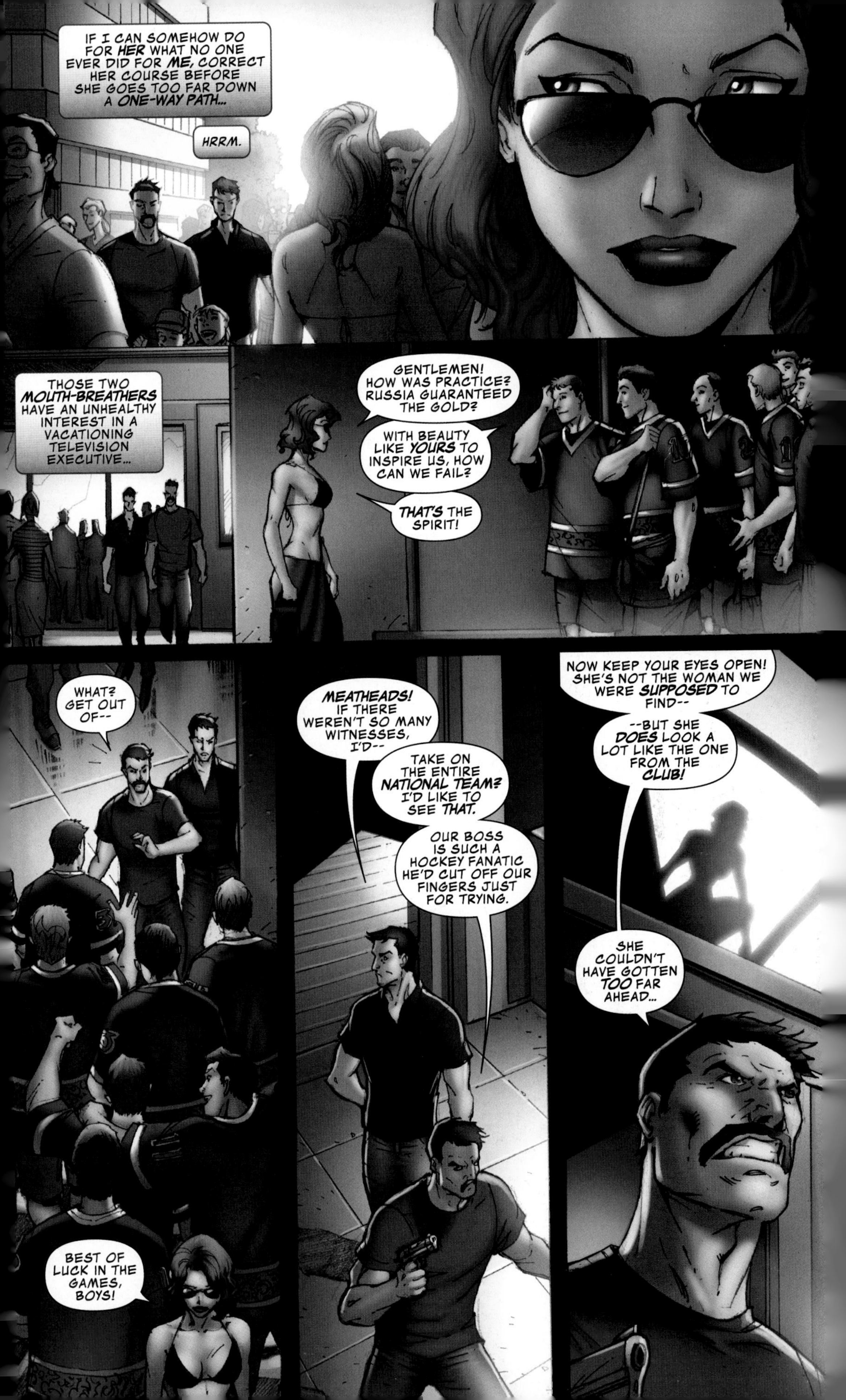

IF I CAN SOMEHOW DO FOR HER WHAT NO ONE EVER DID FOR ME, CORRECT HER COURSE BEFORE SHE GOES TOO FAR DOWN A ONE-WAY PATH...
HRRM.
THOSE TWO MOUTH-BREATHERS HAVE AN UNHEALTHY INTEREST IN A VACATIONING TELEVISION EXECUTIVE...
GENTLEMEN! HOW WAS PRACTICE? RUSSIA GUARANTEED THE GOLD?
WITH BEAUTY LIKE YOURS TO INSPIRE US, HOW CAN WE FAIL?
THAT'S THE SPIRIT!
WHAT? GET OUT OF--
BEST OF LUCK IN THE GAMES, BOYS!
MEATHEADS! IF THERE WEREN'T SO MANY WITNESSES, I'D--
TAKE ON THE ENTIRE NATIONAL TEAM? I'D LIKE TO SEE THAT.
OUR BOSS IS SUCH A HOCKEY FANATIC HE'D CUT OFF OUR FINGERS JUST FOR TRYING.
NOW KEEP YOUR EYES OPEN! SHE'S NOT THE WOMAN WE WERE SUPPOSED TO FIND--
--BUT SHE DOES LOOK A LOT LIKE THE ONE FROM THE CLUB!
SHE COULDN'T HAVE GOTTEN TOO FAR AHEAD...

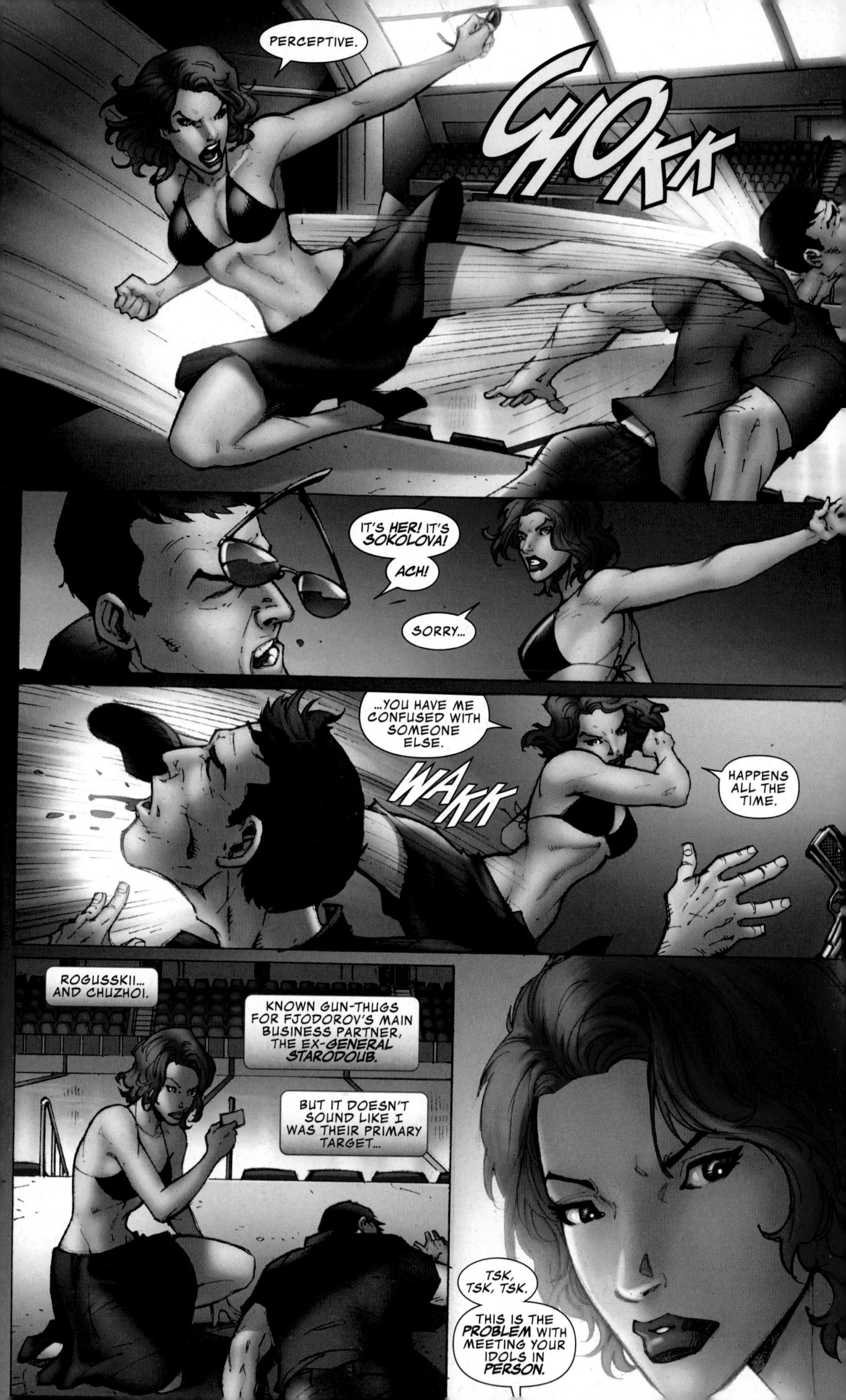
PERCEPTIVE.
CHOKK
IT'S HER! IT'S SOKOLOVA!
ACH!
SORRY...
...YOU HAVE ME CONFUSED WITH SOMEONE ELSE.
WAKK
HAPPENS ALL THE TIME.
ROGUSSKII... AND CHUZHOI.
KNOWN GUN-THUGS FOR FJODOROV'S MAIN BUSINESS PARTNER, THE EX-GENERAL STARODOUB.
BUT IT DOESN'T SOUND LIKE I WAS THEIR PRIMARY TARGET...
TSK, TSK, TSK.
THIS IS THE PROBLEM WITH MEETING YOUR IDOLS IN PERSON.

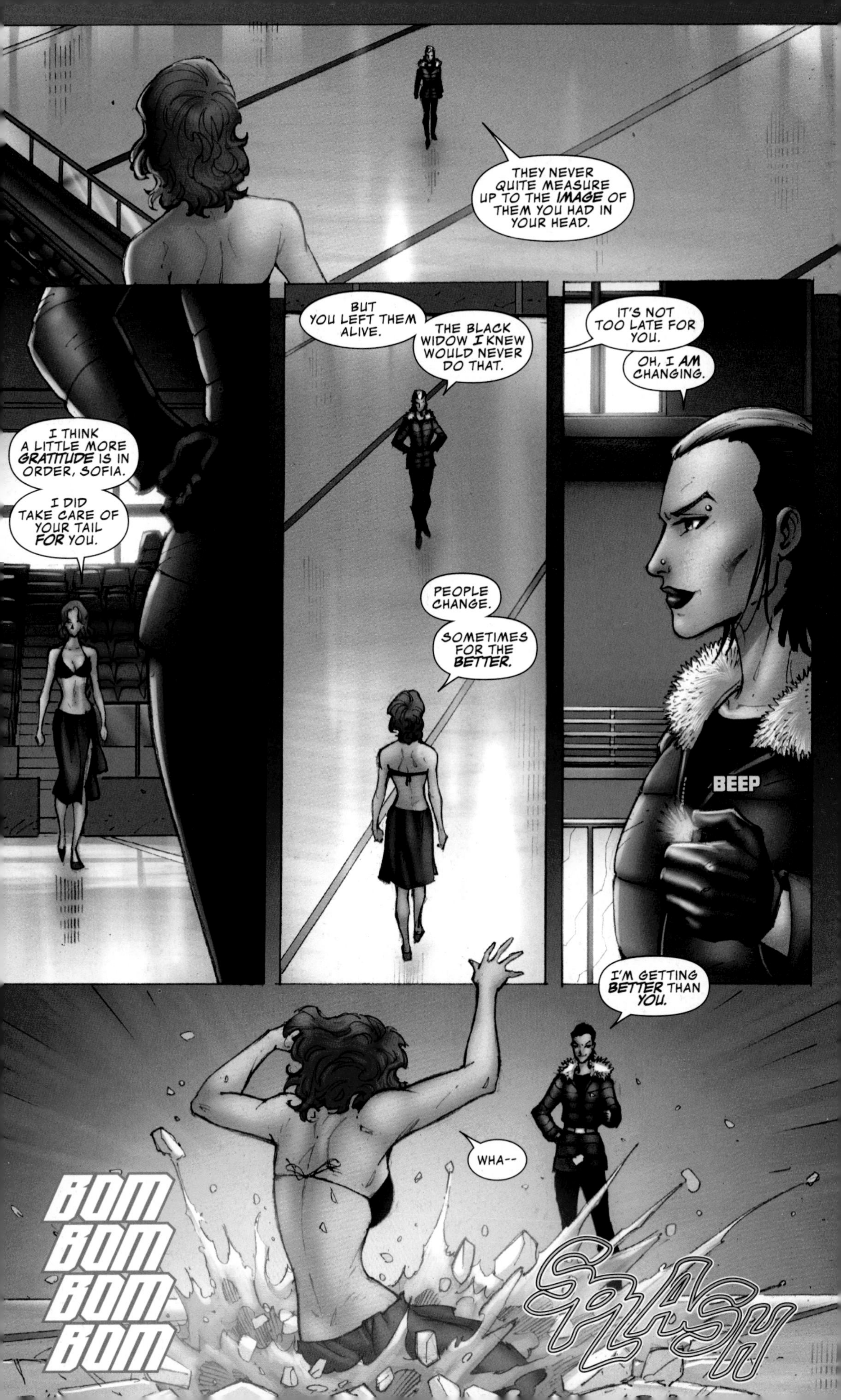
THEY NEVER QUITE MEASURE UP TO THE IMAGE OF THEM YOU HAD IN YOUR HEAD.
I THINK A LITTLE MORE GRATITUDE IS IN ORDER, SOFIA.
I DID TAKE CARE OF YOUR TAIL FOR YOU.
BUT YOU LEFT THEM ALIVE.
THE BLACK WIDOW I KNEW WOULD NEVER DO THAT.
PEOPLE CHANGE.
SOMETIMES FOR THE BETTER.
IT'S NOT TOO LATE FOR YOU.
OH, I AM CHANGING.
BEEP
I'M GETTING BETTER THAN YOU.
WHA--
BOM BOM BOM BOM
SPLASH

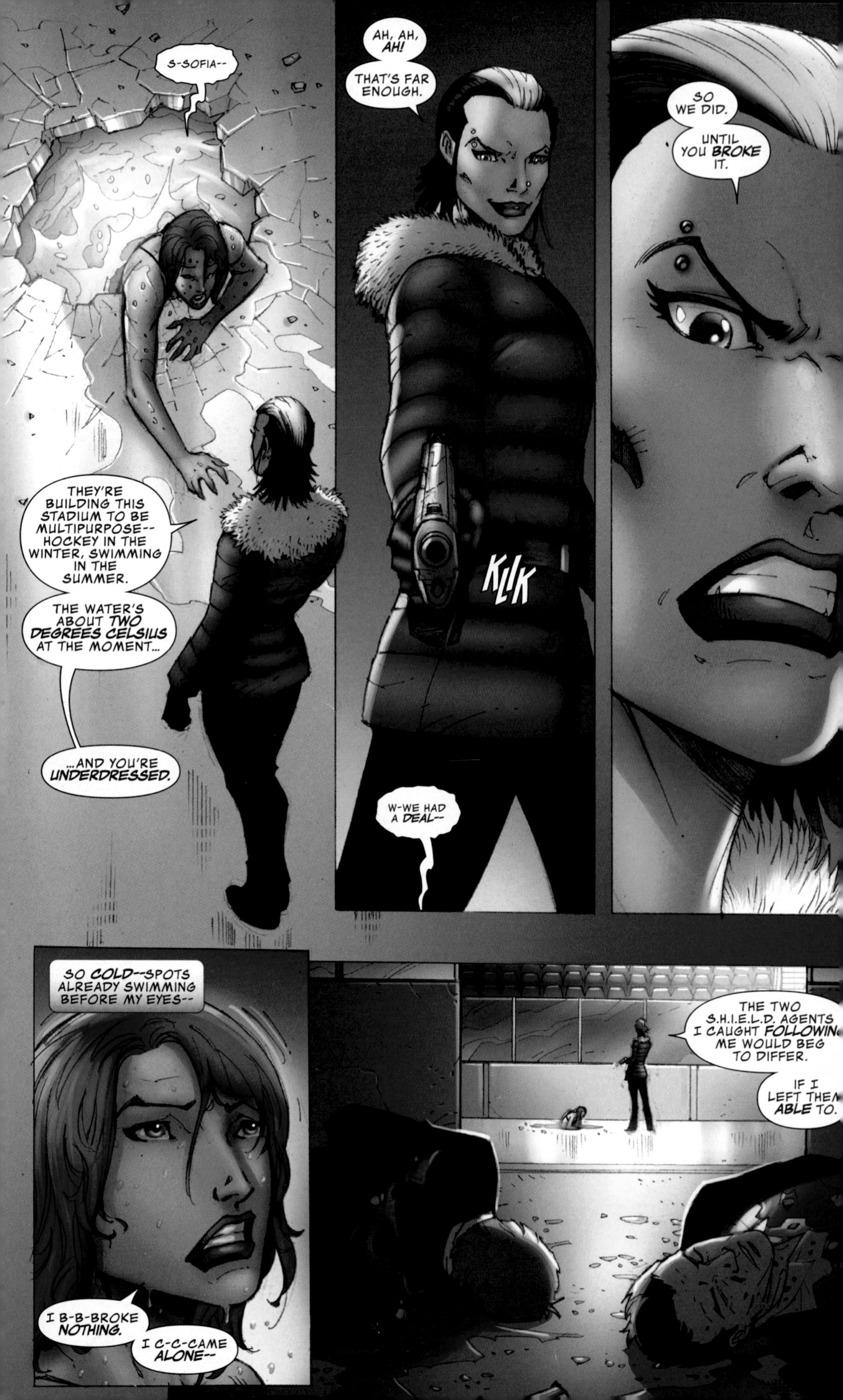
S-SOFIA--
THEY'RE BUILDING THIS STADIUM TO BE MULTIPURPOSE-- HOCKEY IN THE WINTER, SWIMMING IN THE SUMMER.
THE WATER'S ABOUT TWO DEGREES CELSIUS AT THE MOMENT...
...AND YOU'RE UNDERDRESSED.
AH, AH, AH!
THAT'S FAR ENOUGH.
KLIK
W-WE HAD A DEAL--
SO WE DID.
UNTIL YOU BROKE IT.
SO COLD--SPOTS ALREADY SWIMMING BEFORE MY EYES--
I B-B-BROKE NOTHING.
I C-C-CAME ALONE--
THE TWO S.H.I.E.L.D. AGENTS I CAUGHT FOLLOWIN' ME WOULD BEG TO DIFFER.
IF I LEFT THEM ABLE TO.

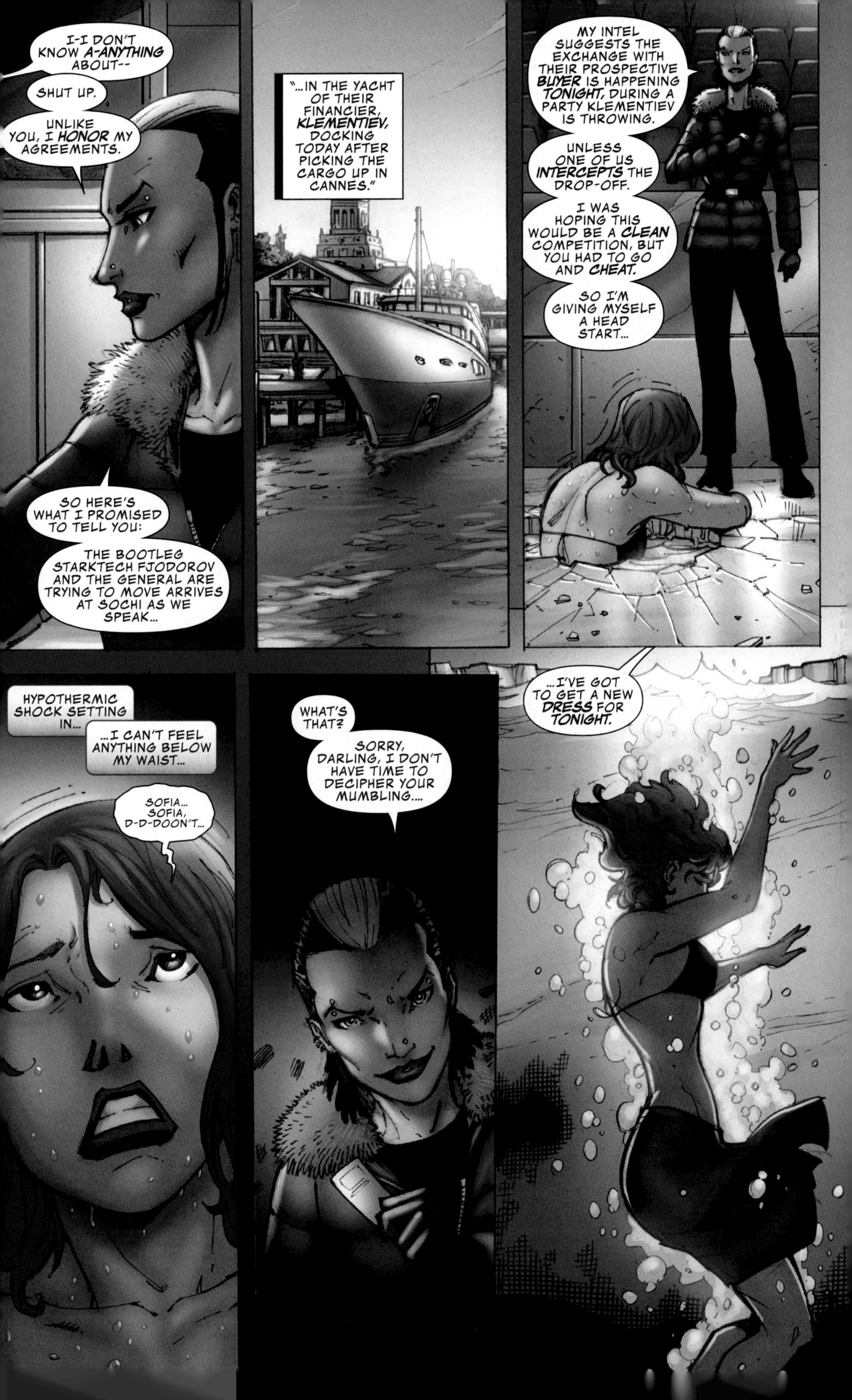
I-I DON'T KNOW A-ANYTHING ABOUT--
SHUT UP.
UNLIKE YOU, I HONOR MY AGREEMENTS.
SO HERE'S WHAT I PROMISED TO TELL YOU:
THE BOOTLEG STARKTECH FJODOROV AND THE GENERAL ARE TRYING TO MOVE ARRIVES AT SOCHI AS WE SPEAK...
"...IN THE YACHT OF THEIR FINANCIER, KLEMENTIEV, DOCKING TODAY AFTER PICKING THE CARGO UP IN CANNES."
MY INTEL SUGGESTS THE EXCHANGE WITH THEIR PROSPECTIVE BUYER IS HAPPENING TONIGHT, DURING A PARTY KLEMENTIEV IS THROWING.
UNLESS ONE OF US INTERCEPTS THE DROP-OFF.
I WAS HOPING THIS WOULD BE A CLEAN COMPETITION, BUT YOU HAD TO GO AND CHEAT.
SO I'M GIVING MYSELF A HEAD START...
HYPOTHERMIC SHOCK SETTING IN...
...I CAN'T FEEL ANYTHING BELOW MY WAIST...
SOFIA... SOFIA, D-D-DOON'T...
WHAT'S THAT?
SORRY, DARLING, I DON'T HAVE TIME TO DECIPHER YOUR MUMBLING....
...I'VE GOT TO GET A NEW DRESS FOR TONIGHT.

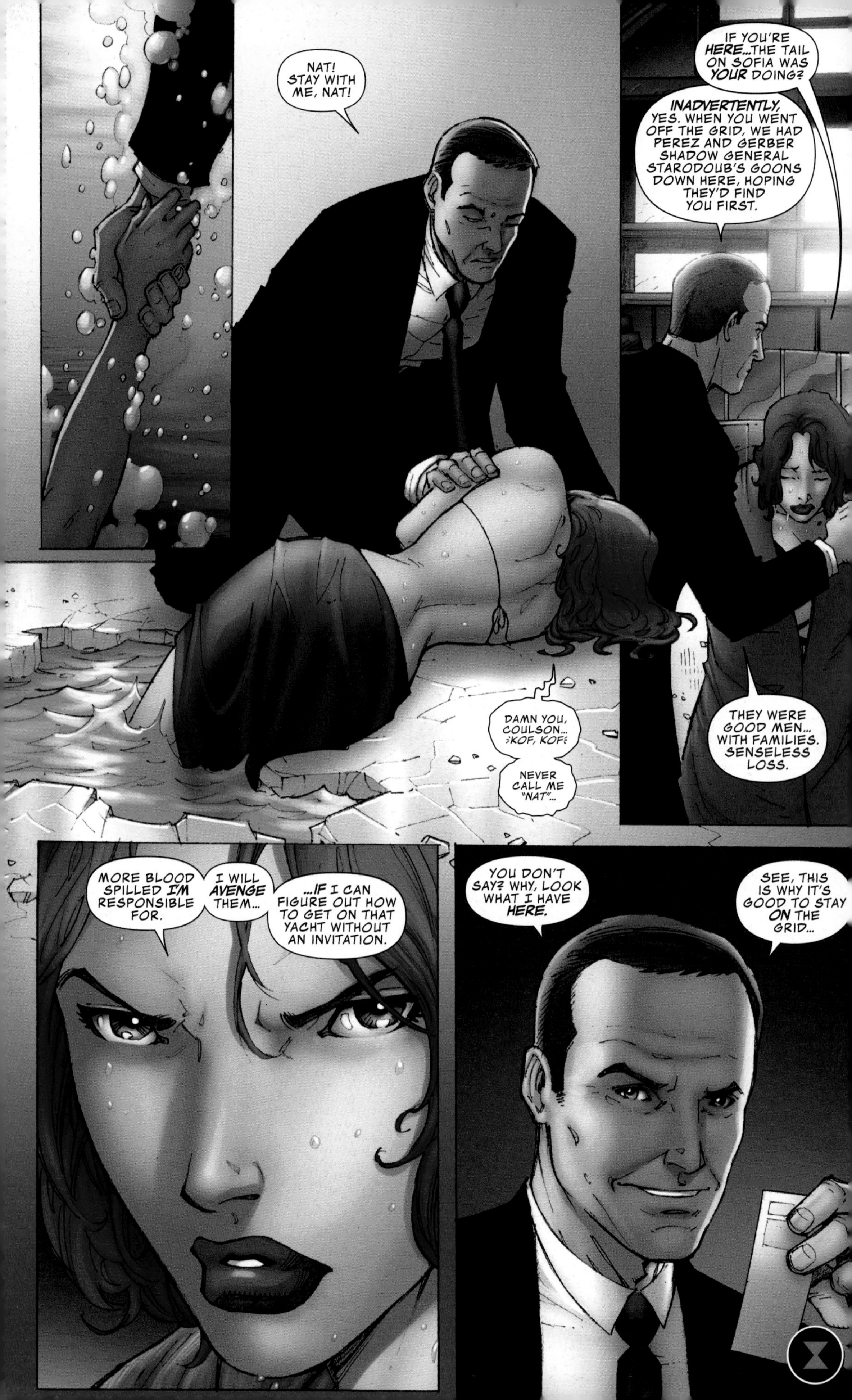
NAT! STAY WITH ME, NAT!
IF YOU'RE HERE...THE TAIL ON SOFIA WAS YOUR DOING?
INADVERTENTLY, YES. WHEN YOU WENT OFF THE GRID, WE HAD PEREZ AND GERBER SHADOW GENERAL STARODOUB'S GOONS DOWN HERE, HOPING THEY'D FIND YOU FIRST.
DAMN YOU, COULSON... KOF, KOF
NEVER CALL ME "NAT"...
THEY WERE GOOD MEN... WITH FAMILIES. SENSELESS LOSS.
MORE BLOOD SPILLED I'M RESPONSIBLE FOR.
I WILL AVENGE THEM...
...IF I CAN FIGURE OUT HOW TO GET ON THAT YACHT WITHOUT AN INVITATION.
YOU DON'T SAY? WHY, LOOK WHAT I HAVE HERE.
SEE, THIS IS WHY IT'S GOOD TO STAY ON THE GRID...

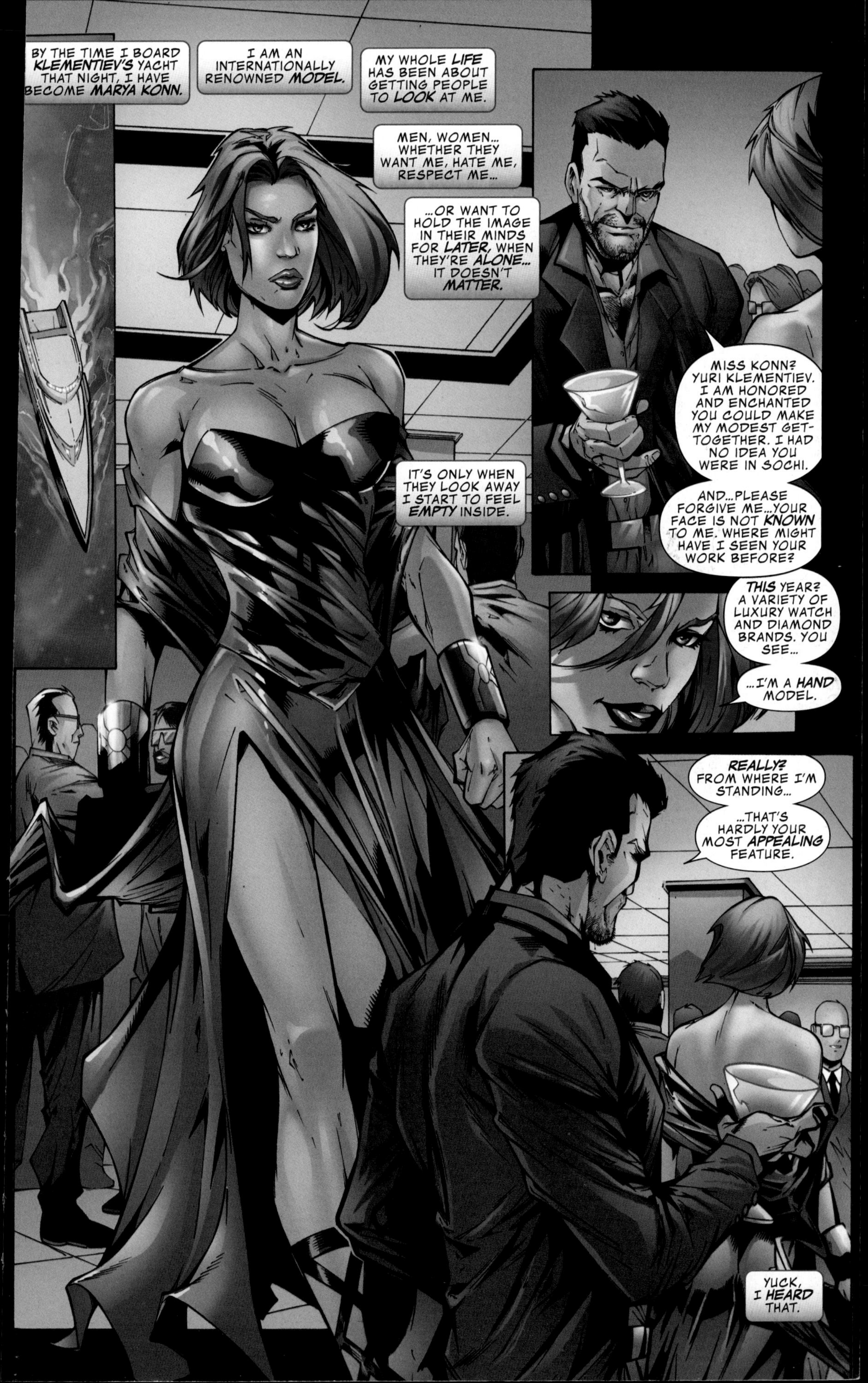
BY THE TIME I BOARD KLEMENTIEV'S YACHT THAT NIGHT, I HAVE BECOME MARYA KONN.
I AM AN INTERNATIONALLY RENOWNED MODEL.
MY WHOLE LIFE HAS BEEN ABOUT GETTING PEOPLE TO LOOK AT ME.
MEN, WOMEN... WHETHER THEY WANT ME, HATE ME, RESPECT ME...
...OR WANT TO HOLD THE IMAGE IN THEIR MINDS FOR LATER, WHEN THEY'RE ALONE... IT DOESN'T MATTER.
IT'S ONLY WHEN THEY LOOK AWAY I START TO FEEL EMPTY INSIDE.
MISS KONN? YURI KLEMENTIEV. I AM HONORED AND ENCHANTED YOU COULD MAKE MY MODEST GET-TOGETHER. I HAD NO IDEA YOU WERE IN SOCHI.
AND...PLEASE FORGIVE ME...YOUR FACE IS NOT KNOWN TO ME. WHERE MIGHT HAVE I SEEN YOUR WORK BEFORE?
THIS YEAR? A VARIETY OF LUXURY WATCH AND DIAMOND BRANDS. YOU SEE...
...I'M A HAND MODEL.
REALLY? FROM WHERE I'M STANDING...
...THAT'S HARDLY YOUR MOST APPEALING FEATURE.
YUCK, I HEARD THAT.

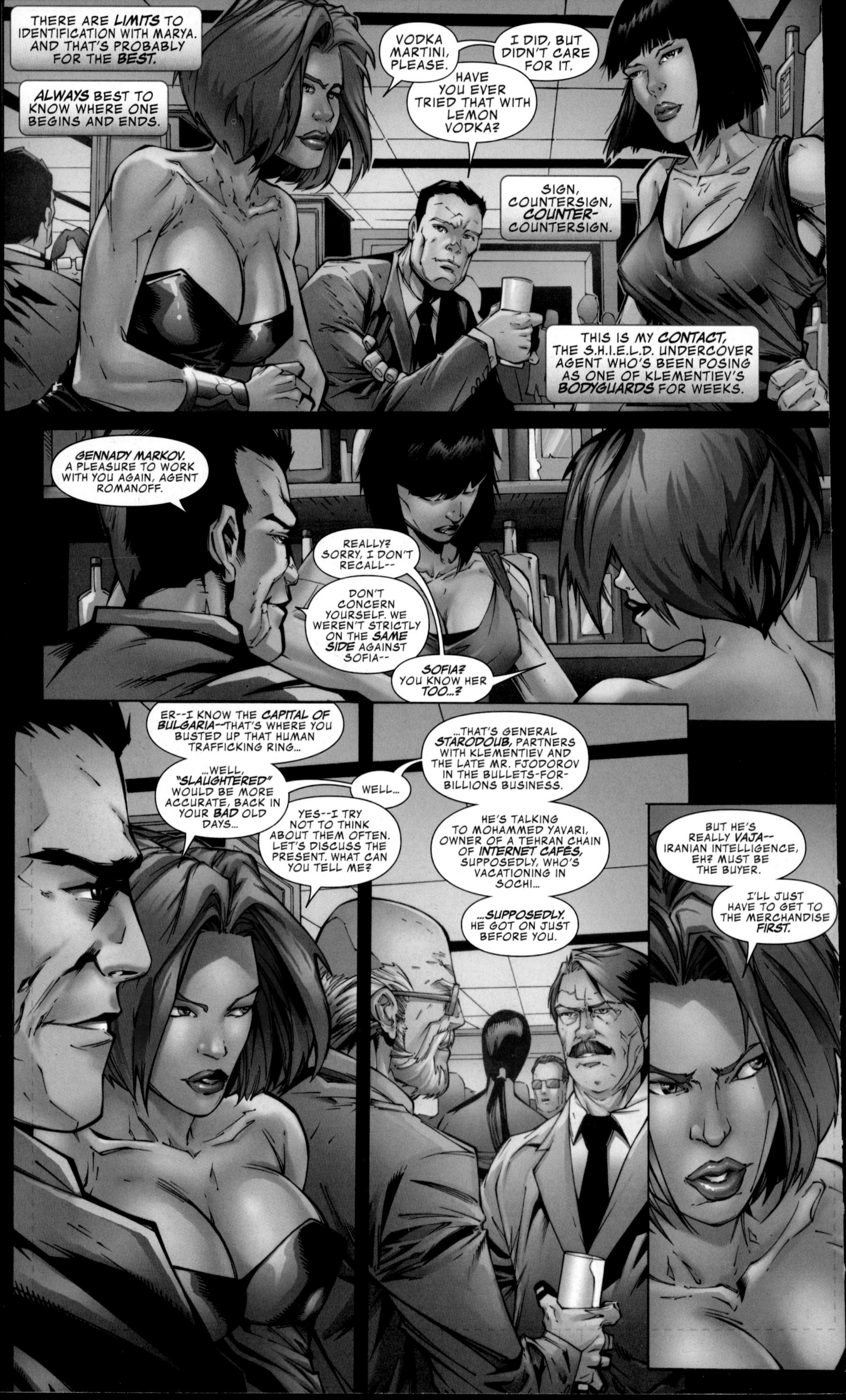
THERE ARE LIMITS TO IDENTIFICATION WITH MARYA. AND THAT'S PROBABLY FOR THE BEST.
ALWAYS BEST TO KNOW WHERE ONE BEGINS AND ENDS.
VODKA MARTINI, PLEASE.
HAVE YOU EVER TRIED THAT WITH LEMON VODKA?
I DID, BUT DIDN'T CARE FOR IT.
SIGN, COUNTERSIGN, COUNTER-COUNTERSIGN.
THIS IS MY CONTACT, THE S.H.I.E.L.D. UNDERCOVER AGENT WHO'S BEEN POSING AS ONE OF KLEMENTIEV'S BODYGUARDS FOR WEEKS.
GENNADY MARKOV. A PLEASURE TO WORK WITH YOU AGAIN, AGENT ROMANOFF.
REALLY? SORRY, I DON'T RECALL--
DON'T CONCERN YOURSELF. WE WEREN'T STRICTLY ON THE SAME SIDE AGAINST SOFIA--
SOFIA? YOU KNOW HER TOO...?
ER--I KNOW THE CAPITAL OF BULGARIA--THAT'S WHERE YOU BUSTED UP THAT HUMAN TRAFFICKING RING...
...WELL, "SLAUGHTERED" WOULD BE MORE ACCURATE, BACK IN YOUR BAD OLD DAYS...
YES--I TRY NOT TO THINK ABOUT THEM OFTEN. LET'S DISCUSS THE PRESENT. WHAT CAN YOU TELL ME?
WELL...
...THAT'S GENERAL STARODOUB, PARTNERS WITH KLEMENTIEV AND THE LATE MR. FJODOROV IN THE BULLETS-FOR-BILLIONS BUSINESS.
HE'S TALKING TO MOHAMMED YAVARI, OWNER OF A TEHRAN CHAIN OF INTERNET CAFÉS, SUPPOSEDLY, WHO'S VACATIONING IN SOCHI...
...SUPPOSEDLY. HE GOT ON JUST BEFORE YOU.
BUT HE'S REALLY VAJA--IRANIAN INTELLIGENCE, EH? MUST BE THE BUYER.
I'LL JUST HAVE TO GET TO THE MERCHANDISE FIRST.

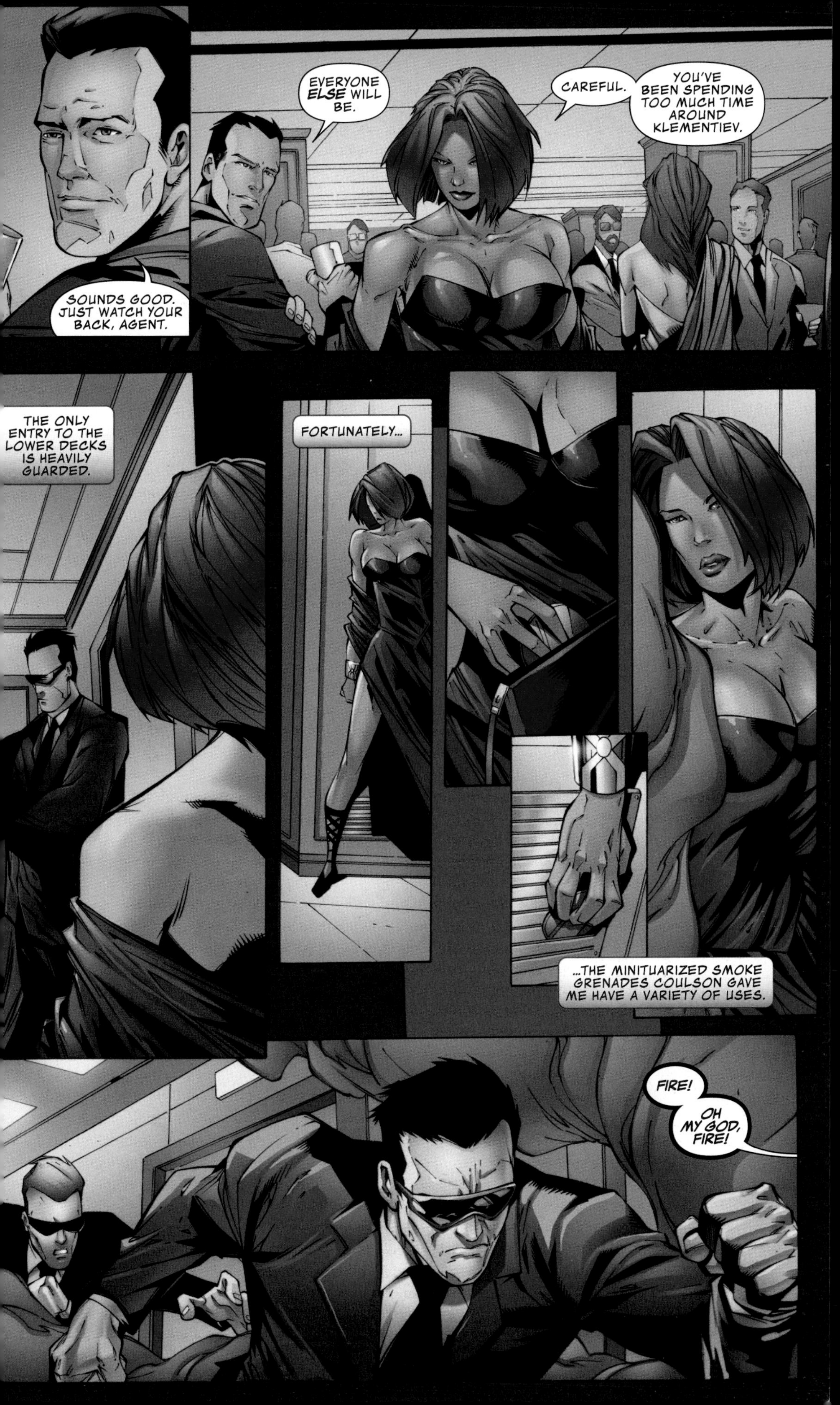
EVERYONE ELSE WILL BE.
CAREFUL.
YOU'VE BEEN SPENDING TOO MUCH TIME AROUND KLEMENTIEV.
SOUNDS GOOD. JUST WATCH YOUR BACK, AGENT.
THE ONLY ENTRY TO THE LOWER DECKS IS HEAVILY GUARDED.
FORTUNATELY...
...THE MINITUARIZED SMOKE GRENADES COULSON GAVE ME HAVE A VARIETY OF USES.
FIRE!
OH MY GOD, FIRE!

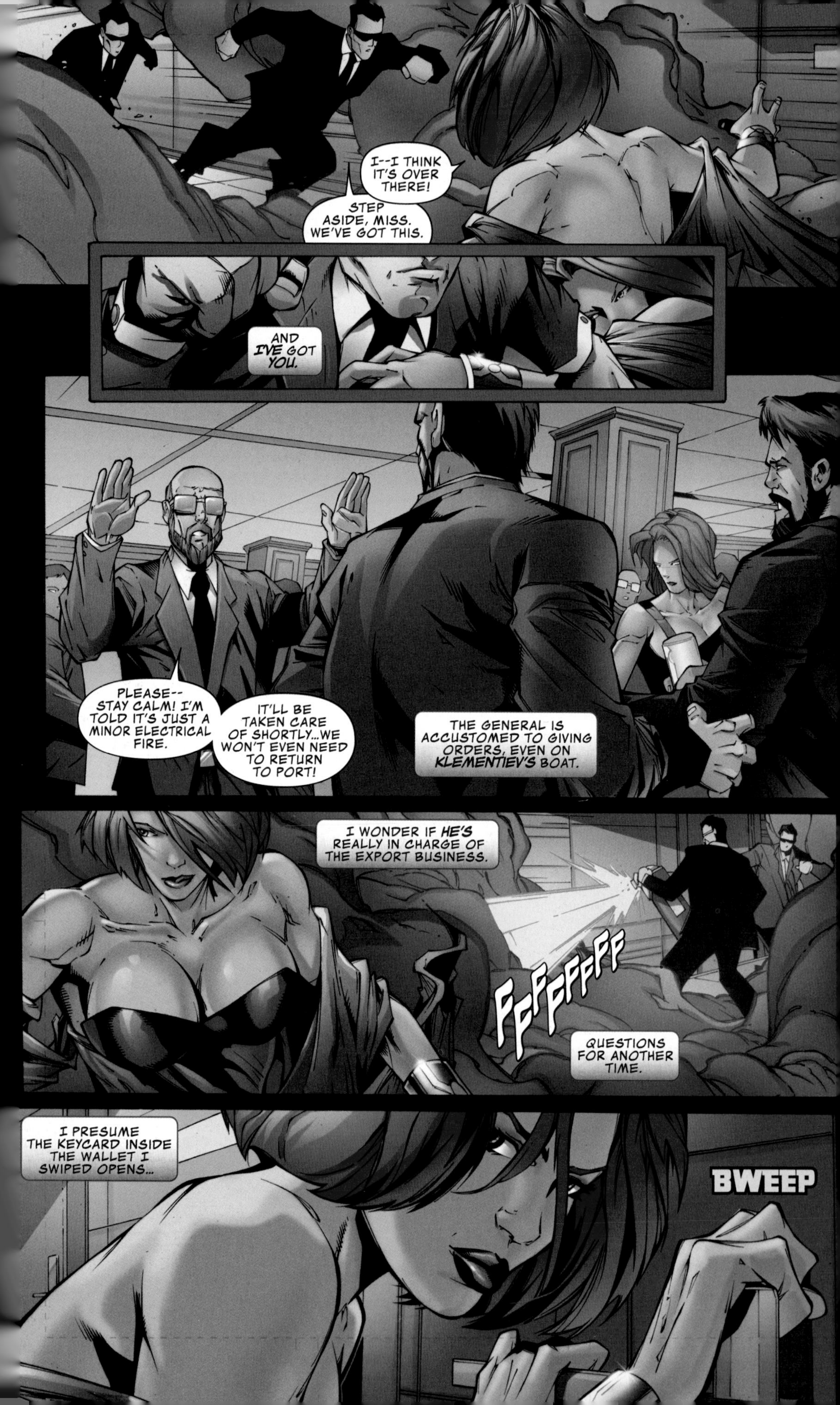
I--I THINK IT'S OVER THERE!
STEP ASIDE, MISS. WE'VE GOT THIS.
AND I'VE GOT YOU.
PLEASE-- STAY CALM! I'M TOLD IT'S JUST A MINOR ELECTRICAL FIRE.
IT'LL BE TAKEN CARE OF SHORTLY...WE WON'T EVEN NEED TO RETURN TO PORT!
THE GENERAL IS ACCUSTOMED TO GIVING ORDERS, EVEN ON KLEMENTIEV'S BOAT.
I WONDER IF HE'S REALLY IN CHARGE OF THE EXPORT BUSINESS.
FFFFFFFF
QUESTIONS FOR ANOTHER TIME.
I PRESUME THE KEYCARD INSIDE THE WALLET I SWIPED OPENS...
BWEEP

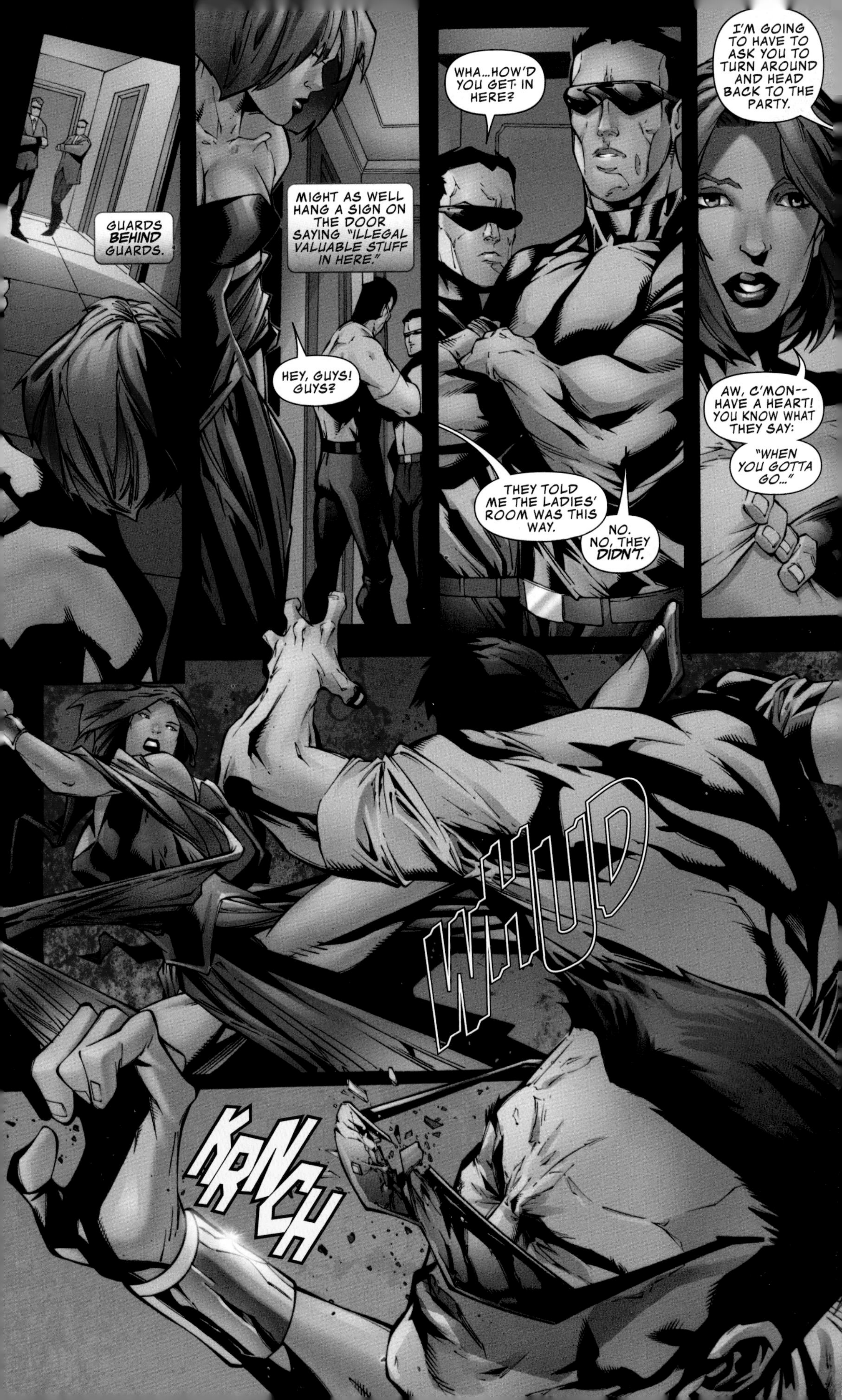
GUARDS BEHIND GUARDS.
MIGHT AS WELL HANG A SIGN ON THE DOOR SAYING "ILLEGAL VALUABLE STUFF IN HERE."
HEY, GUYS! GUYS?
WHA...HOW'D YOU GET IN HERE?
THEY TOLD ME THE LADIES' ROOM WAS THIS WAY.
NO. NO, THEY DIDN'T.
I'M GOING TO HAVE TO ASK YOU TO TURN AROUND AND HEAD BACK TO THE PARTY.
AW, C'MON-- HAVE A HEART! YOU KNOW WHAT THEY SAY:
"WHEN YOU GOTTA GO..."
WHUD
KRNCH

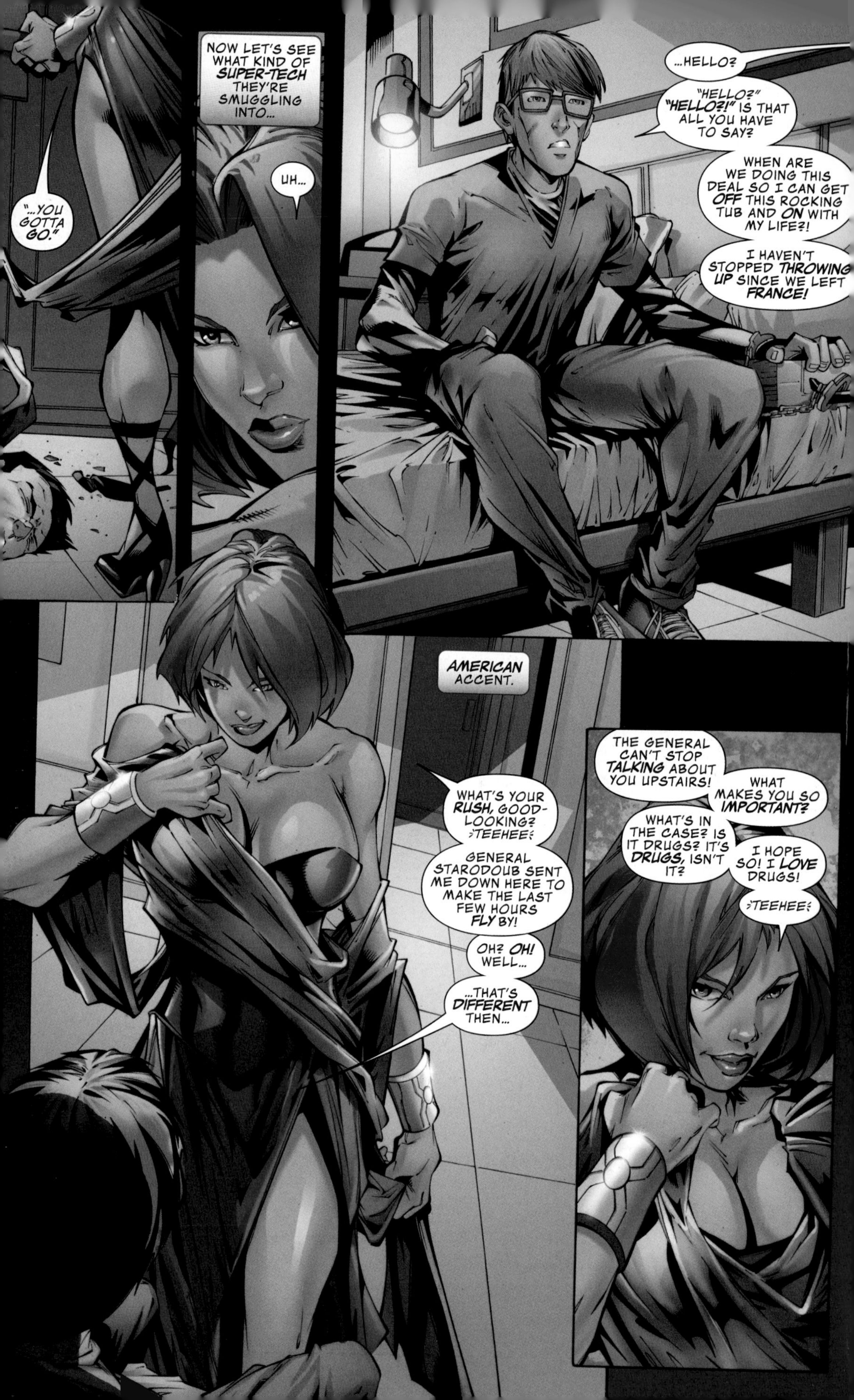
"...YOU GOTTA GO."
NOW LET'S SEE WHAT KIND OF SUPER-TECH THEY'RE SMUGGLING INTO...
UH...
...HELLO?
"HELLO?" "HELLO?!" IS THAT ALL YOU HAVE TO SAY?
WHEN ARE WE DOING THIS DEAL SO I CAN GET OFF THIS ROCKING TUB AND ON WITH MY LIFE?!
I HAVEN'T STOPPED THROWING UP SINCE WE LEFT FRANCE!
AMERICAN ACCENT.
WHAT'S YOUR RUSH, GOOD-LOOKING? >TEEHEE<
GENERAL STARODOUB SENT ME DOWN HERE TO MAKE THE LAST FEW HOURS FLY BY!
OH? OH! WELL...
...THAT'S DIFFERENT THEN...
THE GENERAL CAN'T STOP TALKING ABOUT YOU UPSTAIRS!
WHAT MAKES YOU SO IMPORTANT?
WHAT'S IN THE CASE? IS IT DRUGS? IT'S DRUGS, ISN'T IT?
I HOPE SO! I LOVE DRUGS!
>TEEHEE<

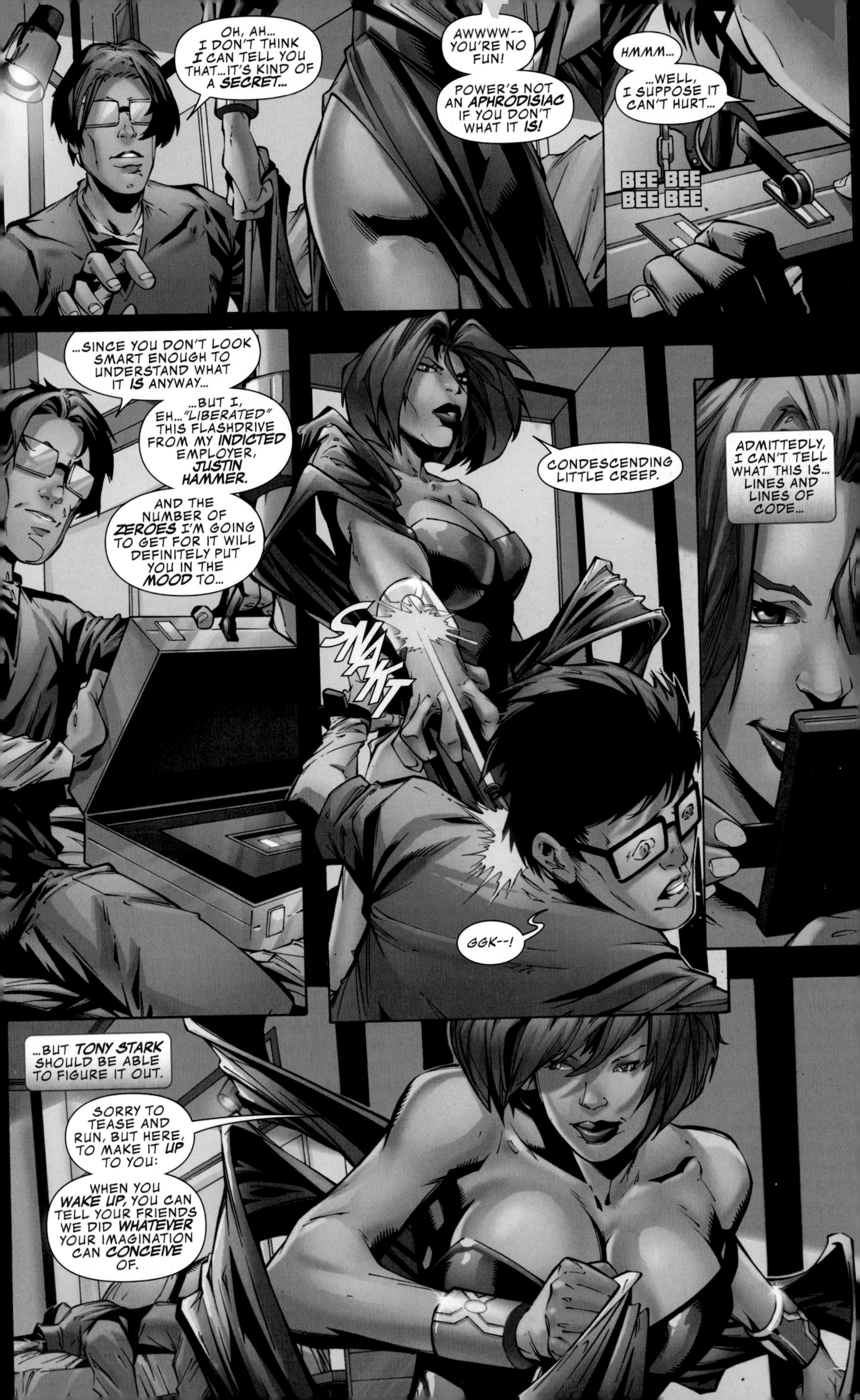

OH, AH... I DON'T THINK I CAN TELL YOU THAT...IT'S KIND OF A SECRET...
AWWWW-- YOU'RE NO FUN!
POWER'S NOT AN APHRODISIAC IF YOU DON'T WHAT IT IS!
HMMM...
...WELL, I SUPPOSE IT CAN'T HURT...
BEE BEE BEE BEE
...SINCE YOU DON'T LOOK SMART ENOUGH TO UNDERSTAND WHAT IT IS ANYWAY...
...BUT I, EH..."LIBERATED" THIS FLASHDRIVE FROM MY INDICTED EMPLOYER, JUSTIN HAMMER.
AND THE NUMBER OF ZEROES I'M GOING TO GET FOR IT WILL DEFINITELY PUT YOU IN THE MOOD TO...
CONDESCENDING LITTLE CREEP.
SNAKT
GGK--!
ADMITTEDLY, I CAN'T TELL WHAT THIS IS... LINES AND LINES OF CODE...
...BUT TONY STARK SHOULD BE ABLE TO FIGURE IT OUT.
SORRY TO TEASE AND RUN, BUT HERE, TO MAKE IT UP TO YOU:
WHEN YOU WAKE UP, YOU CAN TELL YOUR FRIENDS WE DID WHATEVER YOUR IMAGINATION CAN CONCEIVE OF.

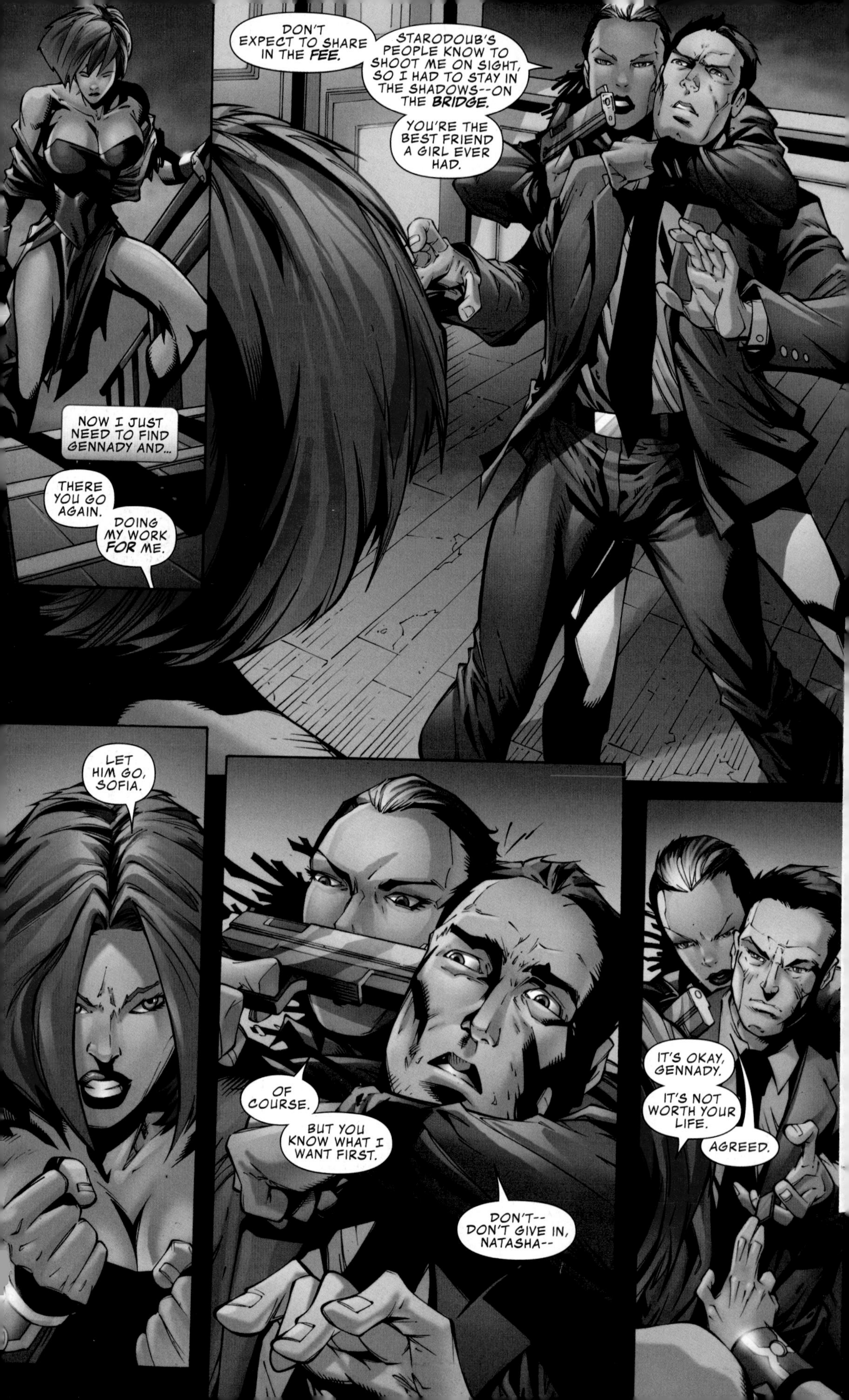
DON'T EXPECT TO SHARE IN THE FEE.
STARODOUB'S PEOPLE KNOW TO SHOOT ME ON SIGHT, SO I HAD TO STAY IN THE SHADOWS--ON THE BRIDGE.
YOU'RE THE BEST FRIEND A GIRL EVER HAD.
NOW I JUST NEED TO FIND GENNADY AND...
THERE YOU GO AGAIN.
DOING MY WORK FOR ME.
LET HIM GO, SOFIA.
OF COURSE.
BUT YOU KNOW WHAT I WANT FIRST.
DON'T-- DON'T GIVE IN, NATASHA--
IT'S OKAY, GENNADY.
IT'S NOT WORTH YOUR LIFE.
AGREED.

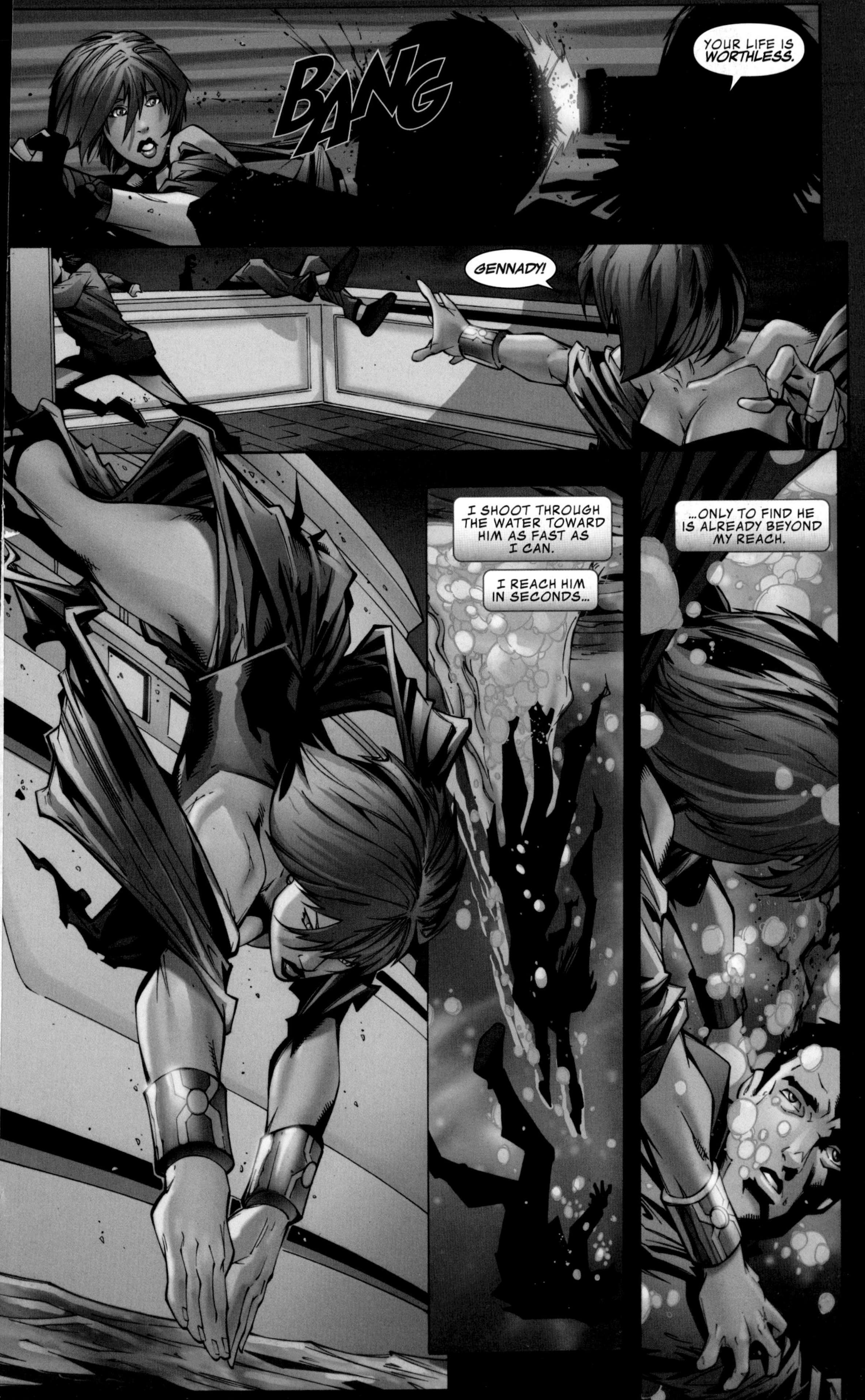
BANG
YOUR LIFE IS WORTHLESS.
GENNADY!
I SHOOT THROUGH THE WATER TOWARD HIM AS FAST AS I CAN.
I REACH HIM IN SECONDS...
...ONLY TO FIND HE IS ALREADY BEYOND MY REACH.

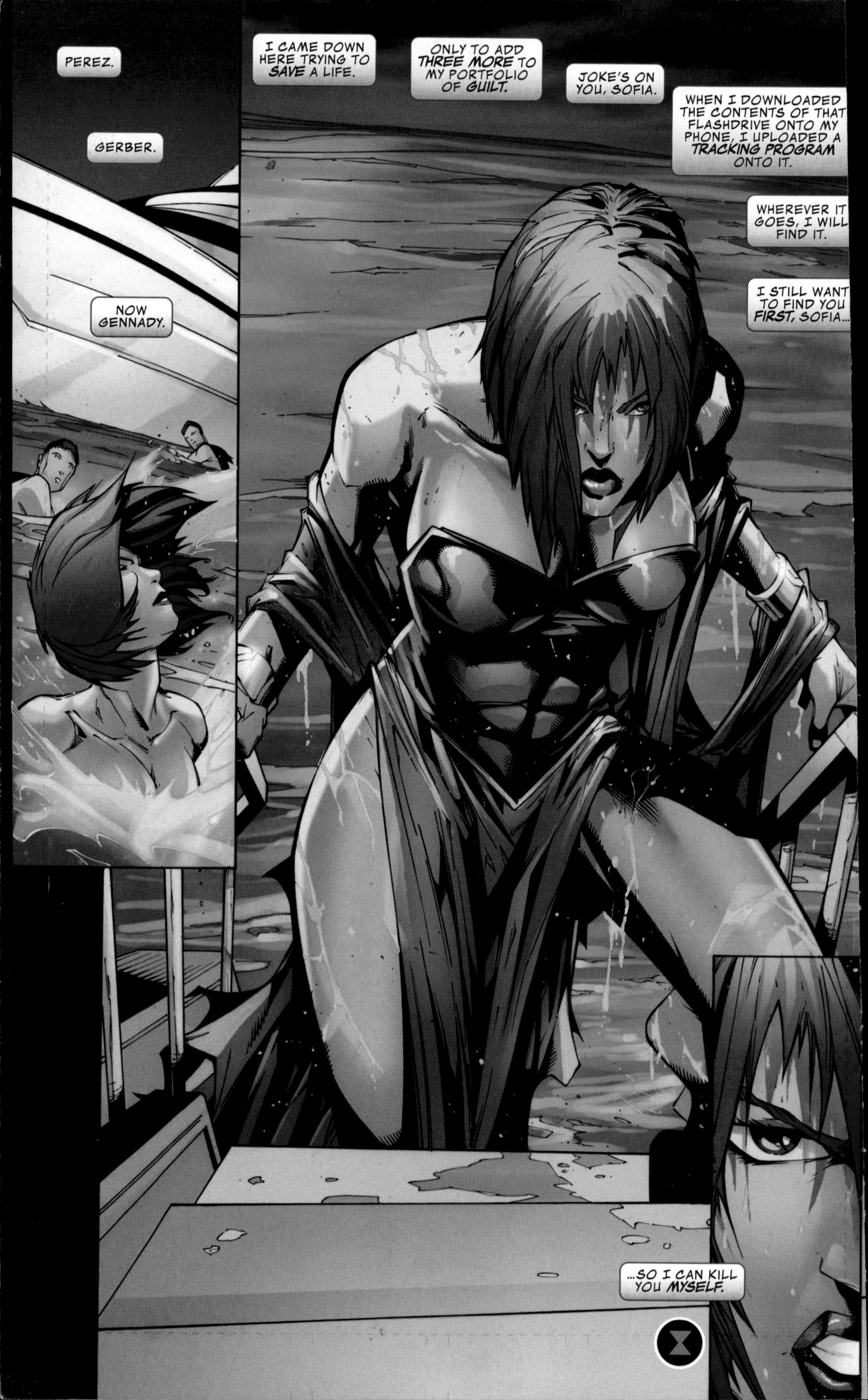
PEREZ.
GERBER.
NOW GENNADY.
I CAME DOWN HERE TRYING TO SAVE A LIFE.
ONLY TO ADD THREE MORE TO MY PORTFOLIO OF GUILT.
JOKE'S ON YOU, SOFIA.
WHEN I DOWNLOADED THE CONTENTS OF THAT FLASHDRIVE ONTO MY PHONE, I UPLOADED A TRACKING PROGRAM ONTO IT.
WHEREVER IT GOES, I WILL FIND IT.
I STILL WANT TO FIND YOU FIRST, SOFIA...
...SO I CAN KILL YOU MYSELF.

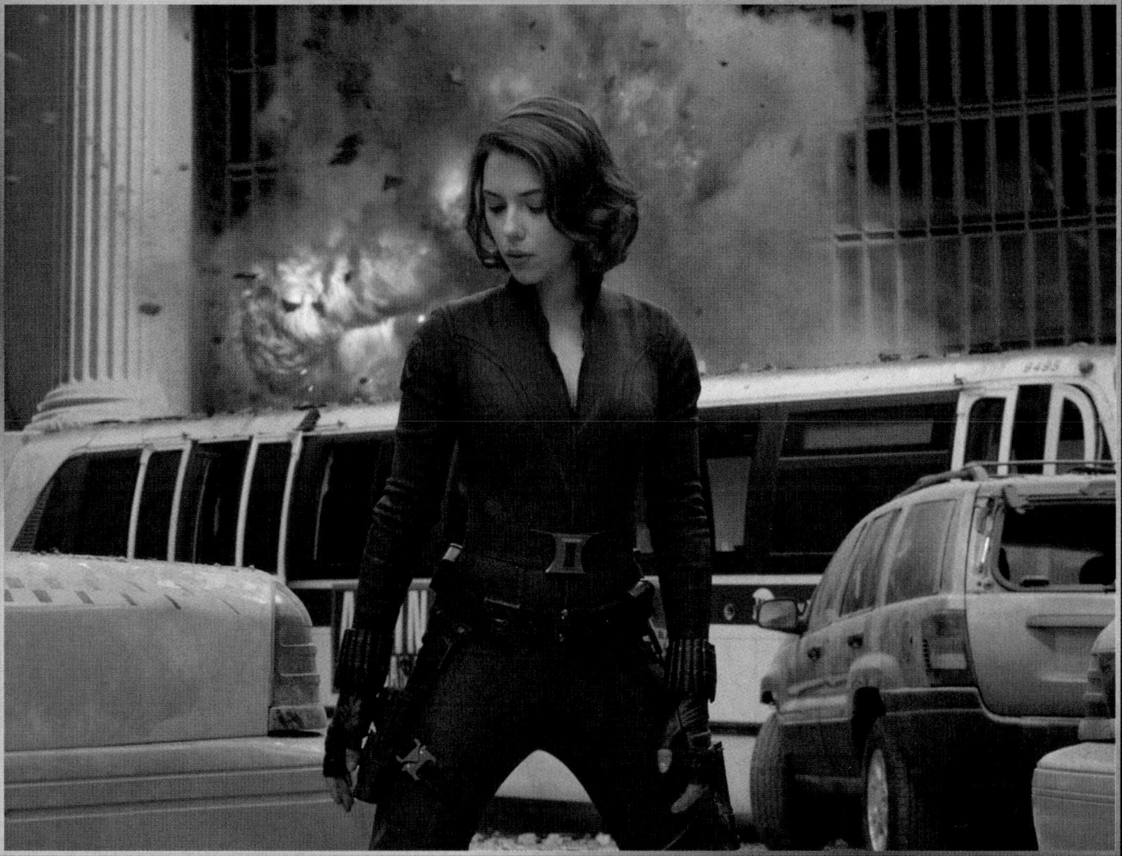

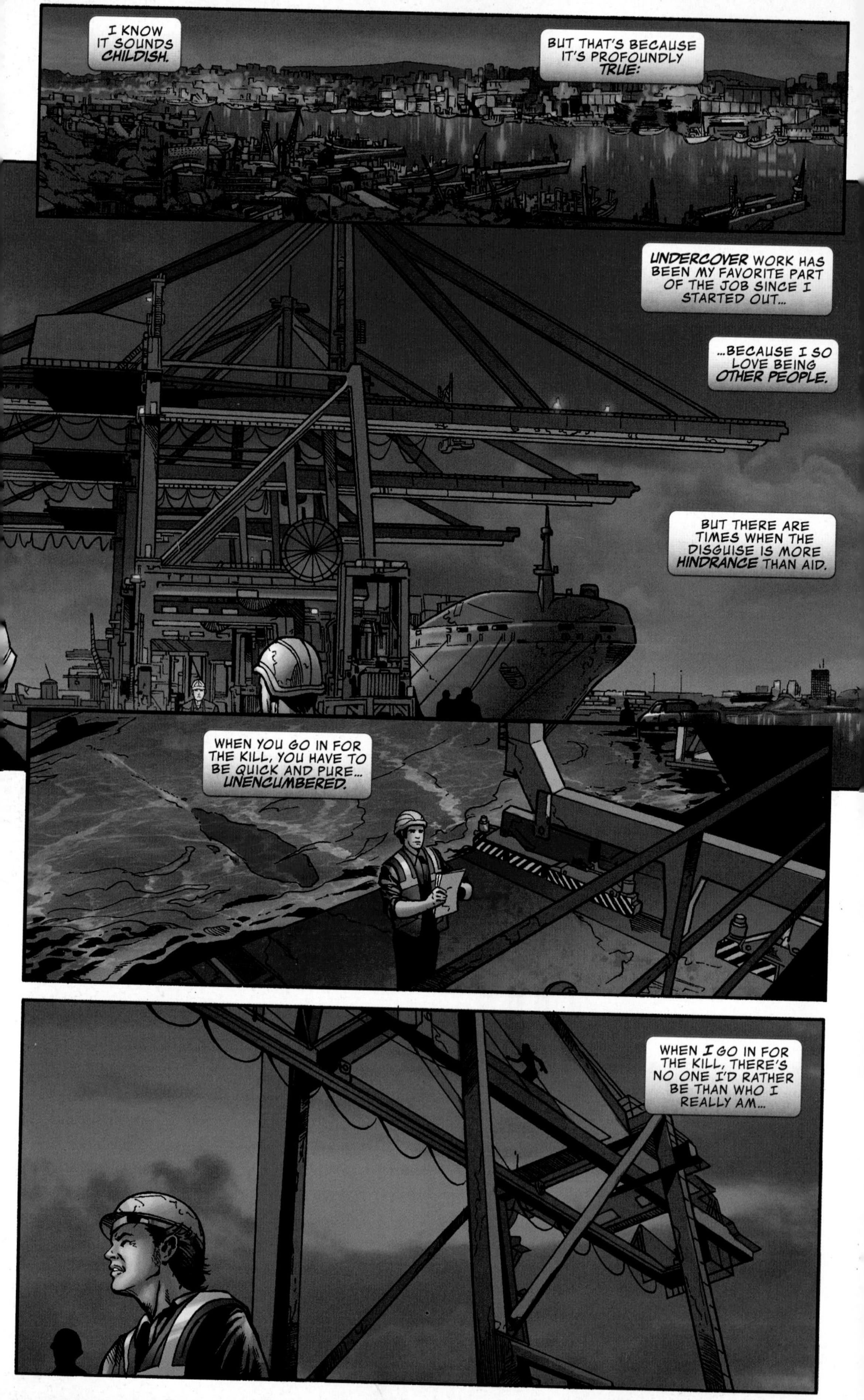
I KNOW IT SOUNDS CHILDISH.
BUT THAT'S BECAUSE IT'S PROFOUNDLY TRUE:
UNDERCOVER WORK HAS BEEN MY FAVORITE PART OF THE JOB SINCE I STARTED OUT...
...BECAUSE I SO LOVE BEING OTHER PEOPLE.
BUT THERE ARE TIMES WHEN THE DISGUISE IS MORE HINDRANCE THAN AID.
WHEN YOU GO IN FOR THE KILL, YOU HAVE TO BE QUICK AND PURE... UNENCUMBERED.
WHEN I GO IN FOR THE KILL, THERE'S NO ONE I'D RATHER BE THAN WHO I REALLY AM...

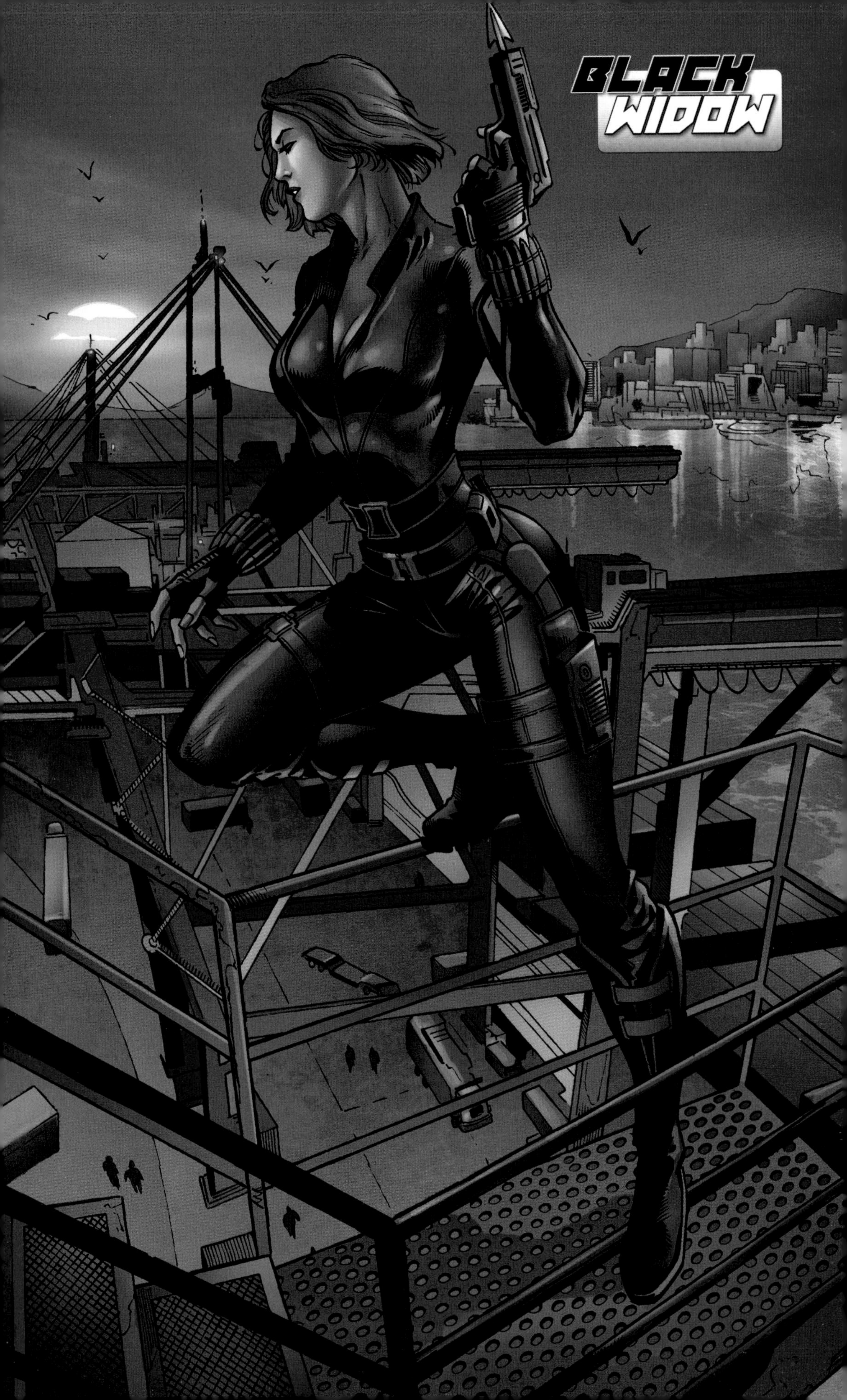
BLACK WIDOW

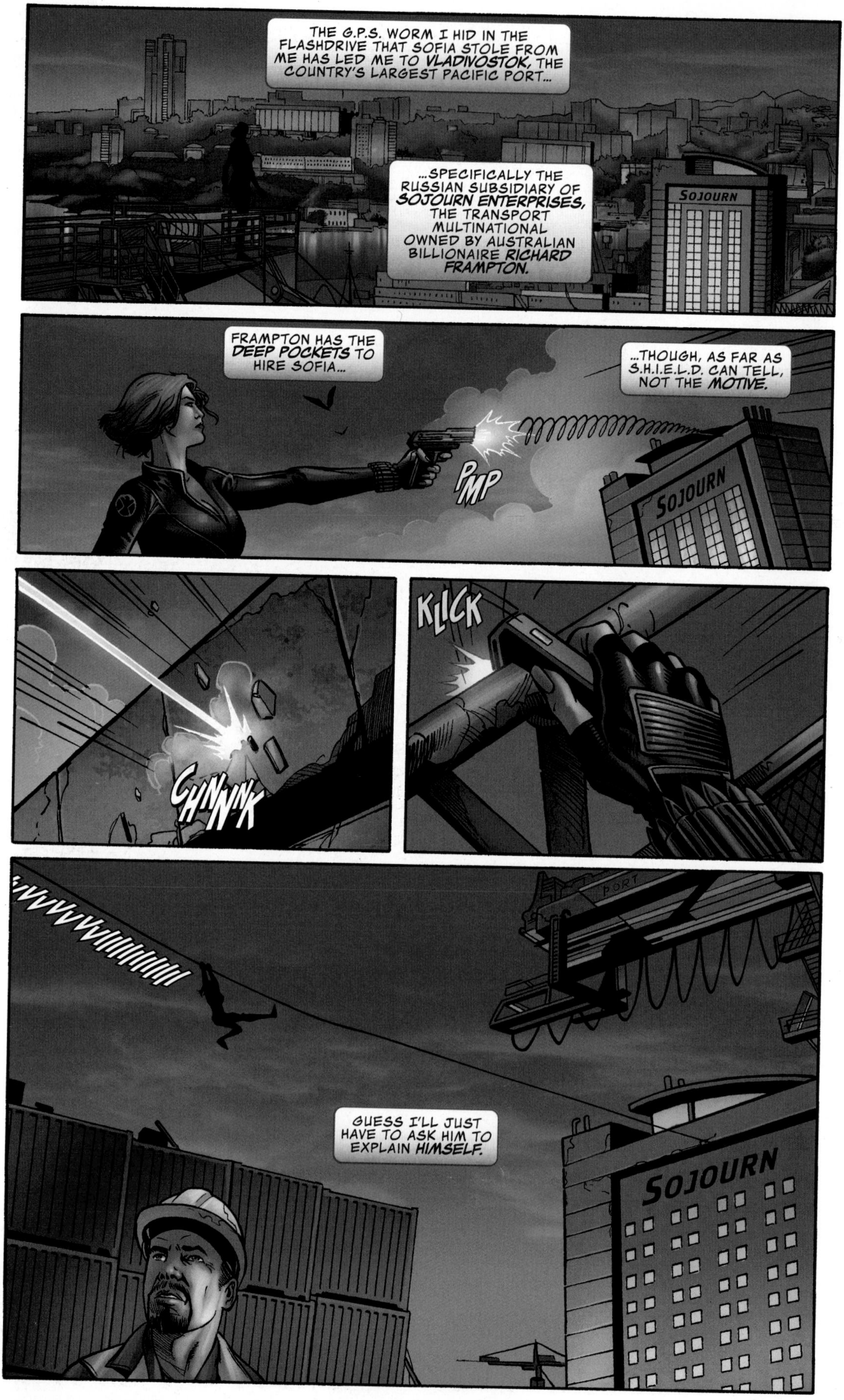
THE G.P.S. WORM I HID IN THE FLASHDRIVE THAT SOFIA STOLE FROM ME HAS LED ME TO VLADIVOSTOK, THE COUNTRY'S LARGEST PACIFIC PORT...
...SPECIFICALLY THE RUSSIAN SUBSIDIARY OF SOJOURN ENTERPRISES, THE TRANSPORT MULTINATIONAL OWNED BY AUSTRALIAN BILLIONAIRE RICHARD FRAMPTON.
SOJOURN
FRAMPTON HAS THE DEEP POCKETS TO HIRE SOFIA...
...THOUGH, AS FAR AS S.H.I.E.L.D. CAN TELL, NOT THE MOTIVE.
PMP
SOJOURN
CHNNNK
KLICK
PORT
GUESS I'LL JUST HAVE TO ASK HIM TO EXPLAIN HIMSELF.
SOJOURN

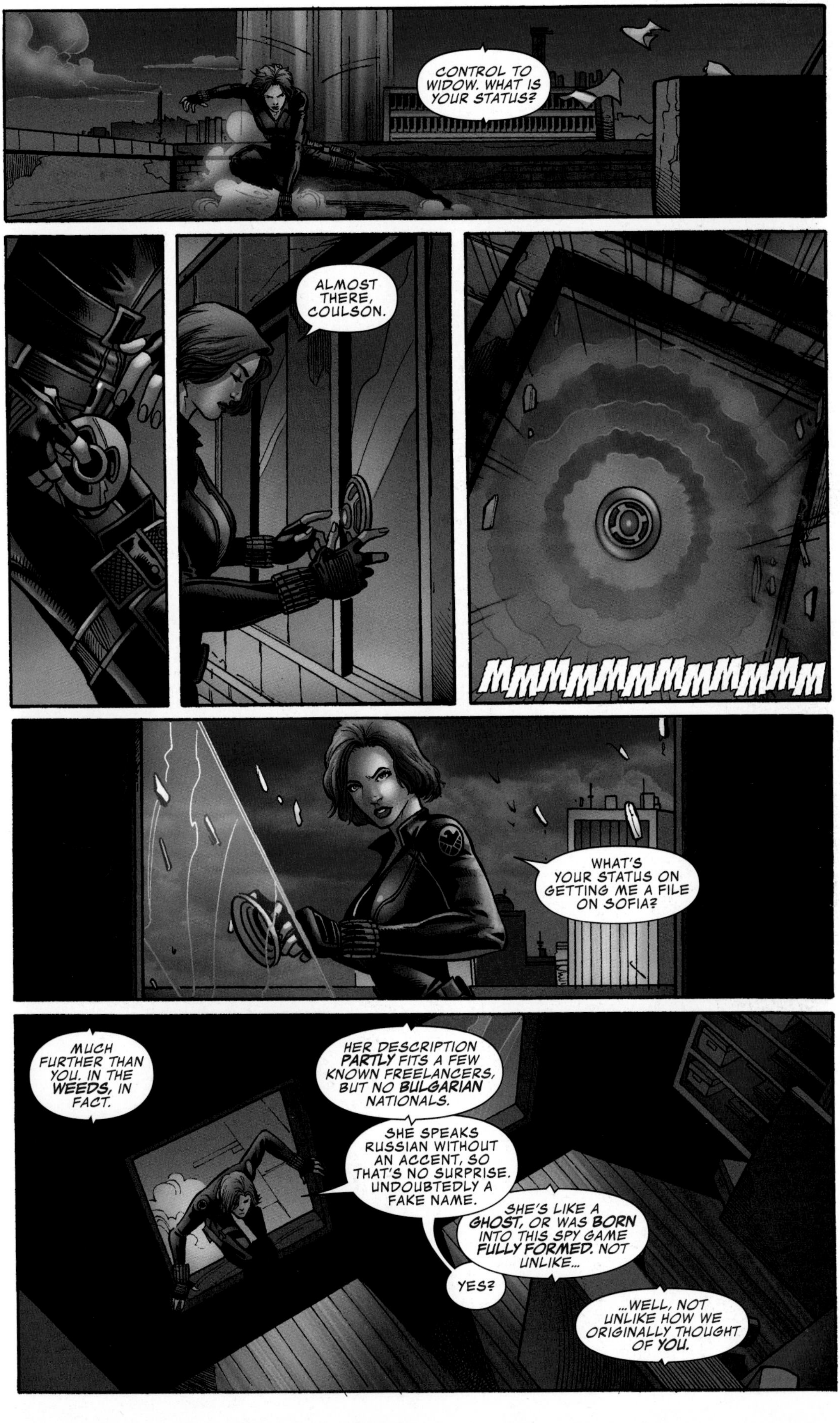
CONTROL TO WIDOW. WHAT IS YOUR STATUS?
ALMOST THERE, COULSON.
MMMMMMMMMMMMMM
WHAT'S YOUR STATUS ON GETTING ME A FILE ON SOFIA?
MUCH FURTHER THAN YOU. IN THE WEEDS, IN FACT.
HER DESCRIPTION PARTLY FITS A FEW KNOWN FREELANCERS, BUT NO BULGARIAN NATIONALS.
SHE SPEAKS RUSSIAN WITHOUT AN ACCENT, SO THAT'S NO SURPRISE. UNDOUBTEDLY A FAKE NAME.
SHE'S LIKE A GHOST, OR WAS BORN INTO THIS SPY GAME FULLY FORMED. NOT UNLIKE...
YES?
...WELL, NOT UNLIKE HOW WE ORIGINALLY THOUGHT OF YOU.

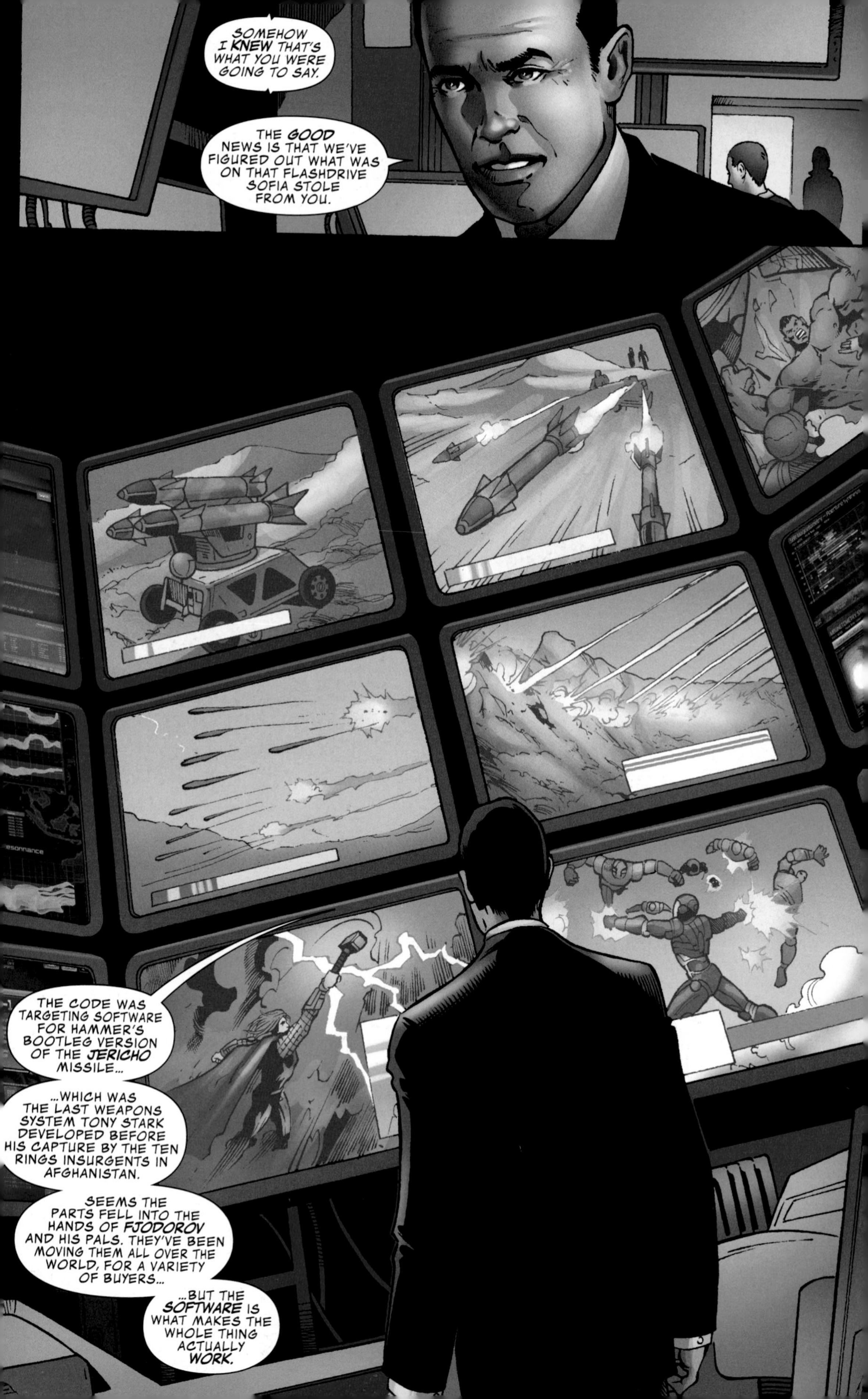
SOMEHOW I KNEW THAT'S WHAT YOU WERE GOING TO SAY.
THE GOOD NEWS IS THAT WE'VE FIGURED OUT WHAT WAS ON THAT FLASHDRIVE SOFIA STOLE FROM YOU.
THE CODE WAS TARGETING SOFTWARE FOR HAMMER'S BOOTLEG VERSION OF THE JERICHO MISSILE...
...WHICH WAS THE LAST WEAPONS SYSTEM TONY STARK DEVELOPED BEFORE HIS CAPTURE BY THE TEN RINGS INSURGENTS IN AFGHANISTAN.
SEEMS THE PARTS FELL INTO THE HANDS OF FJODOROV AND HIS PALS. THEY'VE BEEN MOVING THEM ALL OVER THE WORLD, FOR A VARIETY OF BUYERS...
...BUT THE SOFTWARE IS WHAT MAKES THE WHOLE THING ACTUALLY WORK.

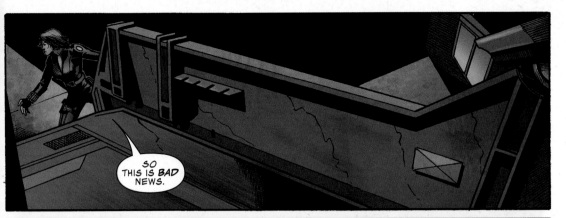

SO THIS IS *BAD* NEWS.

ER...FOR THE *WORLD*, SURE.

BUT AT LEAST *WE* KNOW WHAT THE BAD GUYS ARE AFTER.

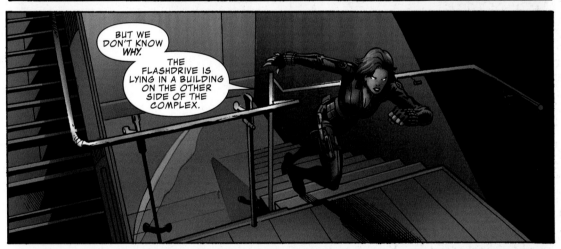

BUT WE DON'T KNOW *WHY*.

THE FLASHDRIVE IS LYING IN A BUILDING ON THE OTHER SIDE OF THE COMPLEX.

HOPEFULLY WE'LL FINALLY FIND SOME ANSWERS THERE.

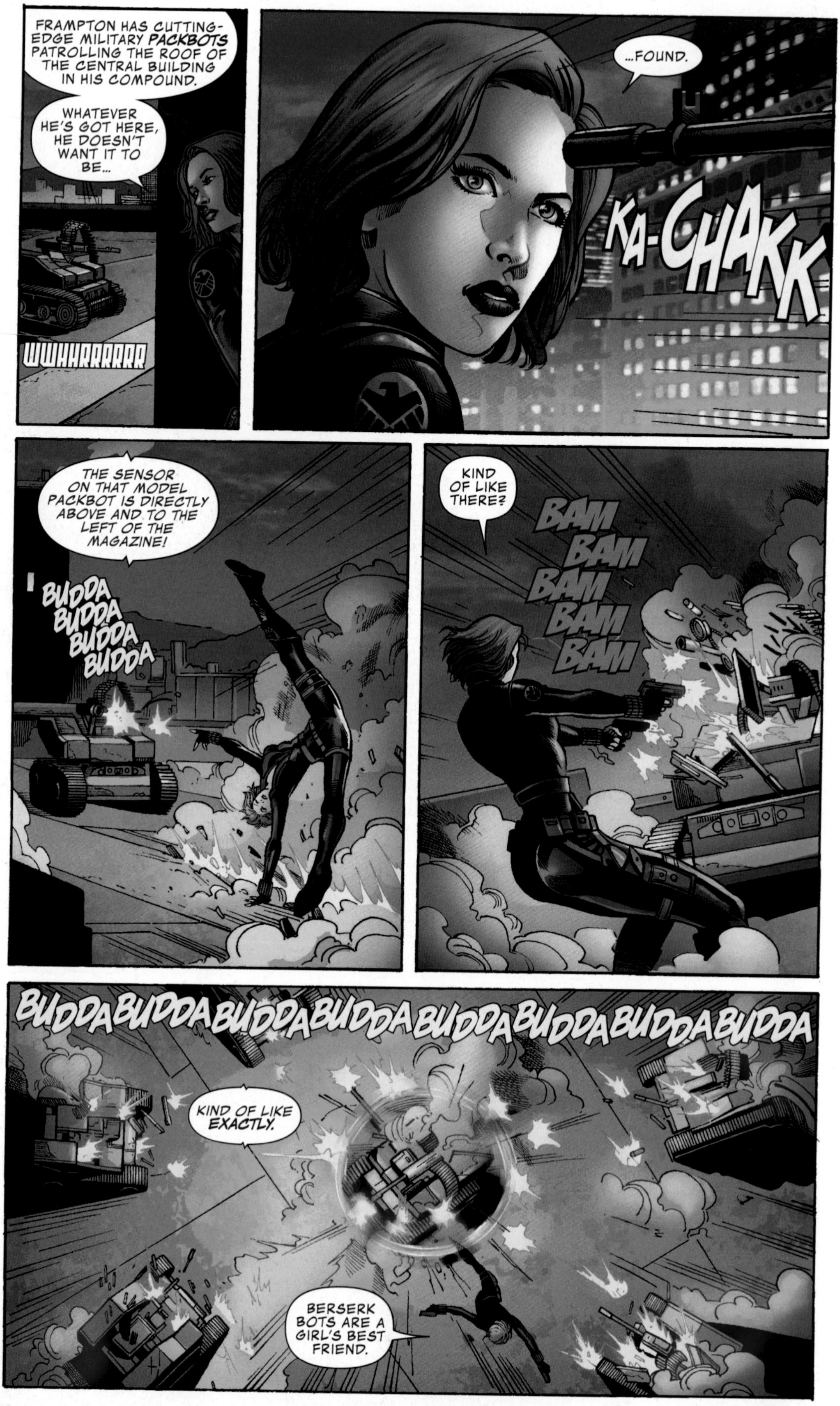
FRAMPTON HAS CUTTING-EDGE MILITARY PACKBOTS PATROLLING THE ROOF OF THE CENTRAL BUILDING IN HIS COMPOUND.
WHATEVER HE'S GOT HERE, HE DOESN'T WANT IT TO BE...
WWHHRRRRRR
...FOUND.
KA-CHAKK
THE SENSOR ON THAT MODEL PACKBOT IS DIRECTLY ABOVE AND TO THE LEFT OF THE MAGAZINE!
BUDDA BUDDA BUDDA BUDDA
KIND OF LIKE THERE?
BAM BAM BAM BAM BAM
BUDDA BUDDA BUDDA BUDDA BUDDA BUDDA BUDDA BUDDA
KIND OF LIKE EXACTLY.
BERSERK BOTS ARE A GIRL'S BEST FRIEND.

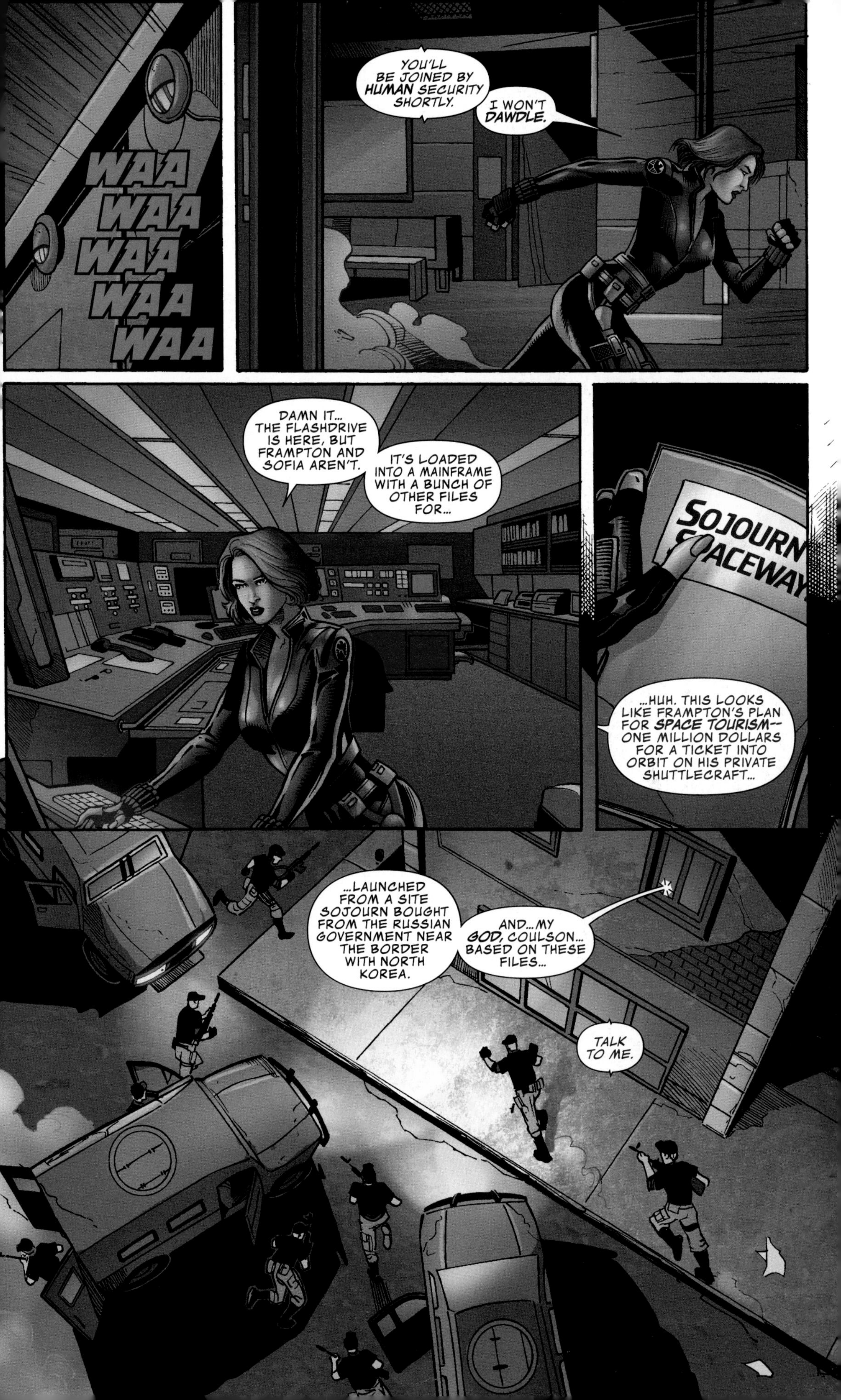
WAA WAA WAA WAA WAA
YOU'LL BE JOINED BY HUMAN SECURITY SHORTLY.
I WON'T DAWDLE.
DAMN IT... THE FLASHDRIVE IS HERE, BUT FRAMPTON AND SOFIA AREN'T.
IT'S LOADED INTO A MAINFRAME WITH A BUNCH OF OTHER FILES FOR...
...HUH. THIS LOOKS LIKE FRAMPTON'S PLAN FOR SPACE TOURISM--ONE MILLION DOLLARS FOR A TICKET INTO ORBIT ON HIS PRIVATE SHUTTLECRAFT...
...LAUNCHED FROM A SITE SOJOURN BOUGHT FROM THE RUSSIAN GOVERNMENT NEAR THE BORDER WITH NORTH KOREA.
AND...MY GOD, COULSON... BASED ON THESE FILES...
TALK TO ME.

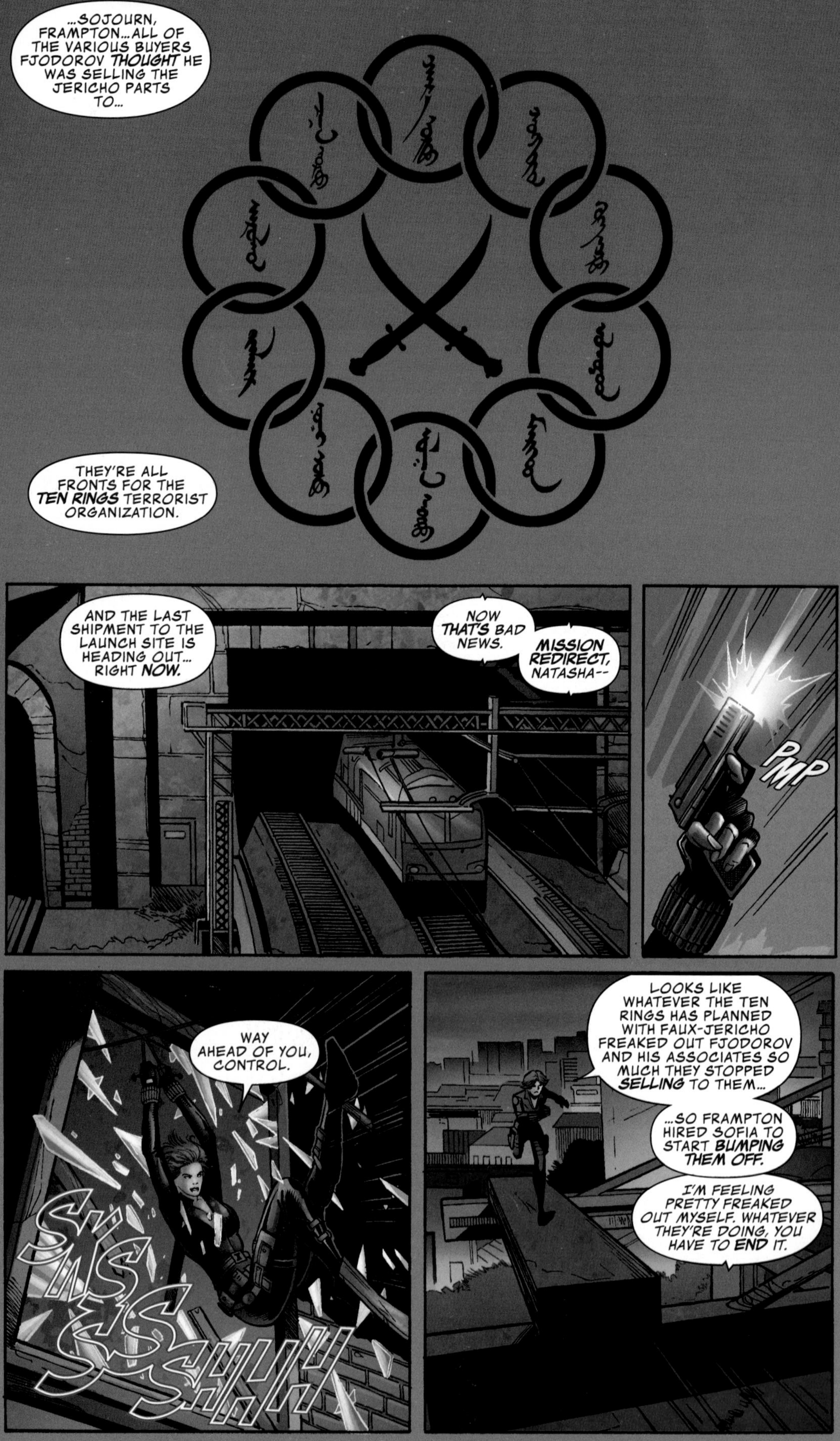
...SOJOURN, FRAMPTON...ALL OF THE VARIOUS BUYERS FJODOROV THOUGHT HE WAS SELLING THE JERICHO PARTS TO...
THEY'RE ALL FRONTS FOR THE TEN RINGS TERRORIST ORGANIZATION.
AND THE LAST SHIPMENT TO THE LAUNCH SITE IS HEADING OUT... RIGHT NOW.
NOW THAT'S BAD NEWS.
MISSION REDIRECT, NATASHA--
PMP
WAY AHEAD OF YOU, CONTROL.
SHSSHHH
LOOKS LIKE WHATEVER THE TEN RINGS HAS PLANNED WITH FAUX-JERICHO FREAKED OUT FJODOROV AND HIS ASSOCIATES SO MUCH THEY STOPPED SELLING TO THEM...
...SO FRAMPTON HIRED SOFIA TO START BUMPING THEM OFF.
I'M FEELING PRETTY FREAKED OUT MYSELF. WHATEVER THEY'RE DOING, YOU HAVE TO END IT.

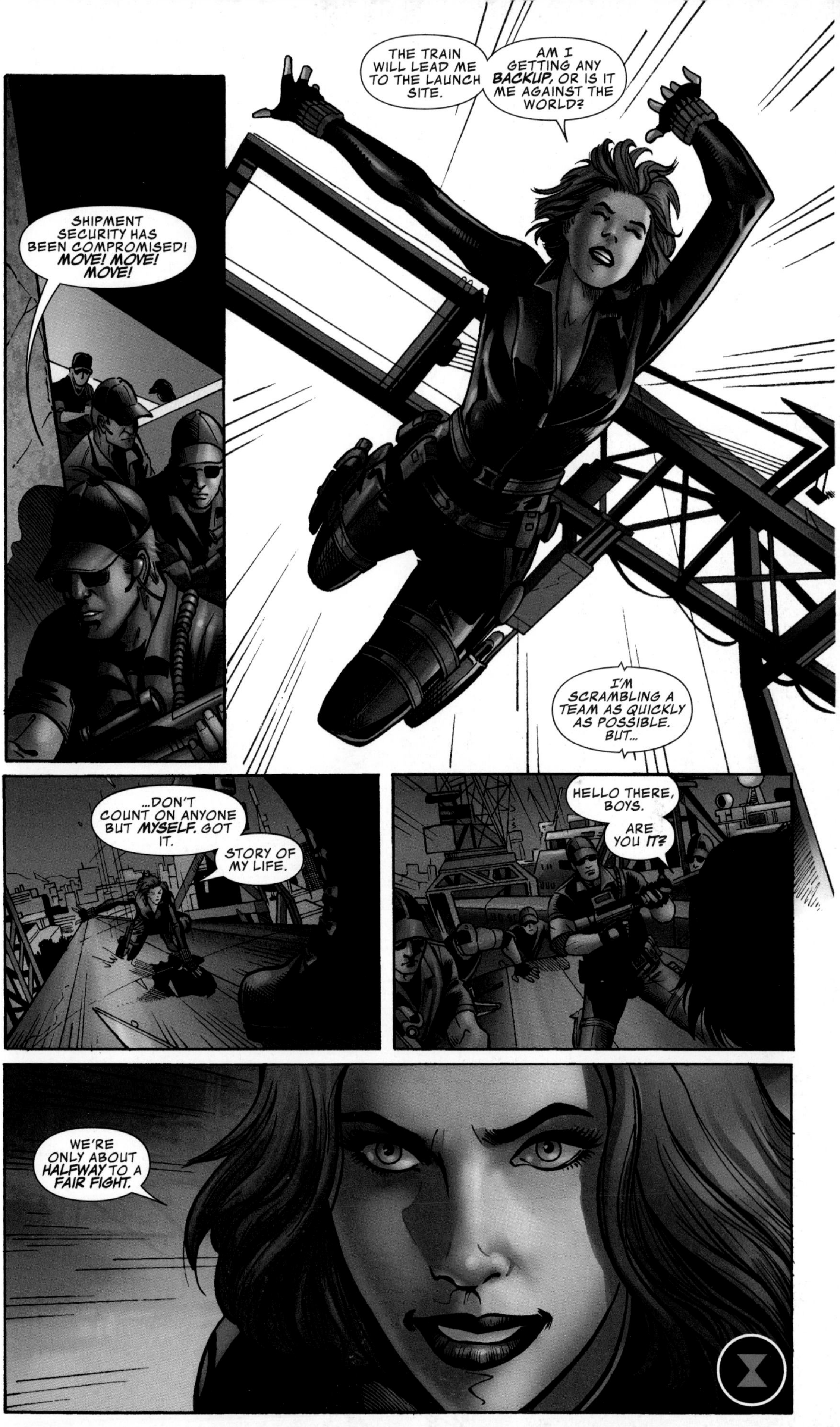
SHIPMENT SECURITY HAS BEEN COMPROMISED! MOVE! MOVE! MOVE!
THE TRAIN WILL LEAD ME TO THE LAUNCH SITE.
AM I GETTING ANY BACKUP, OR IS IT ME AGAINST THE WORLD?
I'M SCRAMBLING A TEAM AS QUICKLY AS POSSIBLE. BUT...
...DON'T COUNT ON ANYONE BUT MYSELF. GOT IT.
STORY OF MY LIFE.
HELLO THERE, BOYS.
ARE YOU IT?
WE'RE ONLY ABOUT HALFWAY TO A FAIR FIGHT.

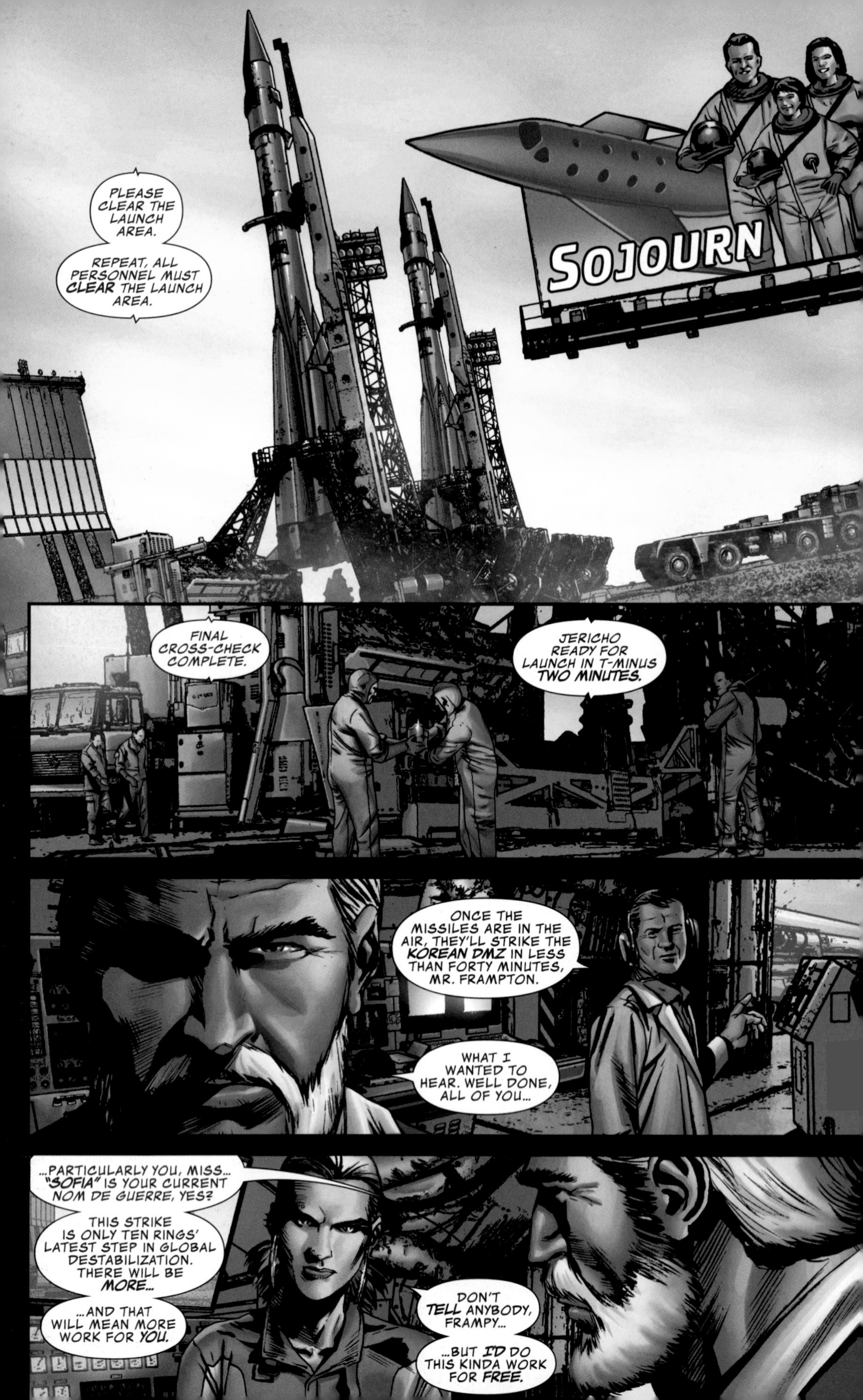
PLEASE CLEAR THE LAUNCH AREA.
REPEAT, ALL PERSONNEL MUST CLEAR THE LAUNCH AREA.
SOJOURN
FINAL CROSS-CHECK COMPLETE.
JERICHO READY FOR LAUNCH IN T-MINUS TWO MINUTES.
ONCE THE MISSILES ARE IN THE AIR, THEY'LL STRIKE THE KOREAN DMZ IN LESS THAN FORTY MINUTES, MR. FRAMPTON.
WHAT I WANTED TO HEAR. WELL DONE, ALL OF YOU...
...PARTICULARLY YOU, MISS... "SOFIA" IS YOUR CURRENT NOM DE GUERRE, YES?
THIS STRIKE IS ONLY TEN RINGS' LATEST STEP IN GLOBAL DESTABILIZATION. THERE WILL BE MORE...
...AND THAT WILL MEAN MORE WORK FOR YOU.
DON'T TELL ANYBODY, FRAMPY...
...BUT I'D DO THIS KINDA WORK FOR FREE.

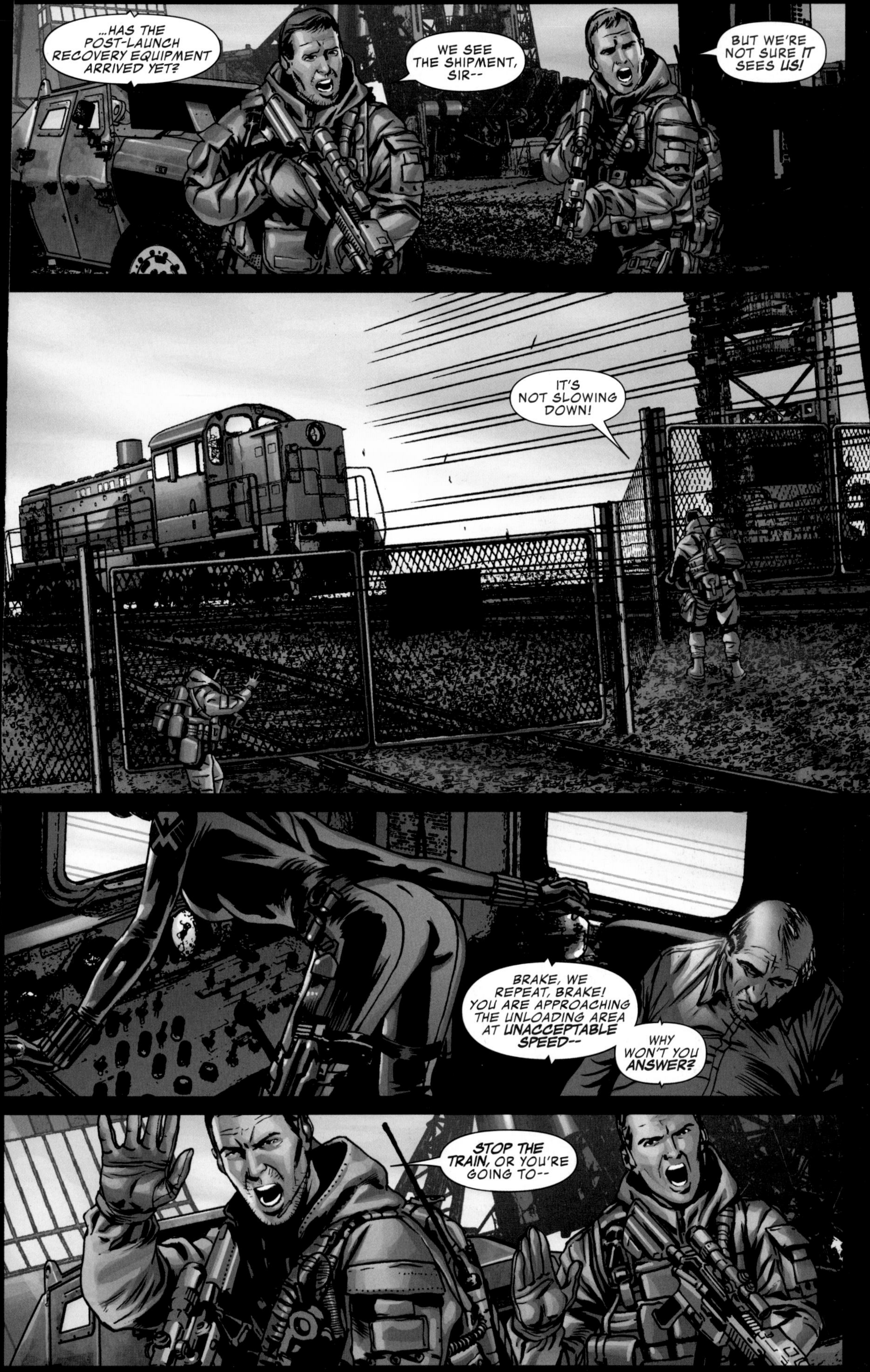
...HAS THE POST-LAUNCH RECOVERY EQUIPMENT ARRIVED YET?
WE SEE THE SHIPMENT, SIR--
BUT WE'RE NOT SURE IT SEES US!
IT'S NOT SLOWING DOWN!
BRAKE, WE REPEAT, BRAKE! YOU ARE APPROACHING THE UNLOADING AREA AT UNACCEPTABLE SPEED--
WHY WON'T YOU ANSWER?
STOP THE TRAIN, OR YOU'RE GOING TO--

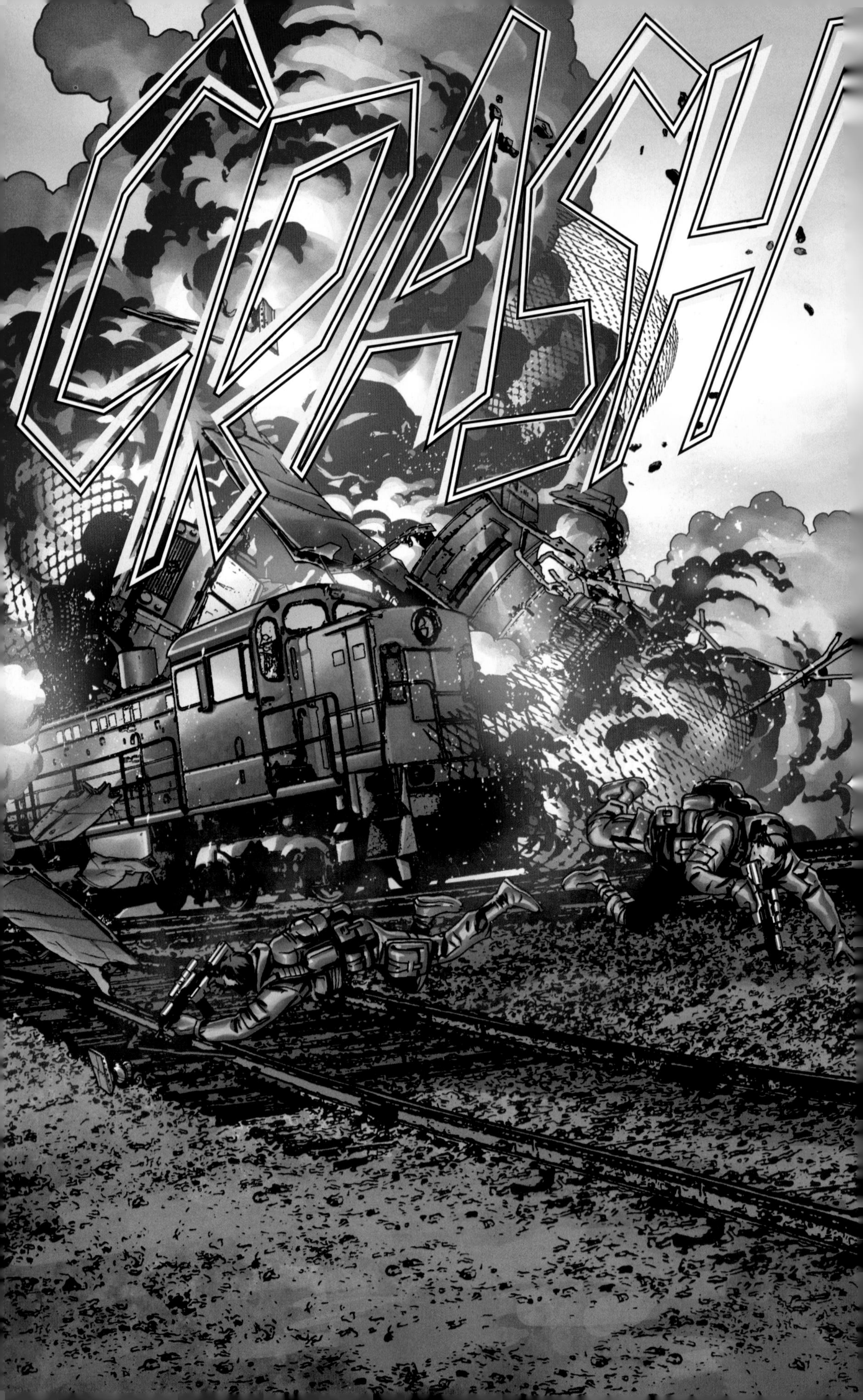
CRASH

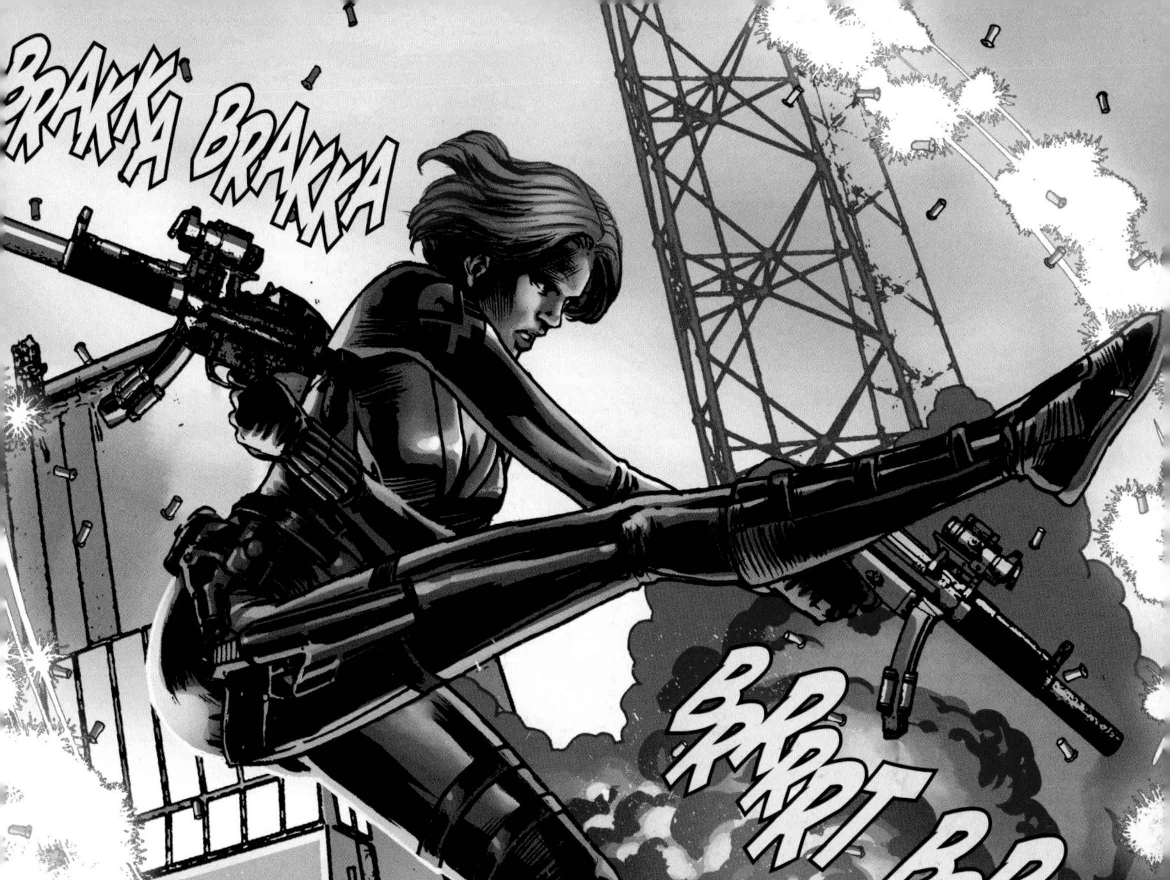
BRAKKA BRAKKA
BRRRT BRRRT
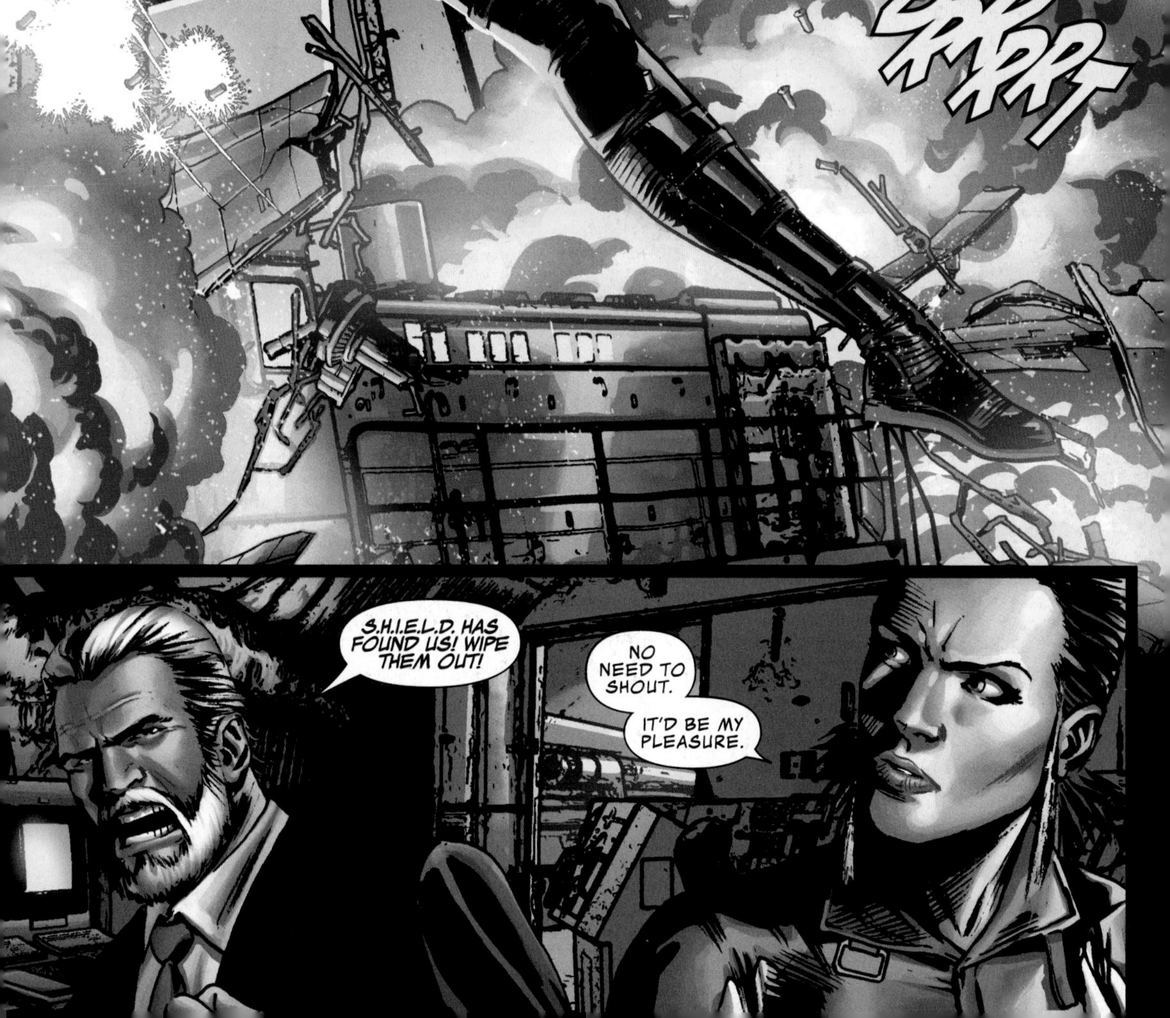
S.H.I.E.L.D. HAS FOUND US! WIPE THEM OUT!
NO NEED TO SHOUT.
IT'D BE MY PLEASURE.

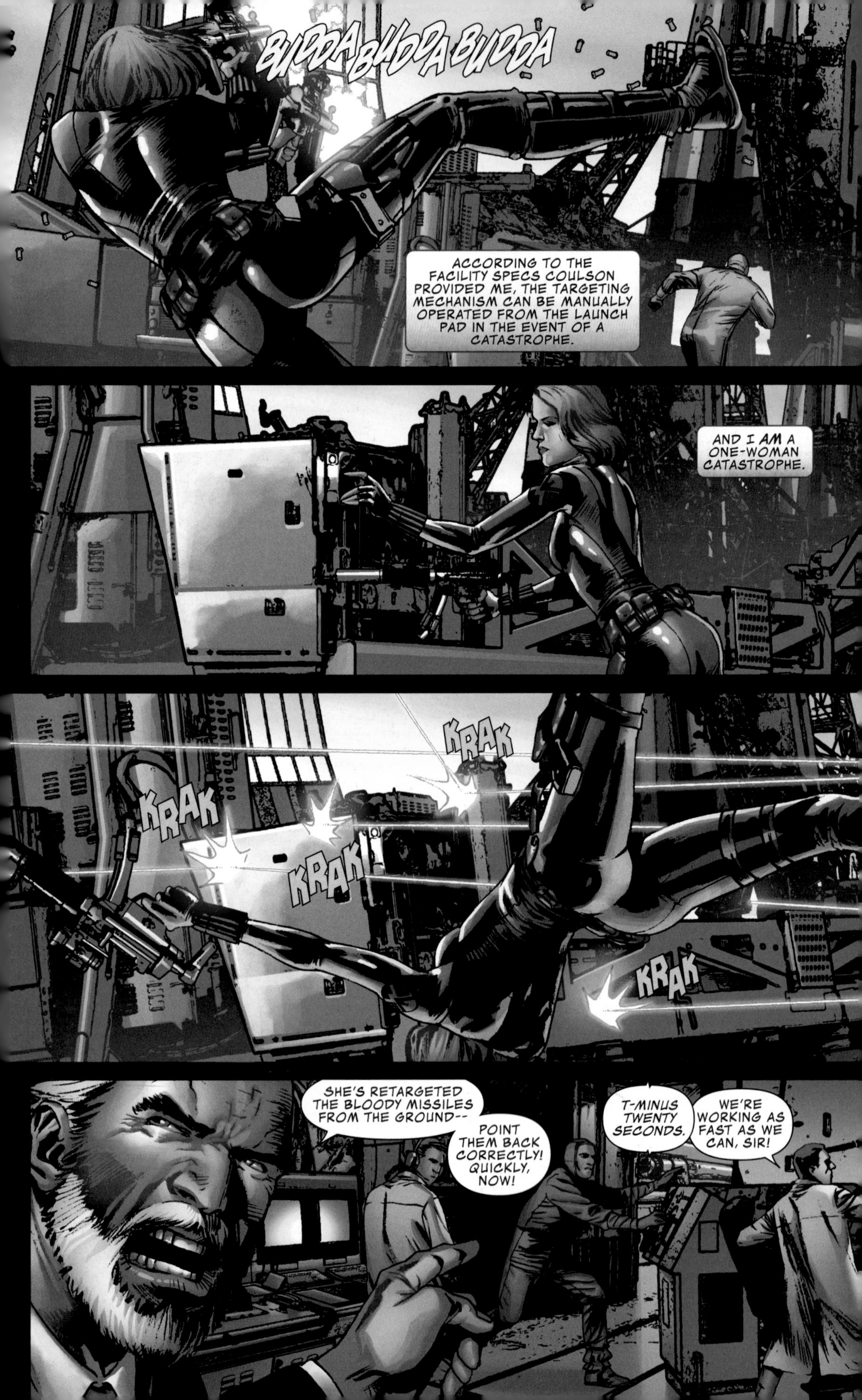
BUDDA BUDDA BUDDA
ACCORDING TO THE FACILITY SPECS COULSON PROVIDED ME, THE TARGETING MECHANISM CAN BE MANUALLY OPERATED FROM THE LAUNCH PAD IN THE EVENT OF A CATASTROPHE.
AND I *AM* A ONE-WOMAN CATASTROPHE.
KRAK
KRAK
KRAK
KRAK
SHE'S RETARGETED THE BLOODY MISSILES FROM THE GROUND--
POINT THEM BACK CORRECTLY! QUICKLY, NOW!
T-MINUS TWENTY SECONDS.
WE'RE WORKING AS FAST AS WE CAN, SIR!

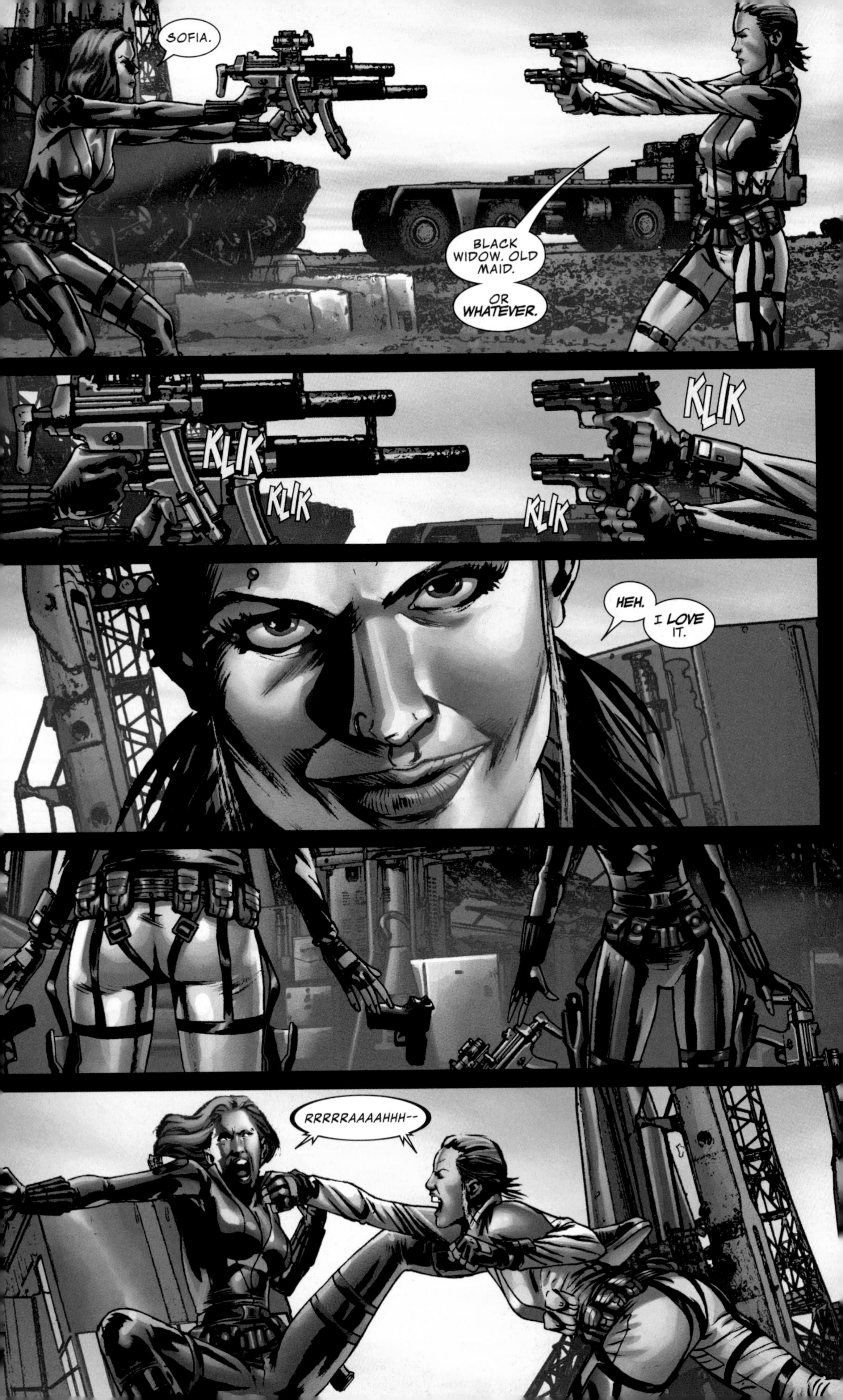
SOFIA.
BLACK WIDOW. OLD MAID.
OR WHATEVER.
KLIK
KLIK
KLIK
KLIK
HEH.
I LOVE IT.
RRRRRAAAAHHH--

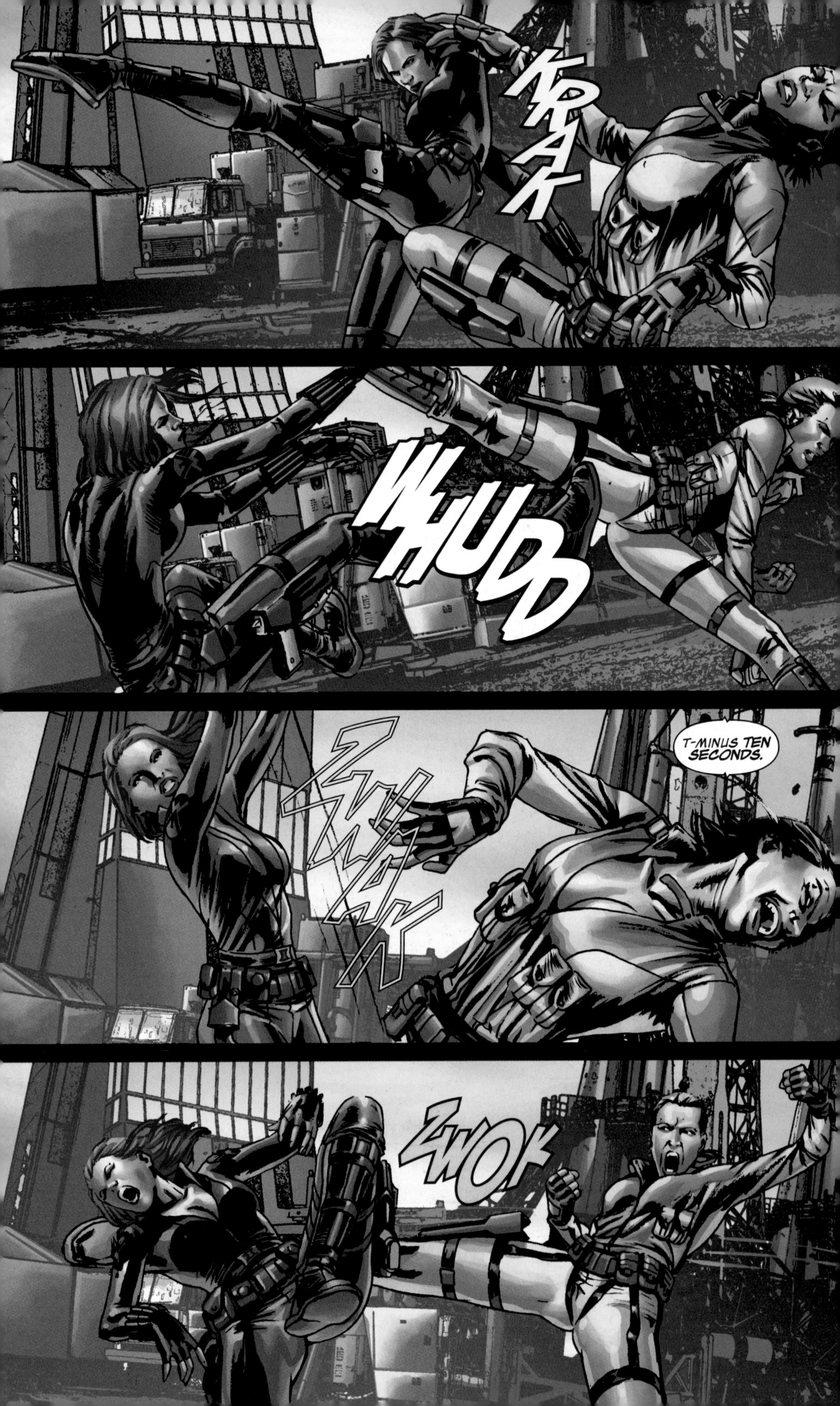
KRAK
WHUDD
T-MINUS TEN SECONDS.
ZWAK
ZWOK

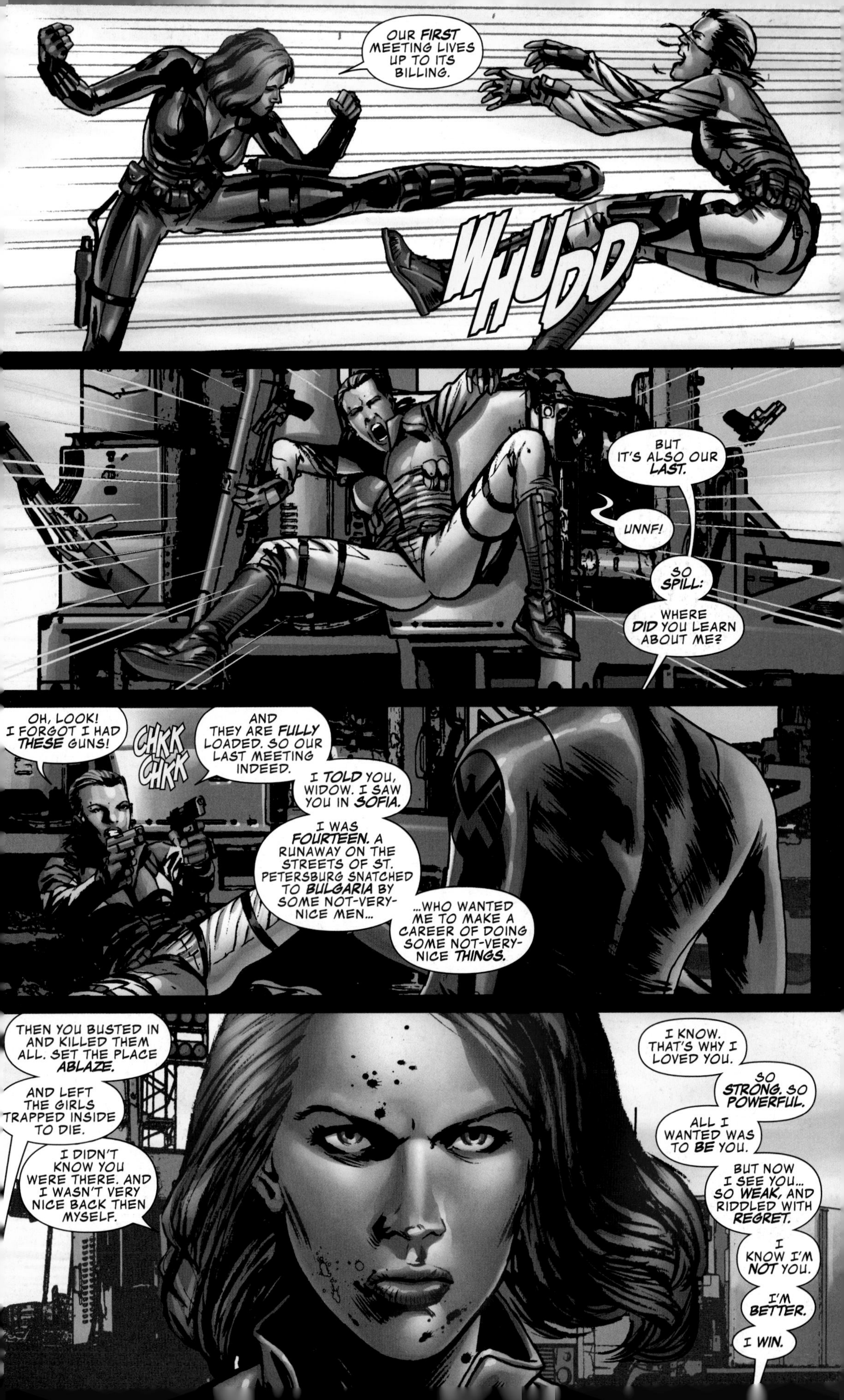
OUR FIRST MEETING LIVES UP TO ITS BILLING.
WHUDD
BUT IT'S ALSO OUR LAST.
UNNF!
SO SPILL:
WHERE DID YOU LEARN ABOUT ME?
OH, LOOK! I FORGOT I HAD THESE GUNS!
CHKK CHKK
AND THEY ARE FULLY LOADED. SO OUR LAST MEETING INDEED.
I TOLD YOU, WIDOW. I SAW YOU IN SOFIA.
I WAS FOURTEEN. A RUNAWAY ON THE STREETS OF ST. PETERSBURG SNATCHED TO BULGARIA BY SOME NOT-VERY-NICE MEN...
...WHO WANTED ME TO MAKE A CAREER OF DOING SOME NOT-VERY-NICE THINGS.
THEN YOU BUSTED IN AND KILLED THEM ALL. SET THE PLACE ABLAZE.
AND LEFT THE GIRLS TRAPPED INSIDE TO DIE.
I DIDN'T KNOW YOU WERE THERE. AND I WASN'T VERY NICE BACK THEN MYSELF.
I KNOW. THAT'S WHY I LOVED YOU.
SO STRONG. SO POWERFUL.
ALL I WANTED WAS TO BE YOU.
BUT NOW I SEE YOU... SO WEAK, AND RIDDLED WITH REGRET.
I KNOW I'M NOT YOU.
I'M BETTER.
I WIN.

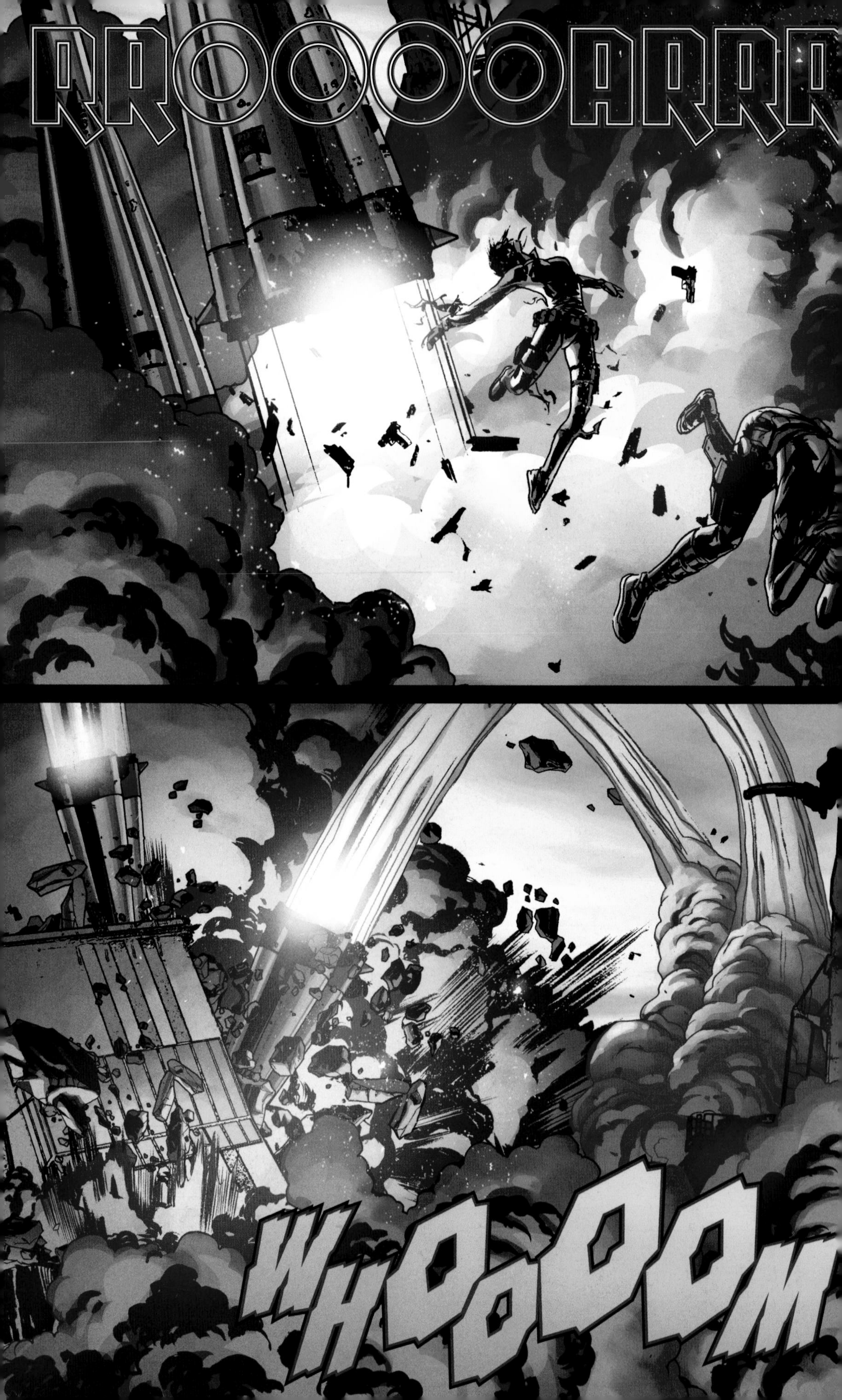
RROOOOARRR
WHOOOOM

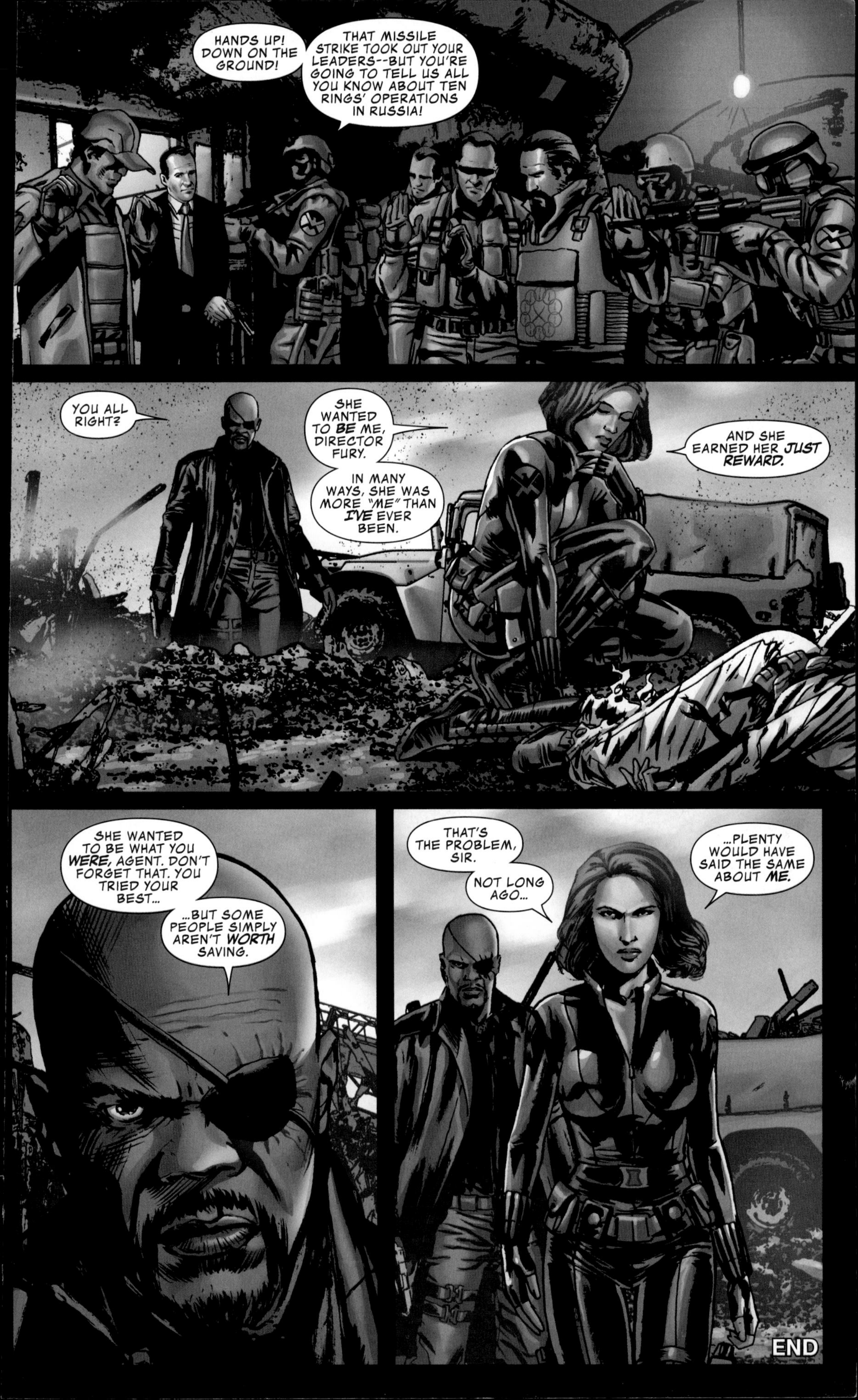
HANDS UP! DOWN ON THE GROUND!
THAT MISSILE STRIKE TOOK OUT YOUR LEADERS--BUT YOU'RE GOING TO TELL US ALL YOU KNOW ABOUT TEN RINGS' OPERATIONS IN RUSSIA!
YOU ALL RIGHT?
SHE WANTED TO BE ME, DIRECTOR FURY.
IN MANY WAYS, SHE WAS MORE "ME" THAN I'VE EVER BEEN.
AND SHE EARNED HER JUST REWARD.
SHE WANTED TO BE WHAT YOU WERE, AGENT. DON'T FORGET THAT. YOU TRIED YOUR BEST...
...BUT SOME PEOPLE SIMPLY AREN'T WORTH SAVING.
THAT'S THE PROBLEM, SIR.
NOT LONG AGO...
...PLENTY WOULD HAVE SAID THE SAME ABOUT ME.
END

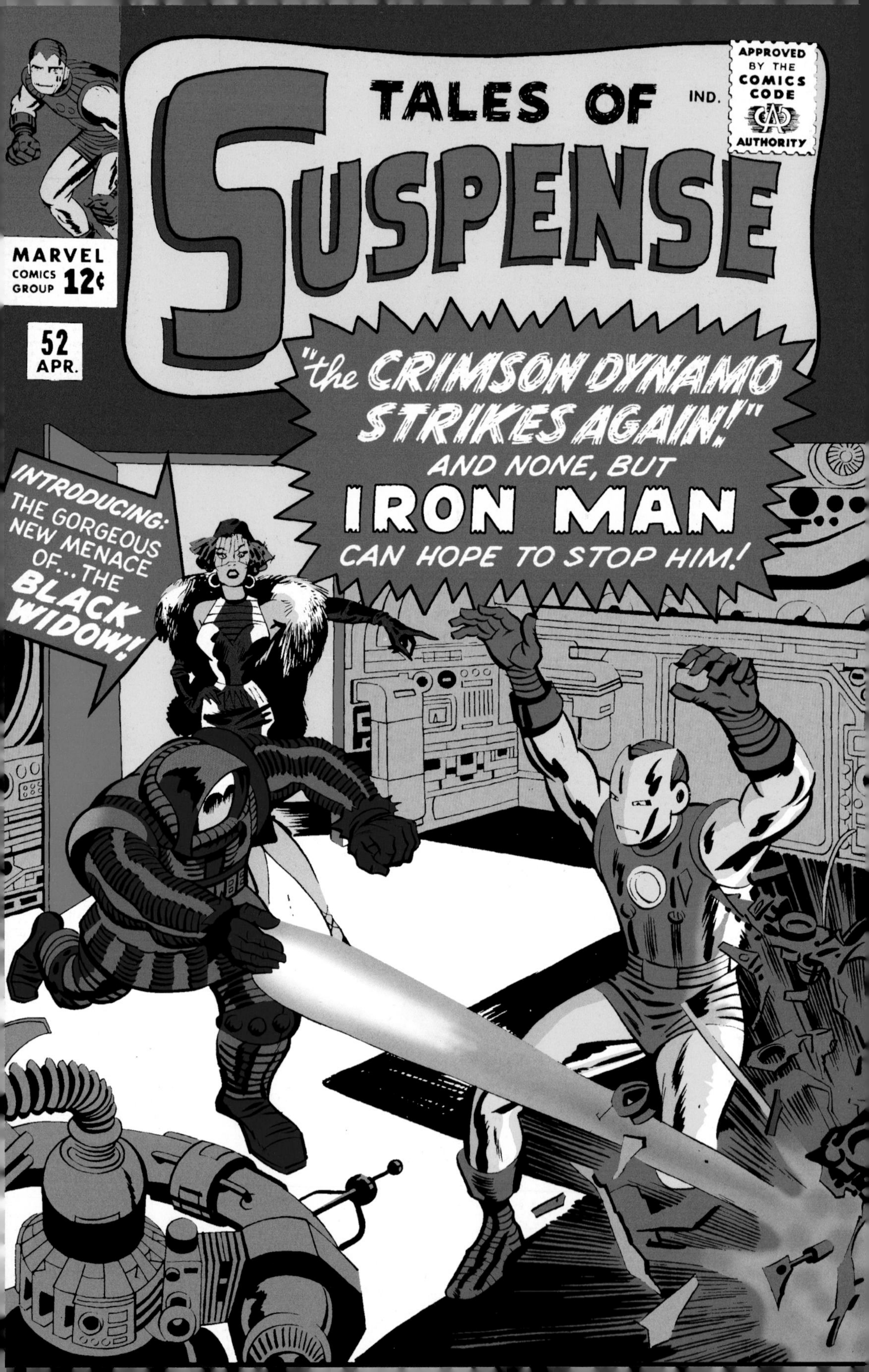

MARVEL COMICS GROUP 12¢
52 APR.
TALES OF SUSPENSE
IND.
APPROVED BY THE COMICS CODE AUTHORITY
"the CRIMSON DYNAMO STRIKES AGAIN!"
AND NONE, BUT IRON MAN CAN HOPE TO STOP HIM!
INTRODUCING: THE GORGEOUS NEW MENACE OF...THE BLACK WIDOW!

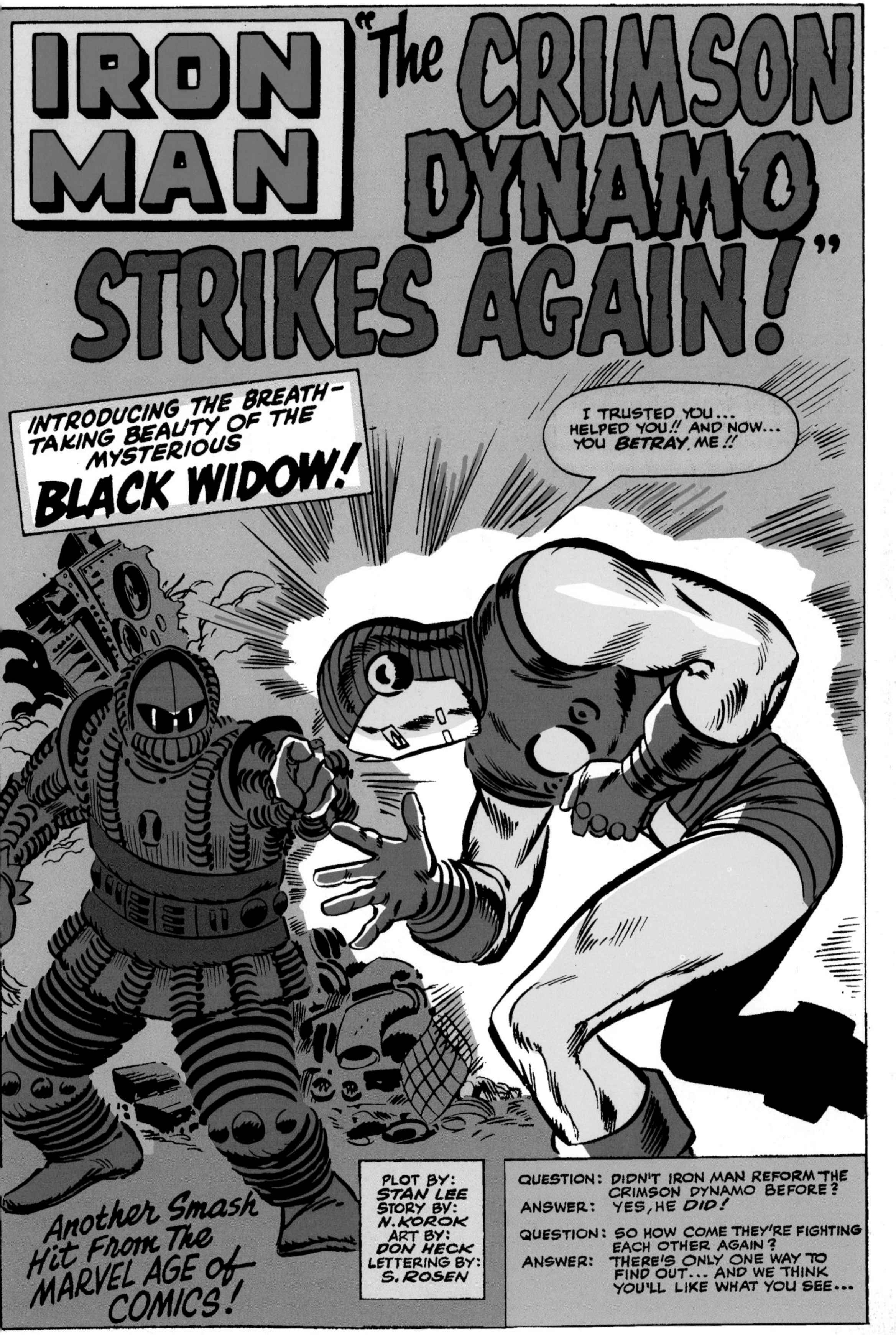
IRON MAN
"The CRIMSON DYNAMO STRIKES AGAIN!"
INTRODUCING THE BREATH-TAKING BEAUTY OF THE MYSTERIOUS BLACK WIDOW!
I TRUSTED YOU... HELPED YOU!! AND NOW... YOU BETRAY ME!!
Another Smash Hit From The MARVEL AGE of COMICS!
PLOT BY: STAN LEE STORY BY: N. KOROK ART BY: DON HECK LETTERING BY: S. ROSEN
QUESTION: DIDN'T IRON MAN REFORM THE CRIMSON DYNAMO BEFORE?
ANSWER: YES, HE DID!
QUESTION: SO HOW COME THEY'RE FIGHTING EACH OTHER AGAIN?
ANSWER: THERE'S ONLY ONE WAY TO FIND OUT... AND WE THINK YOU'LL LIKE WHAT YOU SEE...

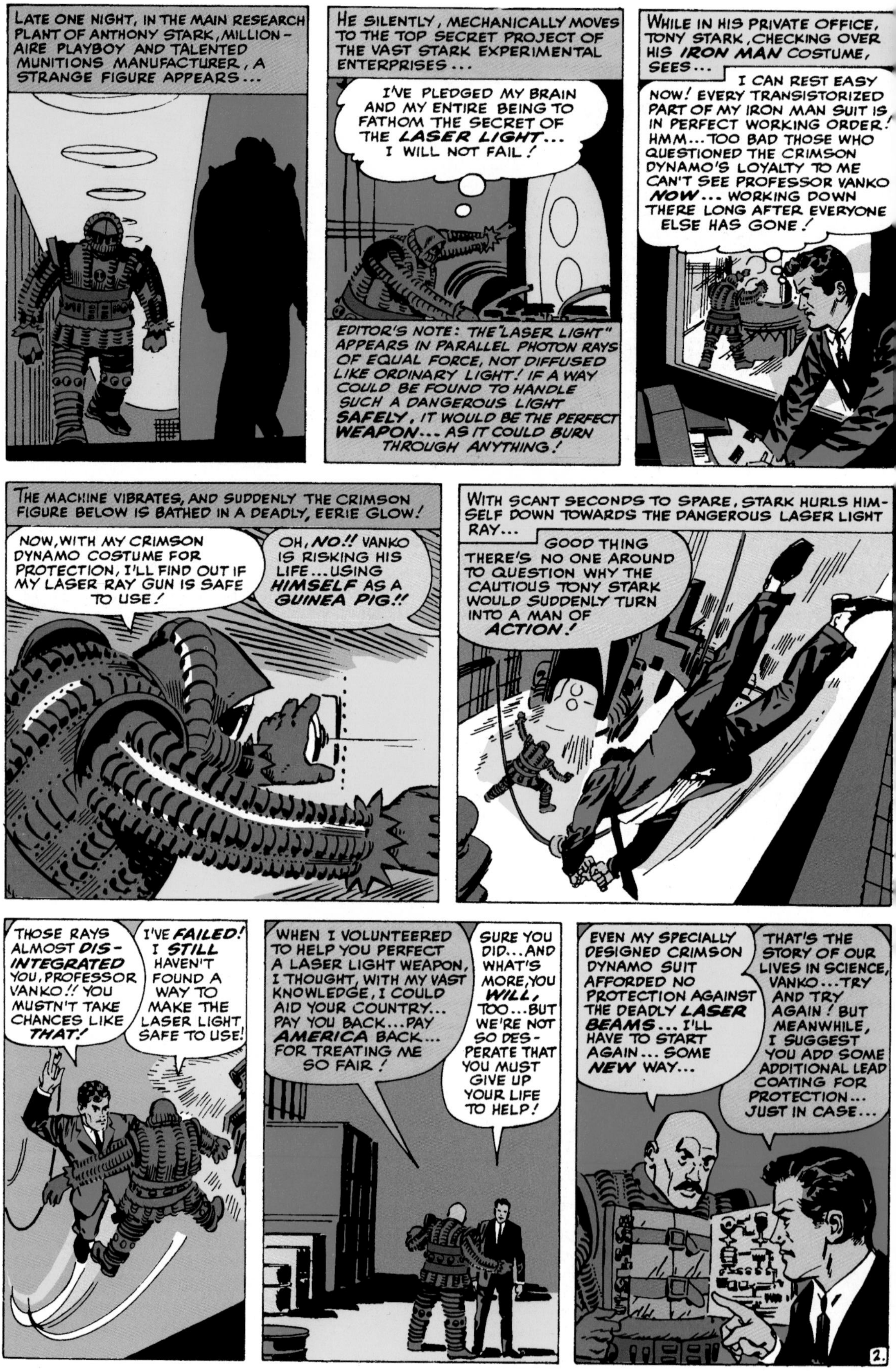

LATE ONE NIGHT, IN THE MAIN RESEARCH PLANT OF ANTHONY STARK, MILLION-AIRE PLAYBOY AND TALENTED MUNITIONS MANUFACTURER, A STRANGE FIGURE APPEARS...
HE SILENTLY, MECHANICALLY MOVES TO THE TOP SECRET PROJECT OF THE VAST STARK EXPERIMENTAL ENTERPRISES...
I'VE PLEDGED MY BRAIN AND MY ENTIRE BEING TO FATHOM THE SECRET OF THE LASER LIGHT... I WILL NOT FAIL!
EDITOR'S NOTE: THE "LASER LIGHT" APPEARS IN PARALLEL PHOTON RAYS OF EQUAL FORCE, NOT DIFFUSED LIKE ORDINARY LIGHT! IF A WAY COULD BE FOUND TO HANDLE SUCH A DANGEROUS LIGHT SAFELY, IT WOULD BE THE PERFECT WEAPON... AS IT COULD BURN THROUGH ANYTHING!
WHILE IN HIS PRIVATE OFFICE, TONY STARK, CHECKING OVER HIS IRON MAN COSTUME, SEES...
I CAN REST EASY NOW! EVERY TRANSISTORIZED PART OF MY IRON MAN SUIT IS IN PERFECT WORKING ORDER! HMM... TOO BAD THOSE WHO QUESTIONED THE CRIMSON DYNAMO'S LOYALTY TO ME CAN'T SEE PROFESSOR VANKO NOW... WORKING DOWN THERE LONG AFTER EVERYONE ELSE HAS GONE!
THE MACHINE VIBRATES, AND SUDDENLY THE CRIMSON FIGURE BELOW IS BATHED IN A DEADLY, EERIE GLOW!
NOW, WITH MY CRIMSON DYNAMO COSTUME FOR PROTECTION, I'LL FIND OUT IF MY LASER RAY GUN IS SAFE TO USE!
OH, NO!! VANKO IS RISKING HIS LIFE... USING HIMSELF AS A GUINEA PIG!!
WITH SCANT SECONDS TO SPARE, STARK HURLS HIM-SELF DOWN TOWARDS THE DANGEROUS LASER LIGHT RAY...
GOOD THING THERE'S NO ONE AROUND TO QUESTION WHY THE CAUTIOUS TONY STARK WOULD SUDDENLY TURN INTO A MAN OF ACTION!
THOSE RAYS ALMOST DIS-INTEGRATED YOU, PROFESSOR VANKO!! YOU MUSTN'T TAKE CHANCES LIKE THAT!
I'VE FAILED! I STILL HAVEN'T FOUND A WAY TO MAKE THE LASER LIGHT SAFE TO USE!
WHEN I VOLUNTEERED TO HELP YOU PERFECT A LASER LIGHT WEAPON, I THOUGHT, WITH MY VAST KNOWLEDGE, I COULD AID YOUR COUNTRY... PAY YOU BACK... PAY AMERICA BACK... FOR TREATING ME SO FAIR!
SURE YOU DID... AND WHAT'S MORE, YOU WILL, TOO... BUT WE'RE NOT SO DES-PERATE THAT YOU MUST GIVE UP YOUR LIFE TO HELP!
EVEN MY SPECIALLY DESIGNED CRIMSON DYNAMO SUIT AFFORDED NO PROTECTION AGAINST THE DEADLY LASER BEAMS... I'LL HAVE TO START AGAIN... SOME NEW WAY...
THAT'S THE STORY OF OUR LIVES IN SCIENCE, VANKO... TRY AND TRY AGAIN! BUT MEANWHILE, I SUGGEST YOU ADD SOME ADDITIONAL LEAD COATING FOR PROTECTION... JUST IN CASE...
2.

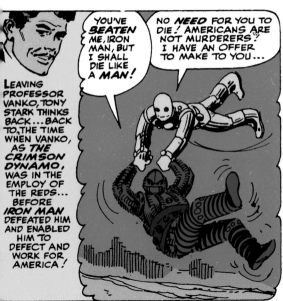

LEAVING PROFESSOR VANKO, TONY STARK THINKS BACK... BACK TO THE TIME WHEN VANKO, AS *THE CRIMSON DYNAMO*, WAS IN THE EMPLOY OF THE REDS... BEFORE *IRON MAN* DEFEATED HIM AND ENABLED HIM TO DEFECT AND WORK FOR AMERICA!

YOU'VE *BEATEN* ME, IRON MAN, BUT I SHALL DIE LIKE A *MAN!*

NO *NEED* FOR YOU TO DIE! AMERICANS ARE NOT MURDERERS! I HAVE AN OFFER TO MAKE TO YOU...

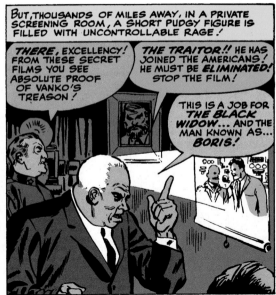

BUT, THOUSANDS OF MILES AWAY, IN A PRIVATE SCREENING ROOM, A SHORT PUDGY FIGURE IS FILLED WITH UNCONTROLLABLE RAGE!

THERE, EXCELLENCY! FROM THESE SECRET FILMS YOU SEE ABSOLUTE PROOF OF VANKO'S TREASON!

THE TRAITOR!! HE HAS JOINED THE AMERICANS! HE MUST BE *ELIMINATED!* STOP THE FILM!

THIS IS A JOB FOR *THE BLACK WIDOW*... AND THE MAN KNOWN AS... *BORIS!*

AND, A SHORT TIME LATER!

YOU SENT FOR ME, COMRADE LEADER?

AND YOU, TOO, BORIS! *COME HERE!* WALK AROUND THE DESK... I WANT TO *SHOW* YOU SOMETHING...

WALK AROUND??

BORIS DOES NOT *WALK AROUND* PUNY OBSTACLES...

...IT IS EASIER TO HURL THEM ASIDE... *SO!!*

THERE ARE YOUR *TARGETS!* THE AMERICAN MUNITIONS-MAKER, *STARK,* AND THE TRAITOR *VANKO!* BUT IT WILL ALSO BE NECESSARY TO DISPOSE OF STARK'S MIGHTY BODYGUARD... *IRON MAN!*

HMM... THAT ANTHONY STARK IS *HANDSOME* AS WELL AS WEALTHY! HE WILL MAKE AN INTERESTING ASSIGNMENT FOR THE BLACK WIDOW!

3.

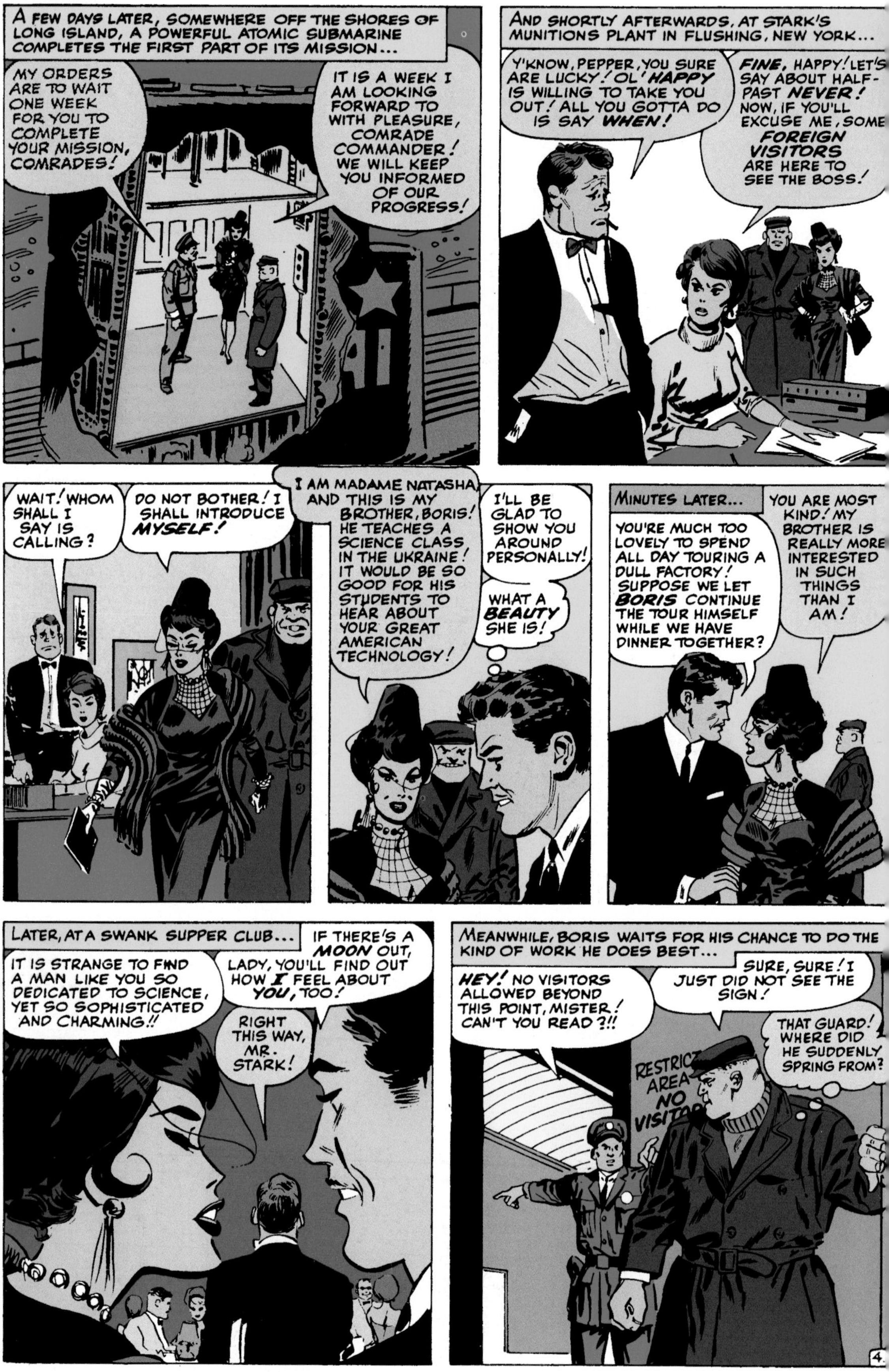

A FEW DAYS LATER, SOMEWHERE OFF THE SHORES OF LONG ISLAND, A POWERFUL ATOMIC SUBMARINE COMPLETES THE FIRST PART OF ITS MISSION...
MY ORDERS ARE TO WAIT ONE WEEK FOR YOU TO COMPLETE YOUR MISSION, COMRADES!
IT IS A WEEK I AM LOOKING FORWARD TO WITH PLEASURE, COMRADE COMMANDER! WE WILL KEEP YOU INFORMED OF OUR PROGRESS!
AND SHORTLY AFTERWARDS, AT STARK'S MUNITIONS PLANT IN FLUSHING, NEW YORK...
Y'KNOW, PEPPER, YOU SURE ARE LUCKY! OL' HAPPY IS WILLING TO TAKE YOU OUT! ALL YOU GOTTA DO IS SAY WHEN!
FINE, HAPPY! LET'S SAY ABOUT HALF-PAST NEVER! NOW, IF YOU'LL EXCUSE ME, SOME FOREIGN VISITORS ARE HERE TO SEE THE BOSS!
WAIT! WHOM SHALL I SAY IS CALLING?
DO NOT BOTHER! I SHALL INTRODUCE MYSELF!
I AM MADAME NATASHA, AND THIS IS MY BROTHER, BORIS! HE TEACHES A SCIENCE CLASS IN THE UKRAINE! IT WOULD BE SO GOOD FOR HIS STUDENTS TO HEAR ABOUT YOUR GREAT AMERICAN TECHNOLOGY!
I'LL BE GLAD TO SHOW YOU AROUND PERSONALLY!
WHAT A BEAUTY SHE IS!
MINUTES LATER...
YOU'RE MUCH TOO LOVELY TO SPEND ALL DAY TOURING A DULL FACTORY! SUPPOSE WE LET BORIS CONTINUE THE TOUR HIMSELF WHILE WE HAVE DINNER TOGETHER?
YOU ARE MOST KIND! MY BROTHER IS REALLY MORE INTERESTED IN SUCH THINGS THAN I AM!
LATER, AT A SWANK SUPPER CLUB...
IT IS STRANGE TO FIND A MAN LIKE YOU SO DEDICATED TO SCIENCE, YET SO SOPHISTICATED AND CHARMING!!
IF THERE'S A MOON OUT, LADY, YOU'LL FIND OUT HOW I FEEL ABOUT YOU, TOO!
RIGHT THIS WAY, MR. STARK!
MEANWHILE, BORIS WAITS FOR HIS CHANCE TO DO THE KIND OF WORK HE DOES BEST...
HEY! NO VISITORS ALLOWED BEYOND THIS POINT, MISTER! CAN'T YOU READ?!!
SURE, SURE! I JUST DID NOT SEE THE SIGN!
THAT GUARD! WHERE DID HE SUDDENLY SPRING FROM?
4

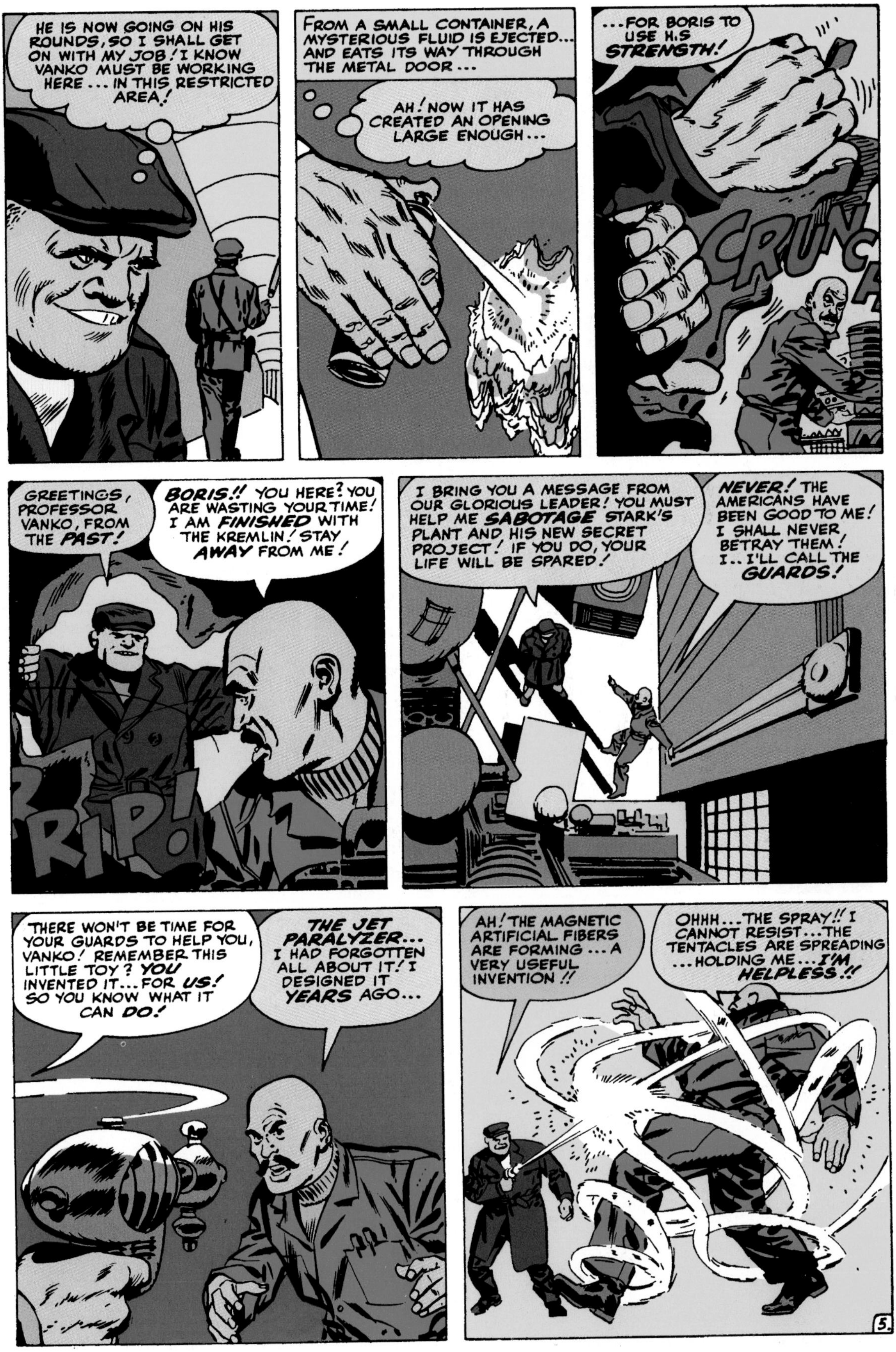
HE IS NOW GOING ON HIS ROUNDS, SO I SHALL GET ON WITH MY JOB! I KNOW VANKO MUST BE WORKING HERE ... IN THIS RESTRICTED AREA!
FROM A SMALL CONTAINER, A MYSTERIOUS FLUID IS EJECTED... AND EATS ITS WAY THROUGH THE METAL DOOR...
AH! NOW IT HAS CREATED AN OPENING LARGE ENOUGH...
...FOR BORIS TO USE H.S STRENGTH!
CRUNCH
GREETINGS, PROFESSOR VANKO, FROM THE PAST!
BORIS!! YOU HERE? YOU ARE WASTING YOUR TIME! I AM FINISHED WITH THE KREMLIN! STAY AWAY FROM ME!
RIP!
I BRING YOU A MESSAGE FROM OUR GLORIOUS LEADER! YOU MUST HELP ME SABOTAGE STARK'S PLANT AND HIS NEW SECRET PROJECT! IF YOU DO, YOUR LIFE WILL BE SPARED!
NEVER! THE AMERICANS HAVE BEEN GOOD TO ME! I SHALL NEVER BETRAY THEM! I.. I'LL CALL THE GUARDS!
THERE WON'T BE TIME FOR YOUR GUARDS TO HELP YOU, VANKO! REMEMBER THIS LITTLE TOY? YOU INVENTED IT... FOR US! SO YOU KNOW WHAT IT CAN DO!
THE JET PARALYZER... I HAD FORGOTTEN ALL ABOUT IT! I DESIGNED IT YEARS AGO...
AH! THE MAGNETIC ARTIFICIAL FIBERS ARE FORMING ... A VERY USEFUL INVENTION!!
OHHH... THE SPRAY!! I CANNOT RESIST... THE TENTACLES ARE SPREADING ...HOLDING ME... I'M HELPLESS!!
5.

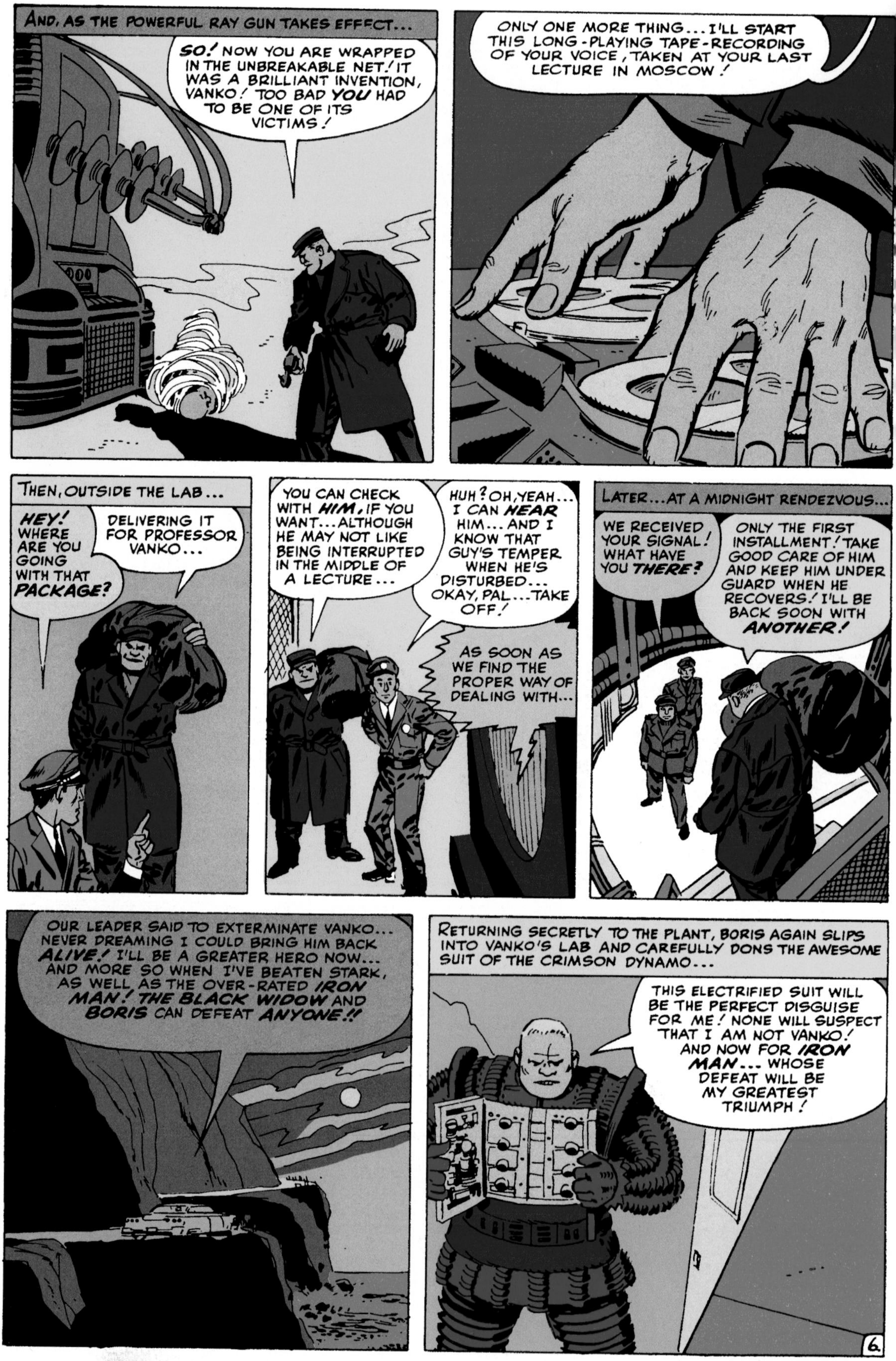
AND, AS THE POWERFUL RAY GUN TAKES EFFECT...
SO! NOW YOU ARE WRAPPED IN THE UNBREAKABLE NET! IT WAS A BRILLIANT INVENTION, VANKO! TOO BAD YOU HAD TO BE ONE OF ITS VICTIMS!
ONLY ONE MORE THING... I'LL START THIS LONG-PLAYING TAPE-RECORDING OF YOUR VOICE, TAKEN AT YOUR LAST LECTURE IN MOSCOW!
THEN, OUTSIDE THE LAB...
HEY! WHERE ARE YOU GOING WITH THAT PACKAGE?
DELIVERING IT FOR PROFESSOR VANKO...
YOU CAN CHECK WITH HIM, IF YOU WANT... ALTHOUGH HE MAY NOT LIKE BEING INTERRUPTED IN THE MIDDLE OF A LECTURE...
HUH? OH, YEAH... I CAN HEAR HIM... AND I KNOW THAT GUY'S TEMPER WHEN HE'S DISTURBED... OKAY, PAL... TAKE OFF!
AS SOON AS WE FIND THE PROPER WAY OF DEALING WITH...
LATER... AT A MIDNIGHT RENDEZVOUS...
WE RECEIVED YOUR SIGNAL! WHAT HAVE YOU THERE?
ONLY THE FIRST INSTALLMENT! TAKE GOOD CARE OF HIM AND KEEP HIM UNDER GUARD WHEN HE RECOVERS! I'LL BE BACK SOON WITH ANOTHER!
OUR LEADER SAID TO EXTERMINATE VANKO... NEVER DREAMING I COULD BRING HIM BACK ALIVE! I'LL BE A GREATER HERO NOW... AND MORE SO WHEN I'VE BEATEN STARK, AS WELL AS THE OVER-RATED IRON MAN! THE BLACK WIDOW AND BORIS CAN DEFEAT ANYONE!!
RETURNING SECRETLY TO THE PLANT, BORIS AGAIN SLIPS INTO VANKO'S LAB AND CAREFULLY DONS THE AWESOME SUIT OF THE CRIMSON DYNAMO...
THIS ELECTRIFIED SUIT WILL BE THE PERFECT DISGUISE FOR ME! NONE WILL SUSPECT THAT I AM NOT VANKO! AND NOW FOR IRON MAN... WHOSE DEFEAT WILL BE MY GREATEST TRIUMPH!
6.

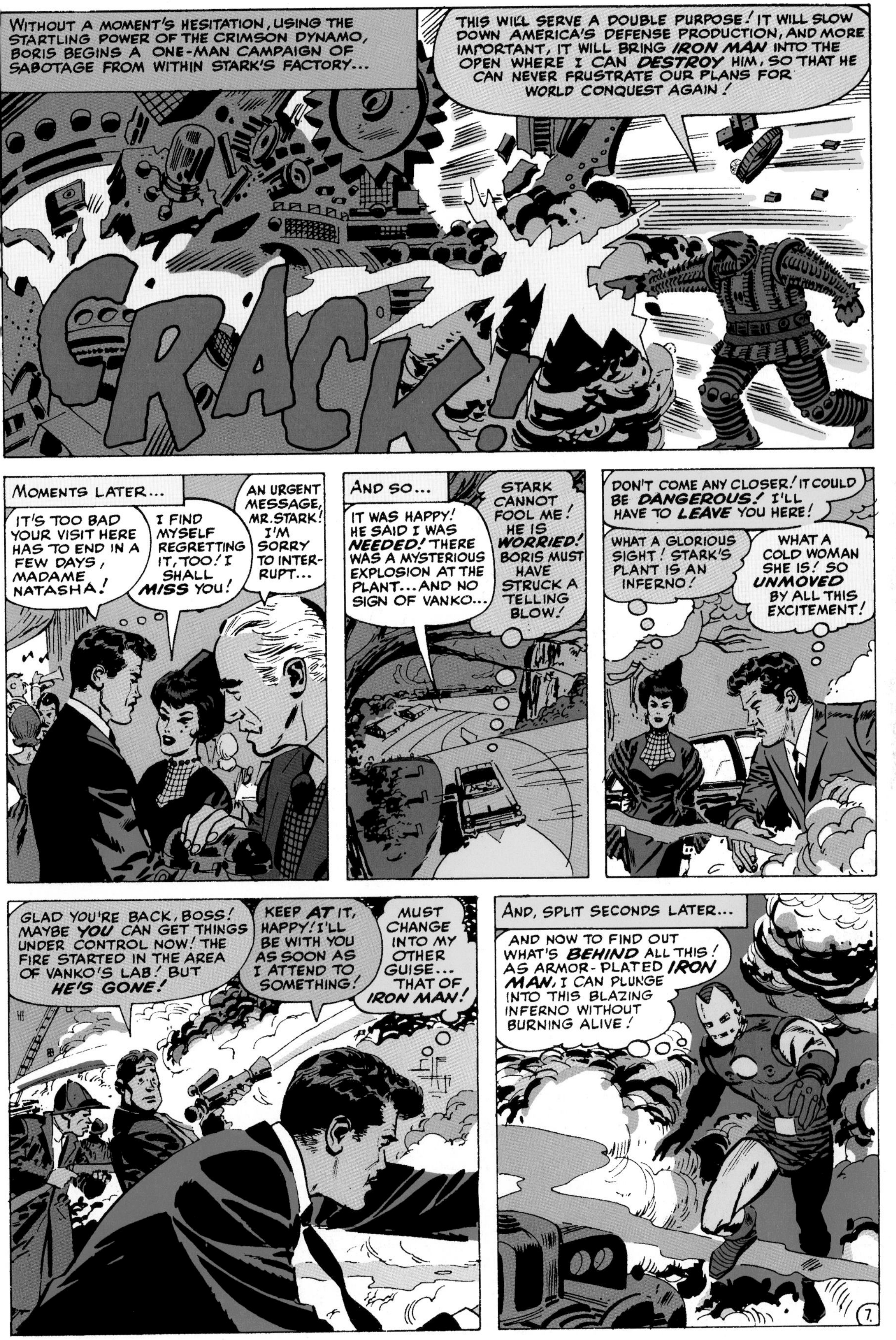
WITHOUT A MOMENT'S HESITATION, USING THE STARTLING POWER OF THE CRIMSON DYNAMO, BORIS BEGINS A ONE-MAN CAMPAIGN OF SABOTAGE FROM WITHIN STARK'S FACTORY...
THIS WILL SERVE A DOUBLE PURPOSE! IT WILL SLOW DOWN AMERICA'S DEFENSE PRODUCTION, AND MORE IMPORTANT, IT WILL BRING IRON MAN INTO THE OPEN WHERE I CAN DESTROY HIM, SO THAT HE CAN NEVER FRUSTRATE OUR PLANS FOR WORLD CONQUEST AGAIN!
CRACK!
MOMENTS LATER...
IT'S TOO BAD YOUR VISIT HERE HAS TO END IN A FEW DAYS, MADAME NATASHA!
I FIND MYSELF REGRETTING IT, TOO! I SHALL MISS YOU!
AN URGENT MESSAGE, MR. STARK! I'M SORRY TO INTERRUPT...
AND SO...
IT WAS HAPPY! HE SAID I WAS NEEDED! THERE WAS A MYSTERIOUS EXPLOSION AT THE PLANT... AND NO SIGN OF VANKO...
STARK CANNOT FOOL ME! HE IS WORRIED! BORIS MUST HAVE STRUCK A TELLING BLOW!
DON'T COME ANY CLOSER! IT COULD BE DANGEROUS! I'LL HAVE TO LEAVE YOU HERE!
WHAT A GLORIOUS SIGHT! STARK'S PLANT IS AN INFERNO!
WHAT A COLD WOMAN SHE IS! SO UNMOVED BY ALL THIS EXCITEMENT!
GLAD YOU'RE BACK, BOSS! MAYBE YOU CAN GET THINGS UNDER CONTROL NOW! THE FIRE STARTED IN THE AREA OF VANKO'S LAB! BUT HE'S GONE!
KEEP AT IT, HAPPY! I'LL BE WITH YOU AS SOON AS I ATTEND TO SOMETHING!
MUST CHANGE INTO MY OTHER GUISE... THAT OF IRON MAN!
AND, SPLIT SECONDS LATER...
AND NOW TO FIND OUT WHAT'S BEHIND ALL THIS! AS ARMOR-PLATED IRON MAN, I CAN PLUNGE INTO THIS BLAZING INFERNO WITHOUT BURNING ALIVE!
7

LOOK! IT'S *IRON MAN!*

HE'S TOO LATE TO STOP THE DAMAGE... BUT HE STILL MAY BE ABLE TO SAVE THE *REST* OF THE FACTORY!

I'VE GOT TO FIND VANKO! HIS WORK WITH THE LASER LIGHT RAY MIGHT HAVE STARTED THIS!

SECONDS LATER...

THE CRIMSON DYNAMO! VANKO! THANK HEAVEN YOU'RE ALL RIGHT! FOLLOW ME! I'LL GET YOU *OUT* OF HERE!

IRON MAN, AT LAST! THE FOOL THINKS I'M VANKO!

CRASH!

WHAT'S *WRONG?* OH, YOU DON'T WANT TO LEAVE THE LASER RAY MACHINE, EH? OKAY, I'LL HELP YOU GET IT *OUT* OF HERE!

I'LL WAIT TILL HE *LIFTS* THE MACHINE! THEN BORIS SHALL *STRIKE!*

LET'S HOPE WE CAN SAVE IT IN TIME! IT WOULD TAKE *YEARS* TO REBUILD IF IT'S DESTROYED!

NOW'S MY CHANCE!... WHILE HE'S COMPLETELY OFF-GUARD!

OHH!

A PERFECT OPPORTUNITY TO USE THE ELECTRICAL CHARGE VANKO PROVIDED IN THIS SUIT!

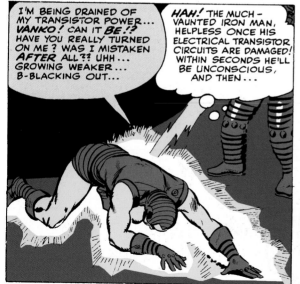

I'M BEING DRAINED OF MY TRANSISTOR POWER... VANKO! CAN IT *BE!?* HAVE YOU REALLY TURNED ON ME? WAS I MISTAKEN *AFTER* ALL?! UHH... GROWING WEAKER... B-BLACKING OUT...

HAH! THE MUCH-VAUNTED IRON MAN, HELPLESS ONCE HIS ELECTRICAL TRANSISTOR CIRCUITS ARE DAMAGED! WITHIN SECONDS HE'LL BE UNCONSCIOUS, AND THEN...

UNDER COVER OF THE THICK BLANKET OF SMOKE, I'LL ESCAPE WITH MY *GREATEST PRIZE!* AND IF I'M SEEN, THE FOOLS WILL THINK I'M *RESCUING* IRON MAN!

8.

LATER, BACK AT THE SUB...

YOU SUBDUED *IRON MAN*, COMRADE? INCREDIBLE! ARE YOU SURE HE'S *TOTALLY HARMLESS?*

COMPLETELY, COMRADE COMMANDER! HE HAS RECEIVED ENOUGH ELECTRIC CURRENT TO DESTROY *TWENTY* MEN!

NOW IRON MAN IS HELPLESS AND LOCKED BEHIND DOORS OF PLATE STEEL! YOU NEED WORRY ABOUT HIM NO LONGER!

SO YOU SAY! BUT I HAVE HEARD *TOO MUCH* OF THIS MAN! I SHALL NOT RELAX UNTIL HE IS OFF MY SHIP AND SAFELY IMPRISONED IN THE HOMELAND!

CL ANK!

MOMENTS LATER...

WHAT A *HERO'S WELCOME* I SHALL RECEIVE WHEN I RETURN! NOW, THE FINAL DETAIL... THE BLACK WIDOW AND I WILL EASILY FINISH OFF ANTHONY STARK... NOW THAT HIS IRON BODY GUARD CANNOT HELP HIM!

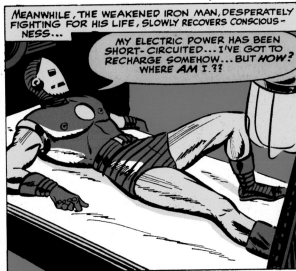

MEANWHILE, THE WEAKENED IRON MAN, DESPERATELY FIGHTING FOR HIS LIFE, SLOWLY RECOVERS CONSCIOUSNESS...

MY ELECTRIC POWER HAS BEEN SHORT-CIRCUITED... I'VE GOT TO RECHARGE SOMEHOW... BUT *HOW?* WHERE *AM* I.??

CAN'T WAIT MUCH LONGER... MUST FIND SOME ELECTRIC CURRENT TO REACTIVATE MY CIRCUITS!! WAIT... THAT LIGHT BULB... OVERHEAD...

SUMMONING ALL HIS REMAINING STRENGTH, IRON MAN SMASHES THE GLASS BULB, AND...

LUCKY I CARRY THIS SPARE EXTENSION CORD FOR ANY EMERGENCIES... AH... I CAN FEEL MY ENERGY... MY VERY LIFE FORCE... FEEDING BACK...

NOW, WITH THE FULL POWER OF IRON MAN, I CAN TEAR THIS PLACE APART, AND... *VANKO!!* WHAT HAVE THEY *DONE* TO YOU? SO IT WAS SOMEONE *ELSE* WHO STRUCK ME DOWN... I SHOULD HAVE *GUESSED!*

9.

IN SECONDS, IRON MAN RIPS OFF THE SYNTHETIC WIRE MESH NET, FREEING VANKO! THEN, SLEDGE-HAMMER FISTS, AIDED BY POWERFUL TRANSISTOR FORCE, BATTER AN ESCAPE ROUTE RIGHT THROUGH THE STEEL SHELL OF THE SUB...

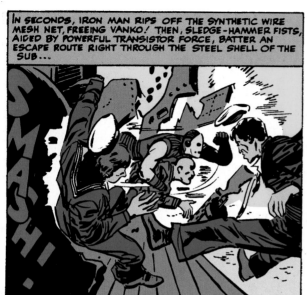

SMASH!

UNTIL... YOU *DID* IT, IRON MAN!! YOU *FREED* US! BUT...ARE YOUR SMALL FLYING JETS POWERFUL ENOUGH TO CARRY *MY* WEIGHT, TOO?

THEY'RE *ULTRA-TURBO JETS,* VANKO! THEY COULD LIFT AN *ELEPHANT,* IF NEED BE! THERE... WE'RE SAFELY OUT OF RANGE NOW!

THEY'VE *ESCAPED!* WE'LL PAY WITH OUR *LIVES* FOR THIS!

IT'S ALL *MY* FAULT FOR INVOLVING YOU IN MY PAST, IRON MAN! MY ENEMIES DO NOT GIVE UP EASILY!

THAT'S WHAT MAKES THEM DANGEROUS, VANKO, BUT WE'LL SHOW THEM *WE* CAN BE EQUALLY DANGEROUS!

THINKING HE'S DEFEATED YOU, BORIS WILL RETURN TO THE FACTORY TO DESTROY OUR LASER RAY WEAPON!!

BORIS! SO HE'S THE ONE!

IRON MAN... *LOOK!* MY CRIMSON DYNAMO COSTUME! IT MUST BE *HIM!*

YOU MUST BE CAREFUL! HE, TOO, IS A *SCIENTIST*...A MAN OF GREAT ABILITY... AND GREATER *STRENGTH!!*

NO, VANKO! THIS IS NO TIME FOR CAUTION!! I'VE *RETURNED,*

IRON MAN! HOW??

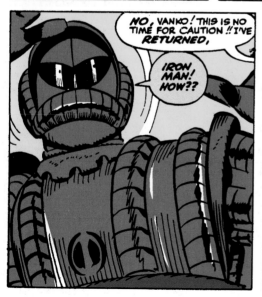

WE'LL PLAY TWENTY QUESTIONS, LATER, YOU TREACHEROUS SPY!! RIGHT NOW, WE'LL FIND OUT HOW GOOD YOU ARE WHEN I'VE GOT *BOTH HANDS FREE!*

CRASH

10.

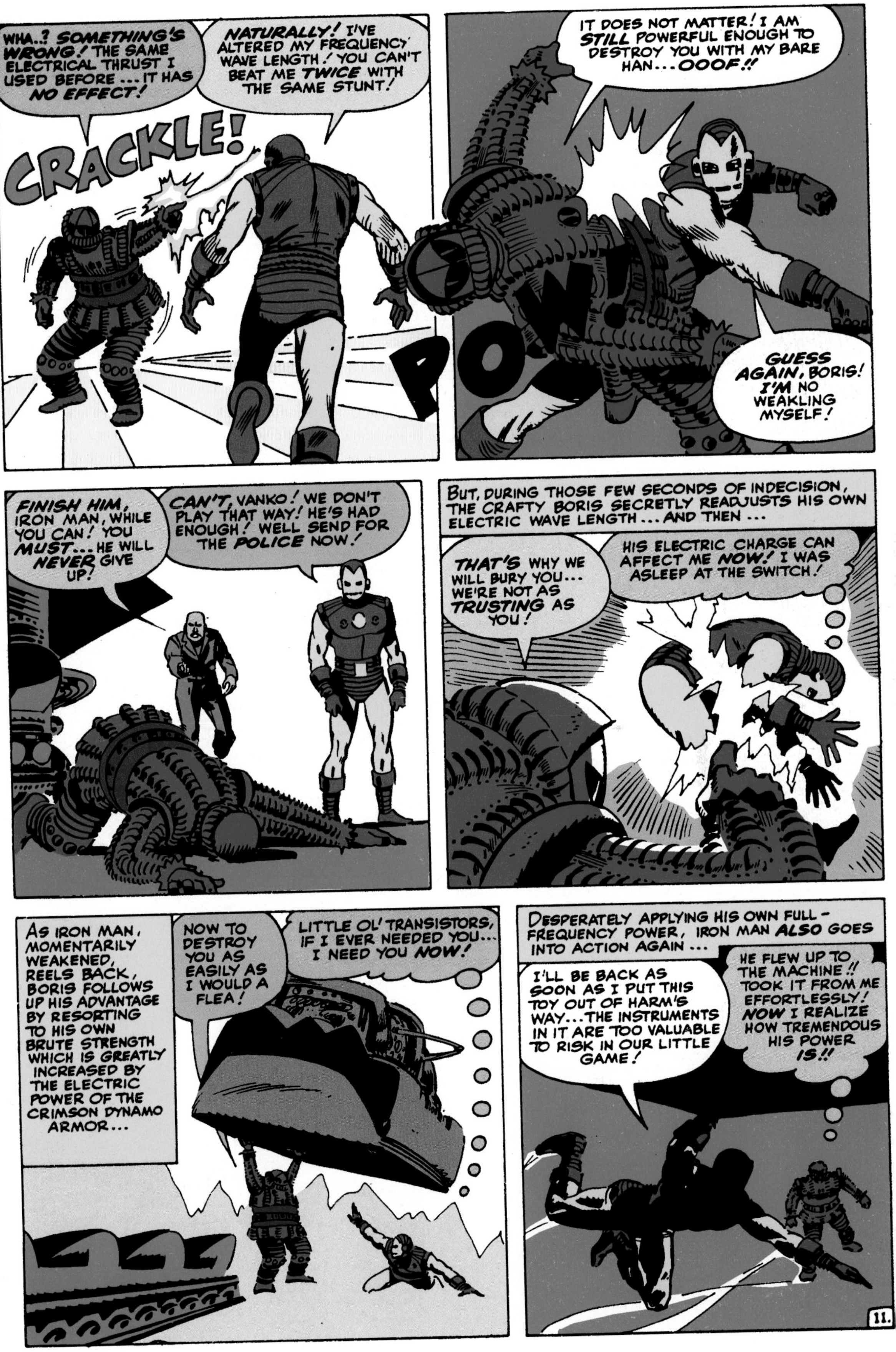
WHA..? SOMETHING'S WRONG! THE SAME ELECTRICAL THRUST I USED BEFORE ... IT HAS NO EFFECT!
NATURALLY! I'VE ALTERED MY FREQUENCY WAVE LENGTH! YOU CAN'T BEAT ME TWICE WITH THE SAME STUNT!
CRACKLE!
IT DOES NOT MATTER! I AM STILL POWERFUL ENOUGH TO DESTROY YOU WITH MY BARE HAN...OOOF!!
POW!
GUESS AGAIN, BORIS! I'M NO WEAKLING MYSELF!
FINISH HIM, IRON MAN, WHILE YOU CAN! YOU MUST... HE WILL NEVER GIVE UP!
CAN'T, VANKO! WE DON'T PLAY THAT WAY! HE'S HAD ENOUGH! WELL SEND FOR THE POLICE NOW!
BUT, DURING THOSE FEW SECONDS OF INDECISION, THE CRAFTY BORIS SECRETLY READJUSTS HIS OWN ELECTRIC WAVE LENGTH... AND THEN ...
THAT'S WHY WE WILL BURY YOU... WE'RE NOT AS TRUSTING AS YOU!
HIS ELECTRIC CHARGE CAN AFFECT ME NOW! I WAS ASLEEP AT THE SWITCH!
AS IRON MAN, MOMENTARILY WEAKENED, REELS BACK, BORIS FOLLOWS UP HIS ADVANTAGE BY RESORTING TO HIS OWN BRUTE STRENGTH WHICH IS GREATLY INCREASED BY THE ELECTRIC POWER OF THE CRIMSON DYNAMO ARMOR...
NOW TO DESTROY YOU AS EASILY AS I WOULD A FLEA!
LITTLE OL' TRANSISTORS, IF I EVER NEEDED YOU... I NEED YOU NOW!
DESPERATELY APPLYING HIS OWN FULL-FREQUENCY POWER, IRON MAN ALSO GOES INTO ACTION AGAIN ...
I'LL BE BACK AS SOON AS I PUT THIS TOY OUT OF HARM'S WAY...THE INSTRUMENTS IN IT ARE TOO VALUABLE TO RISK IN OUR LITTLE GAME!
HE FLEW UP TO THE MACHINE!! TOOK IT FROM ME EFFORTLESSLY! NOW I REALIZE HOW TREMENDOUS HIS POWER IS!!
11.

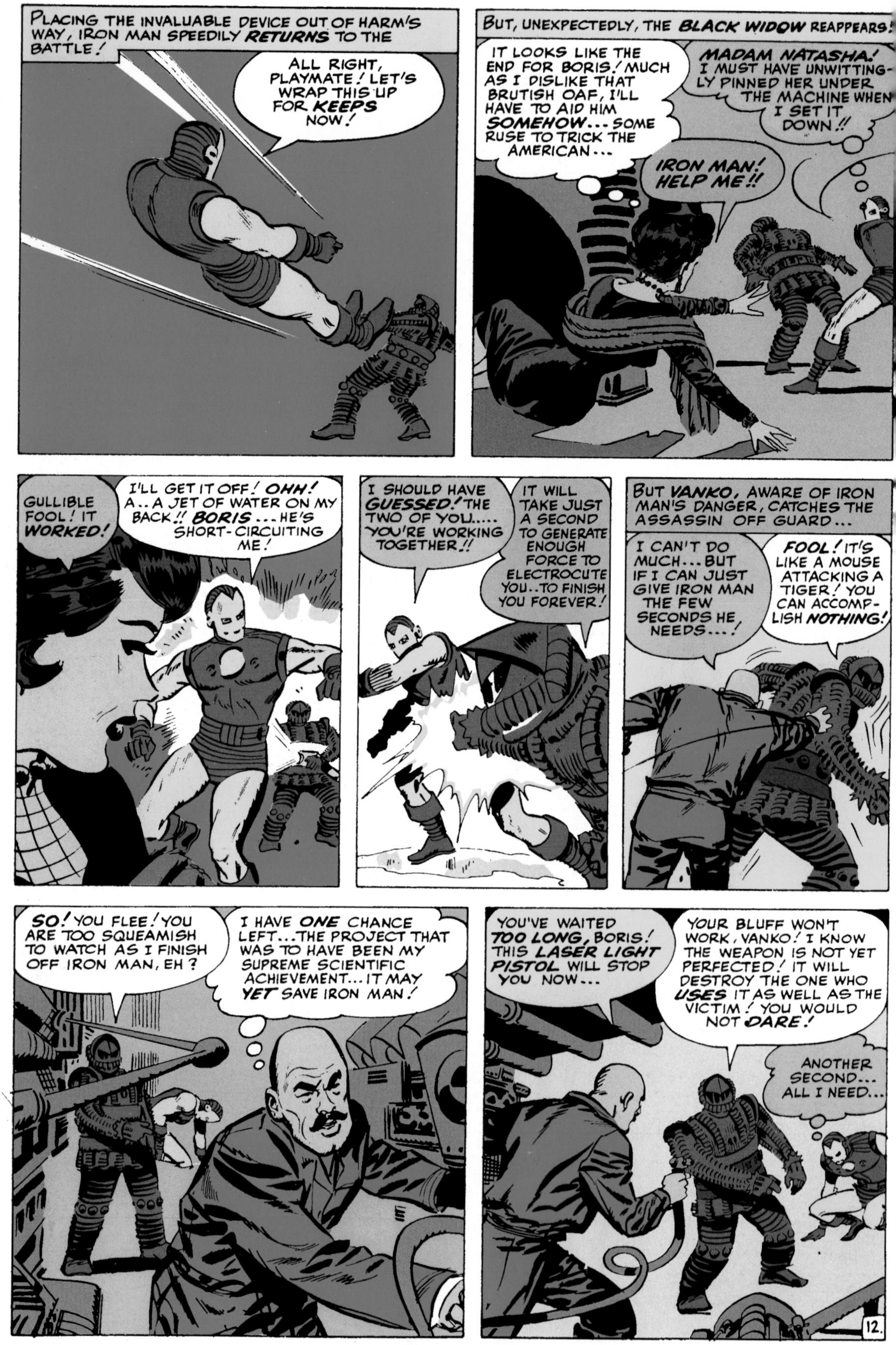
PLACING THE INVALUABLE DEVICE OUT OF HARM'S WAY, IRON MAN SPEEDILY RETURNS TO THE BATTLE!
ALL RIGHT, PLAYMATE! LET'S WRAP THIS UP FOR KEEPS NOW!
BUT, UNEXPECTEDLY, THE BLACK WIDOW REAPPEARS!
IT LOOKS LIKE THE END FOR BORIS! MUCH AS I DISLIKE THAT BRUTISH OAF, I'LL HAVE TO AID HIM SOMEHOW... SOME RUSE TO TRICK THE AMERICAN...
MADAM NATASHA! I MUST HAVE UNWITTINGLY PINNED HER UNDER THE MACHINE WHEN I SET IT DOWN!!
IRON MAN! HELP ME!!
GULLIBLE FOOL! IT WORKED!
I'LL GET IT OFF! OHH! A.. A JET OF WATER ON MY BACK!! BORIS... HE'S SHORT-CIRCUITING ME!
I SHOULD HAVE GUESSED! THE TWO OF YOU..... YOU'RE WORKING TOGETHER!!
IT WILL TAKE JUST A SECOND TO GENERATE ENOUGH FORCE TO ELECTROCUTE YOU..TO FINISH YOU FOREVER!
BUT VANKO, AWARE OF IRON MAN'S DANGER, CATCHES THE ASSASSIN OFF GUARD...
I CAN'T DO MUCH... BUT IF I CAN JUST GIVE IRON MAN THE FEW SECONDS HE NEEDS...!
FOOL! IT'S LIKE A MOUSE ATTACKING A TIGER! YOU CAN ACCOMPLISH NOTHING!
SO! YOU FLEE! YOU ARE TOO SQUEAMISH TO WATCH AS I FINISH OFF IRON MAN, EH?
I HAVE ONE CHANCE LEFT... THE PROJECT THAT WAS TO HAVE BEEN MY SUPREME SCIENTIFIC ACHIEVEMENT... IT MAY YET SAVE IRON MAN!
YOU'VE WAITED TOO LONG, BORIS! THIS LASER LIGHT PISTOL WILL STOP YOU NOW...
YOUR BLUFF WON'T WORK, VANKO! I KNOW THE WEAPON IS NOT YET PERFECTED! IT WILL DESTROY THE ONE WHO USES IT AS WELL AS THE VICTIM! YOU WOULD NOT DARE!
ANOTHER SECOND... ALL I NEED...
12.

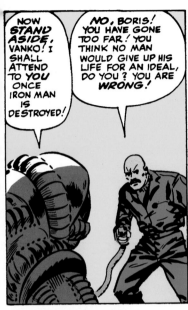

NOW **STAND ASIDE**, VANKO! I SHALL ATTEND TO **YOU** ONCE IRON MAN IS DESTROYED!

NO, BORIS! YOU HAVE GONE TOO FAR! YOU THINK NO MAN WOULD GIVE UP HIS LIFE FOR AN IDEAL, DO YOU? YOU ARE **WRONG!**

I WOULD DARE **ANYTHING** FOR THIS COUNTRY... WHICH HAS BEEN SO **GOOD** TO ME!

WORDS! WORDS! WORDS! NOW OUT OF MY WAY, OLD MAN!

NO! VANKO.. **DON'T!**

NOT JUST WORDS, BORIS... **BUT DEEDS!** IS THERE ANY MORE FITTING WAY TO GLORIFY MY GREATEST PROJECT THAN TO DESTROY AN ENEMY OF FREEDOM WITH IT?!!

NO!! YOU ARE MAD! **YOU** WILL DIE ALSO... **STOP!!**

I MUST ESCAPE IN THE CONFUSION! WE HAVE **FAILED!**

BOOM!

LATER... POOR VANKO! HE SACRIFICED HIS LIFE TO PROVE HIS LOYALTY TO OUR NATION! HE SHALL NEVER BE FORGOTTEN!

THEN, AFTER RESUMING HIS TRUE IDENTITY AS ANTHONY STARK ...

HEY, BOSS! WE JUST GOT SOME HOT REPORTS ON THAT PHONY SISTER OF BORIS! SHE'S A REAL MATA HARI, CALLED **THE BLACK WIDOW!** WHY DON'T WE GO **AFTER** HER??

WHY BOTHER, HAPPY? SHE'S FAILED IN HER MISSION! WHERE CAN SHE GO? WHERE CAN SHE **HIDE?** IN A WAY, I **PITY** HER! ALL THAT BEAUTY OUTSIDE... BUT **INSIDE**... **NOTHING!!**

YET, WHAT OF THE BEAUTIFUL, DANGEROUSLY IRRESISTIBLE BLACK WIDOW? SHE IS STILL AT LARGE, ON SOME FOG-FILLED STREET IN SOME CROWDED CITY... LONELY... ABANDONED... ALWAYS HIDING! HER CONSTANT COMPANION... **FEAR!**

I MUST KEEP MOVING... I KNOW TOO WELL THE PENALTY FOR FAILURE!!

BUT, TIME IS LONG, AND UNENDING... AND FATE WORKS IN MYSTERIOUS WAYS! NEXT ISSUE THE BLACK WIDOW **RETURNS**, MORE DEADLY THAN EVER! SO DON'T MISS THE GREAT **TALES OF SUSPENSE #53**, WHERE ANOTHER THRILLING **IRON MAN** ADVENTURE AWAITS YOU!

The End

#2 COVER PROCESS BY ADI GRANOV

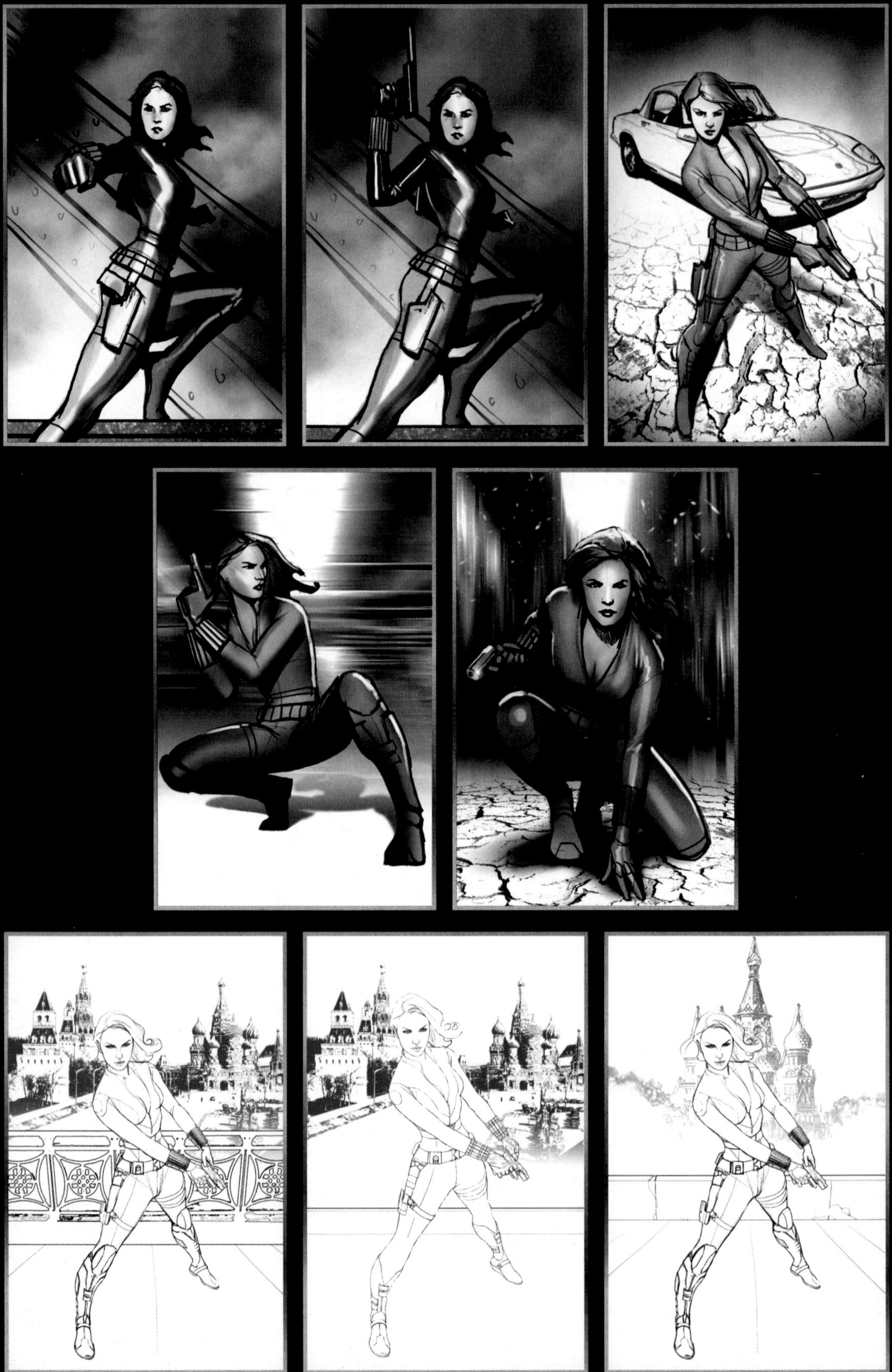

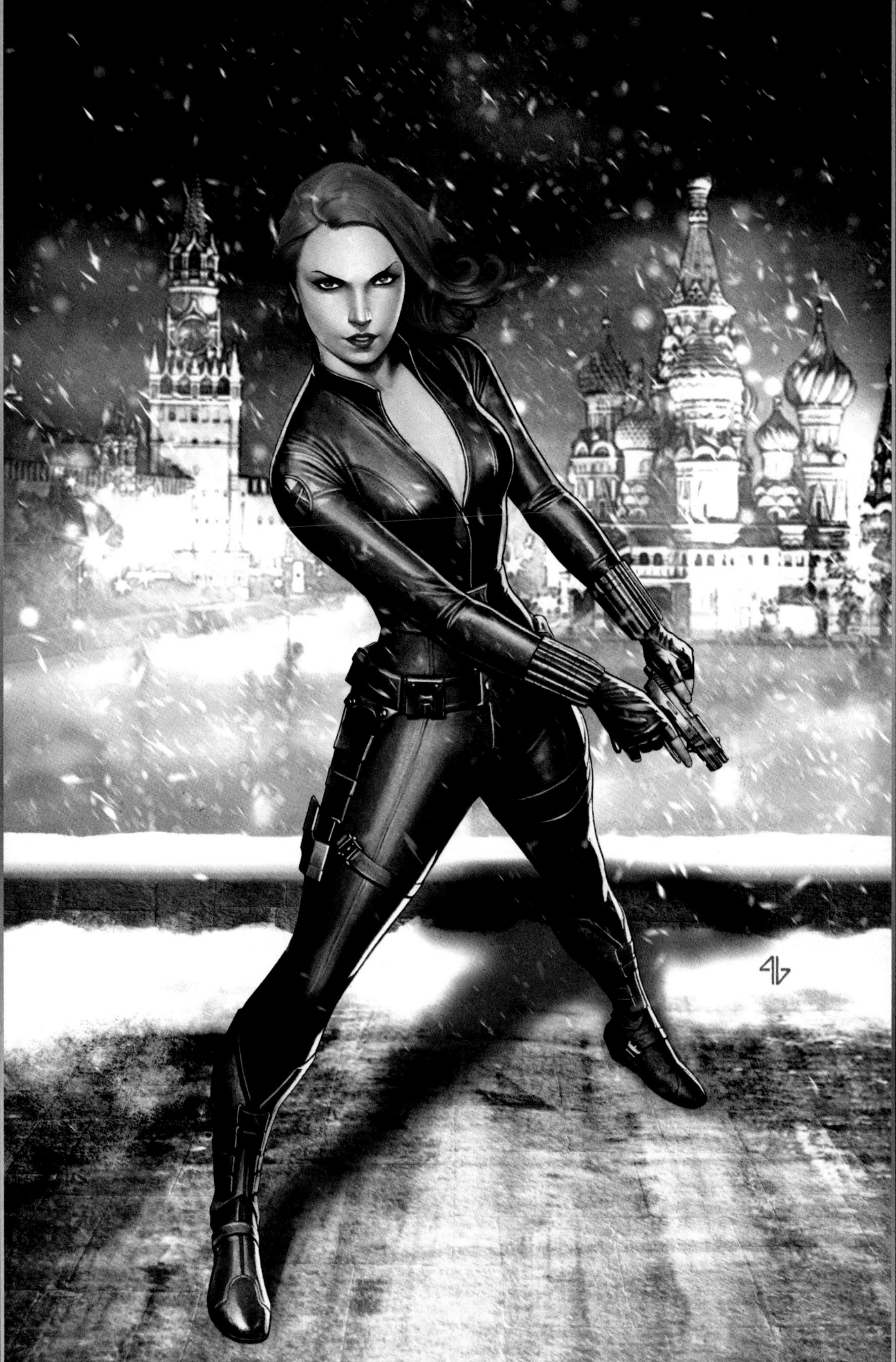

CHAPTER 1 PAGE 1 PROCESS

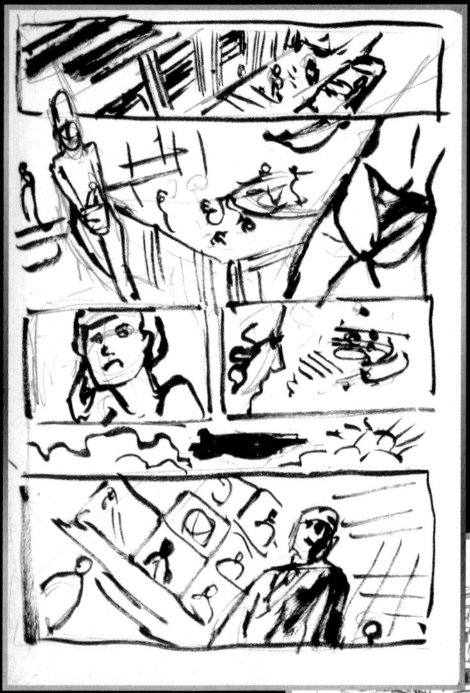

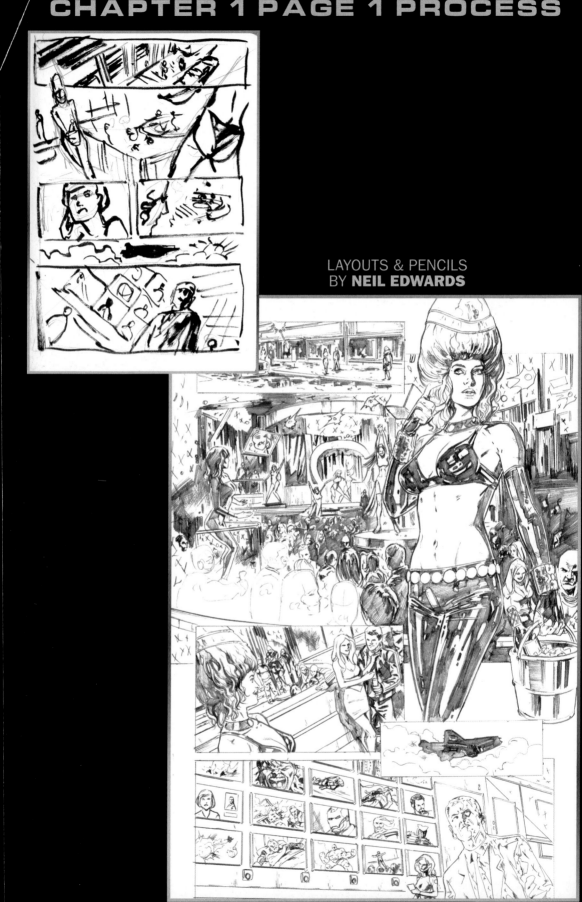

LAYOUTS & PENCILS
BY **NEIL EDWARDS**

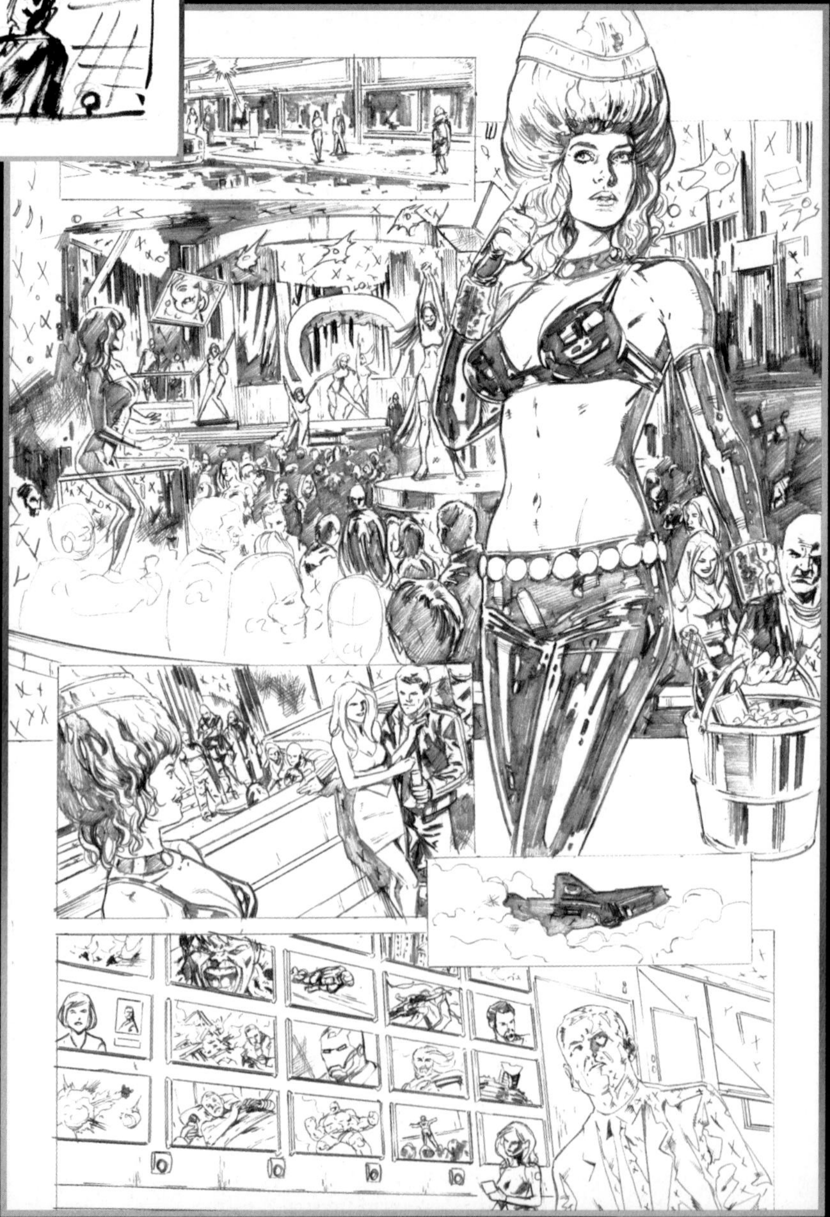

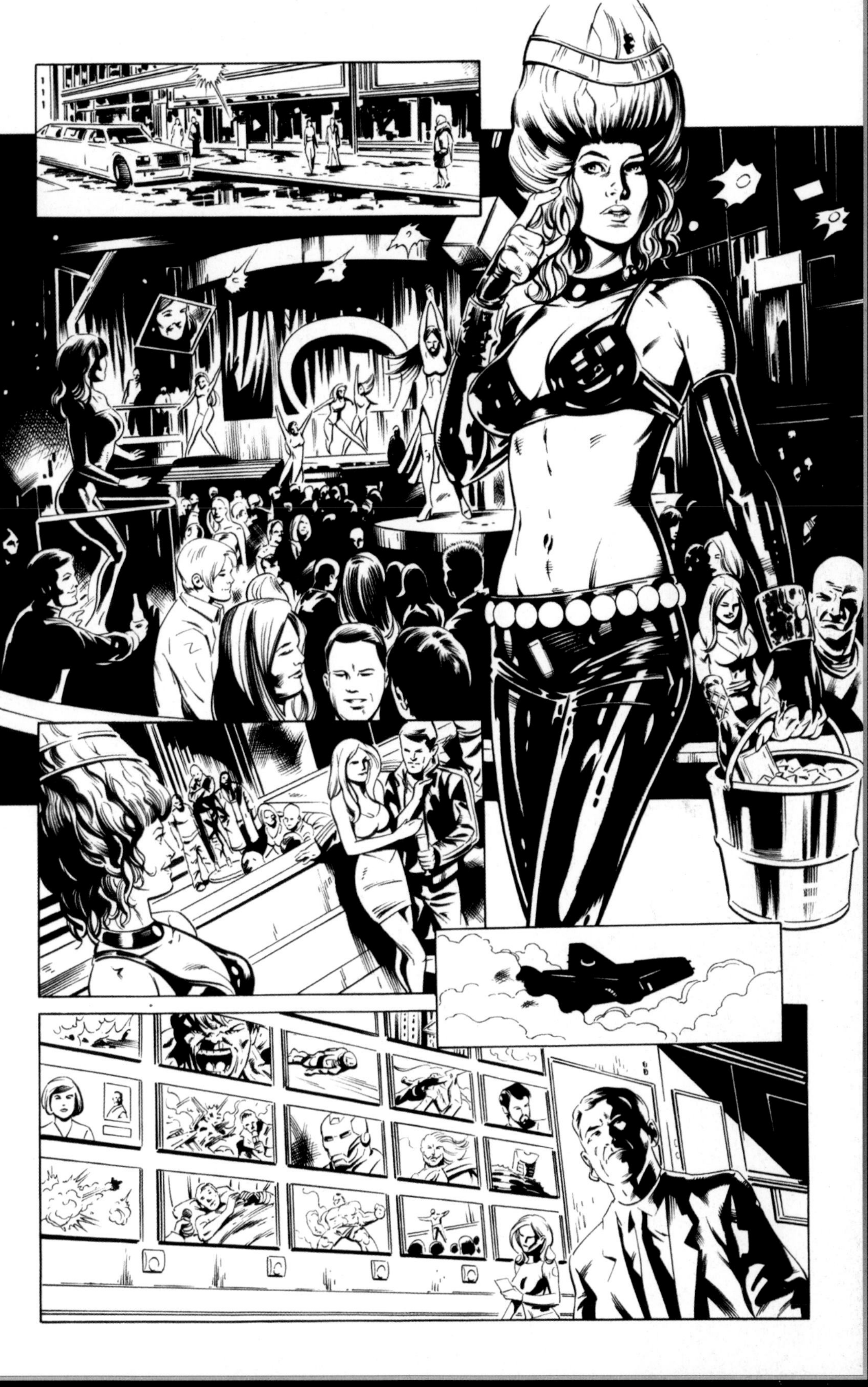

INKS BY **RICK MAGYAR**

CHAPTER 1 PAGE 10 PROCESS

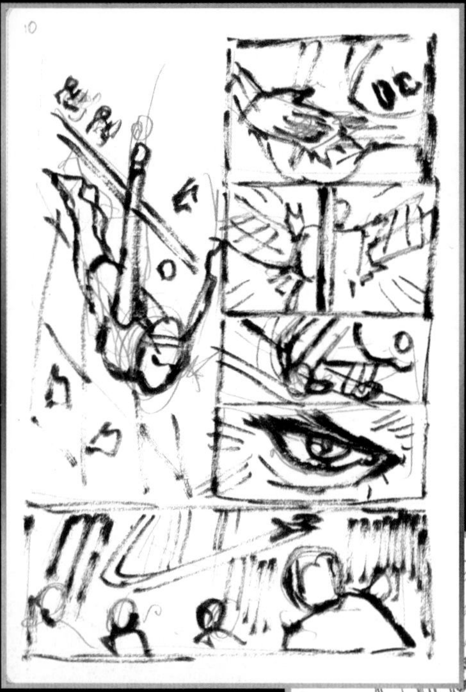

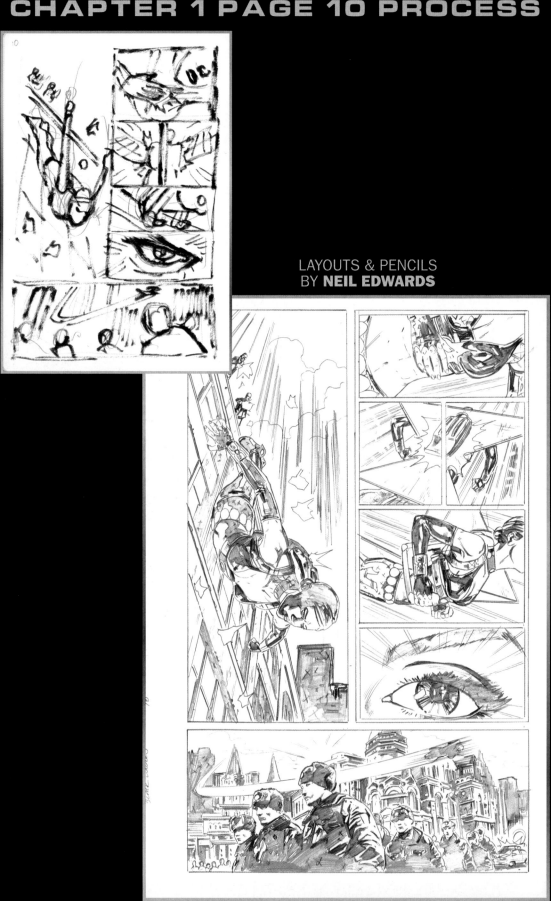

LAYOUTS & PENCILS
BY **NEIL EDWARDS**

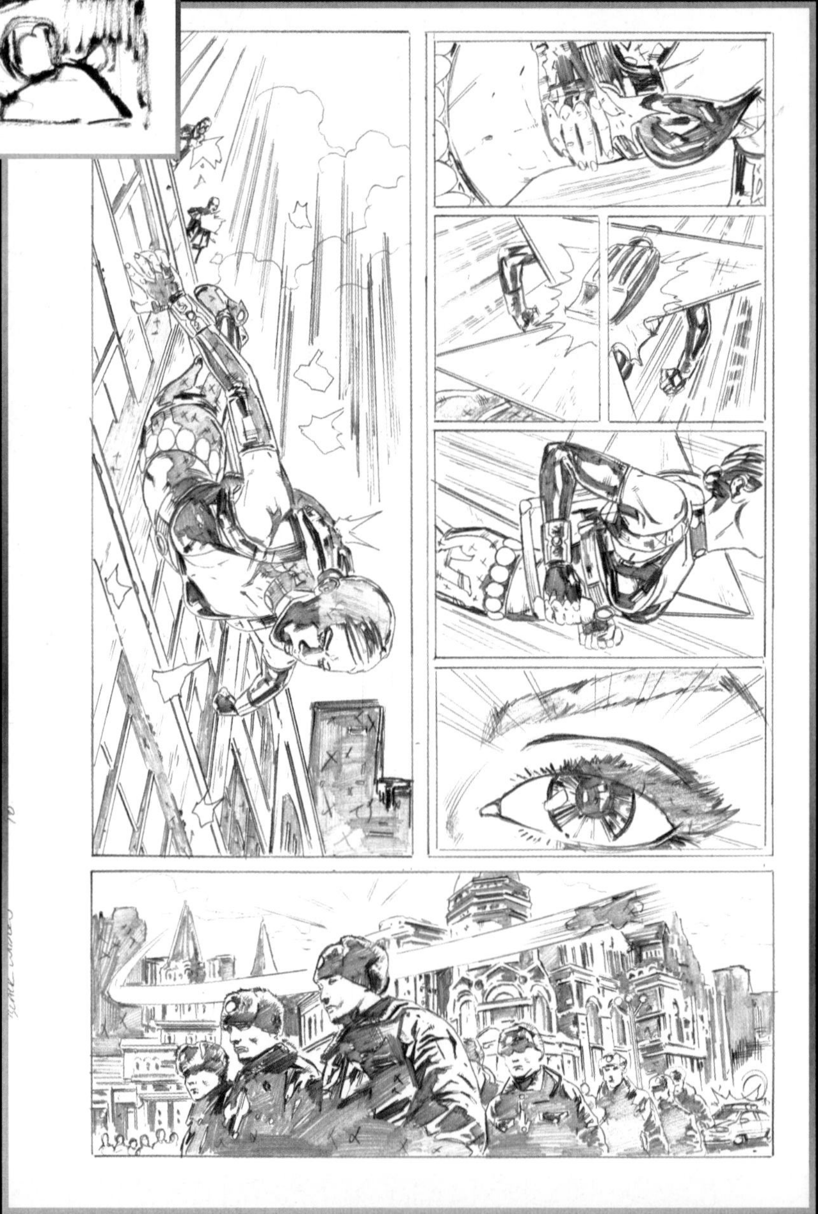

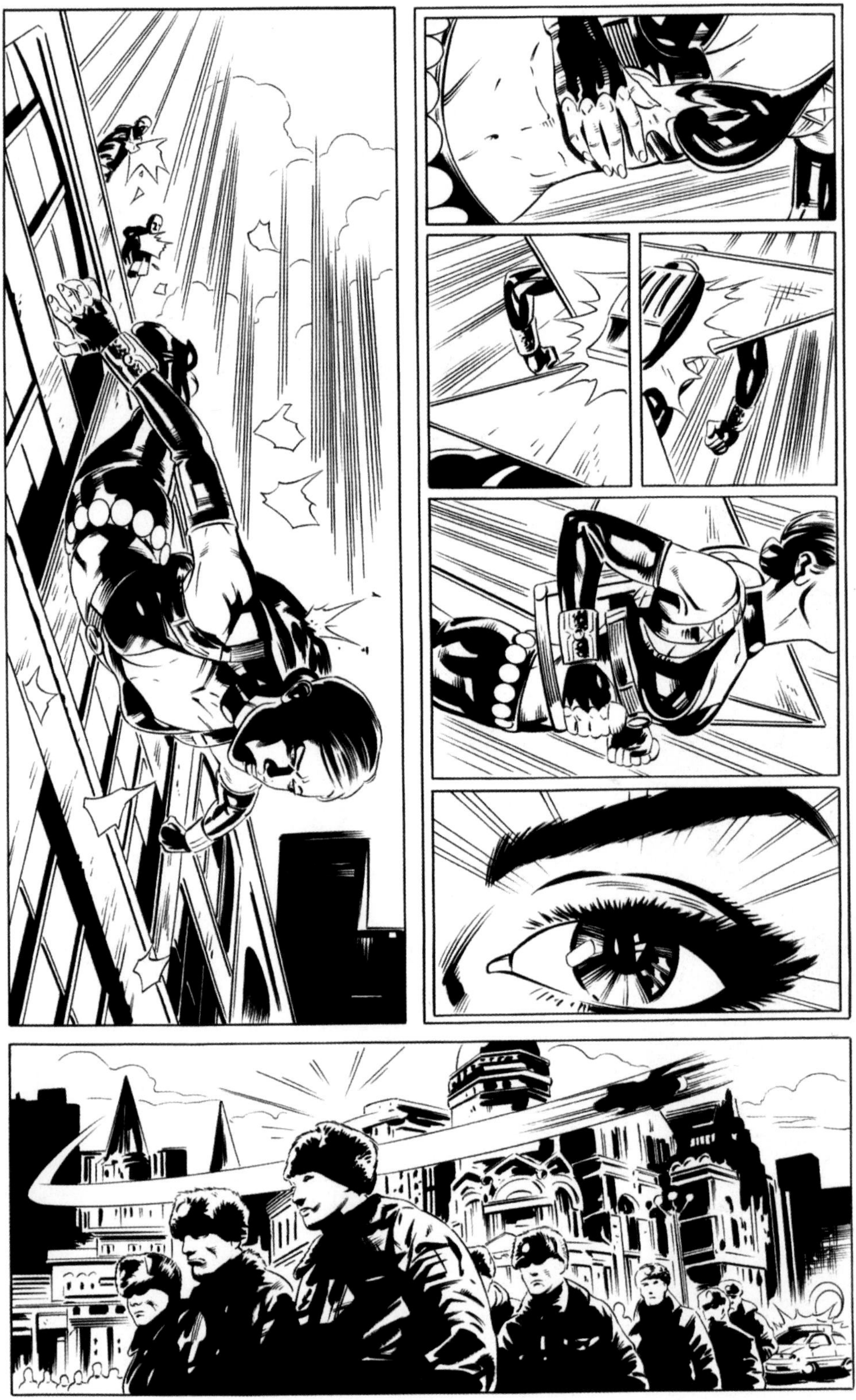

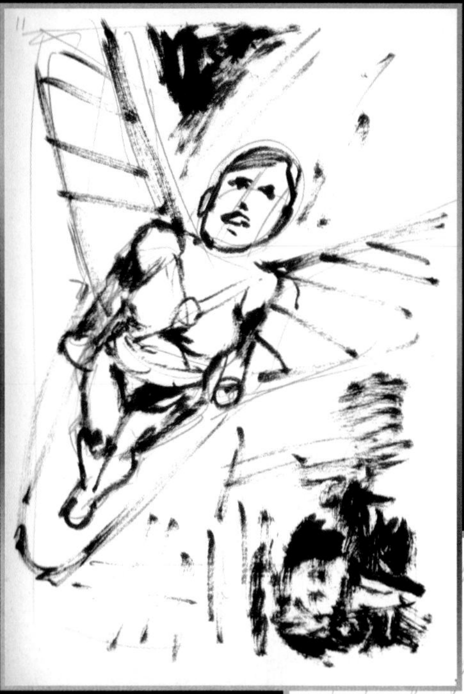

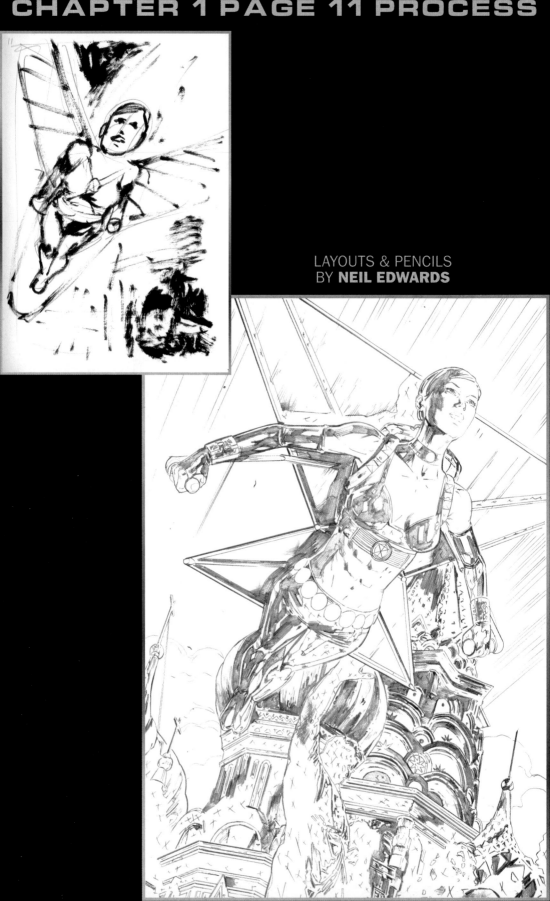

LAYOUTS & PENCILS
BY **NEIL EDWARDS**

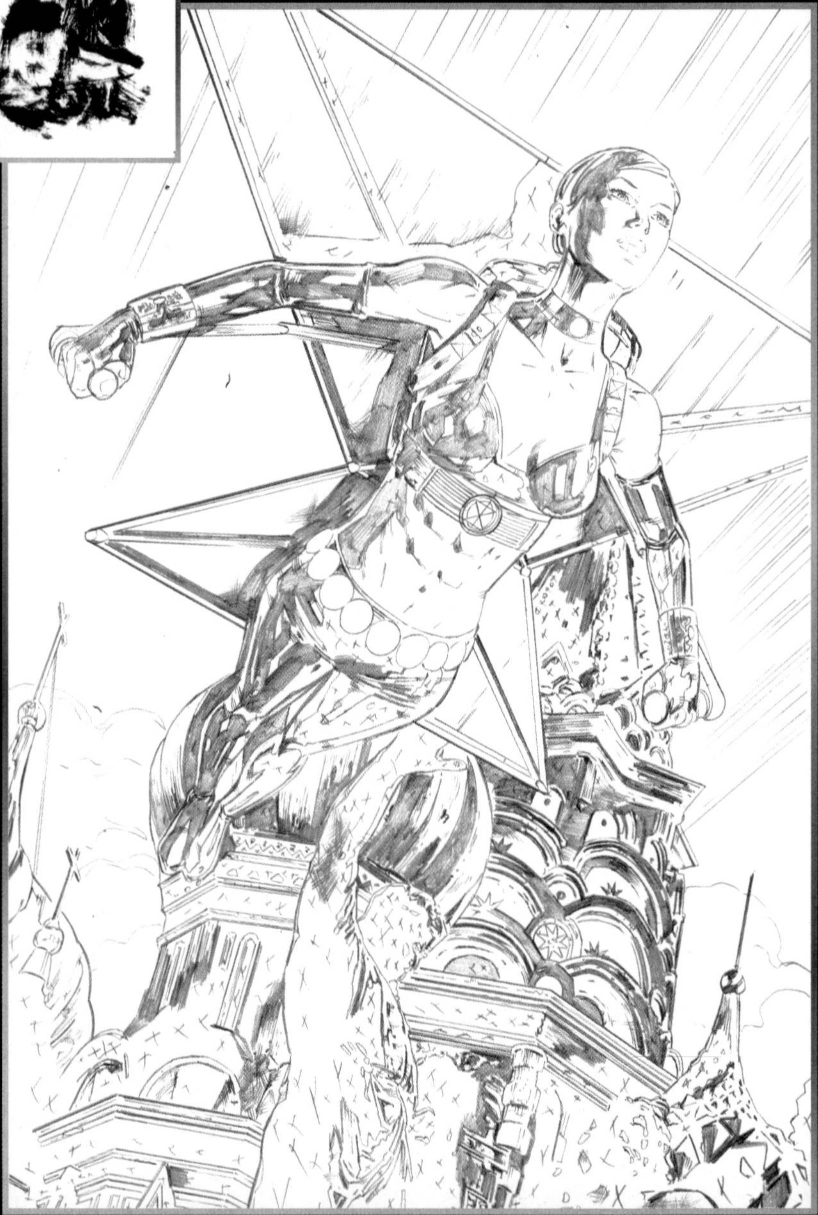

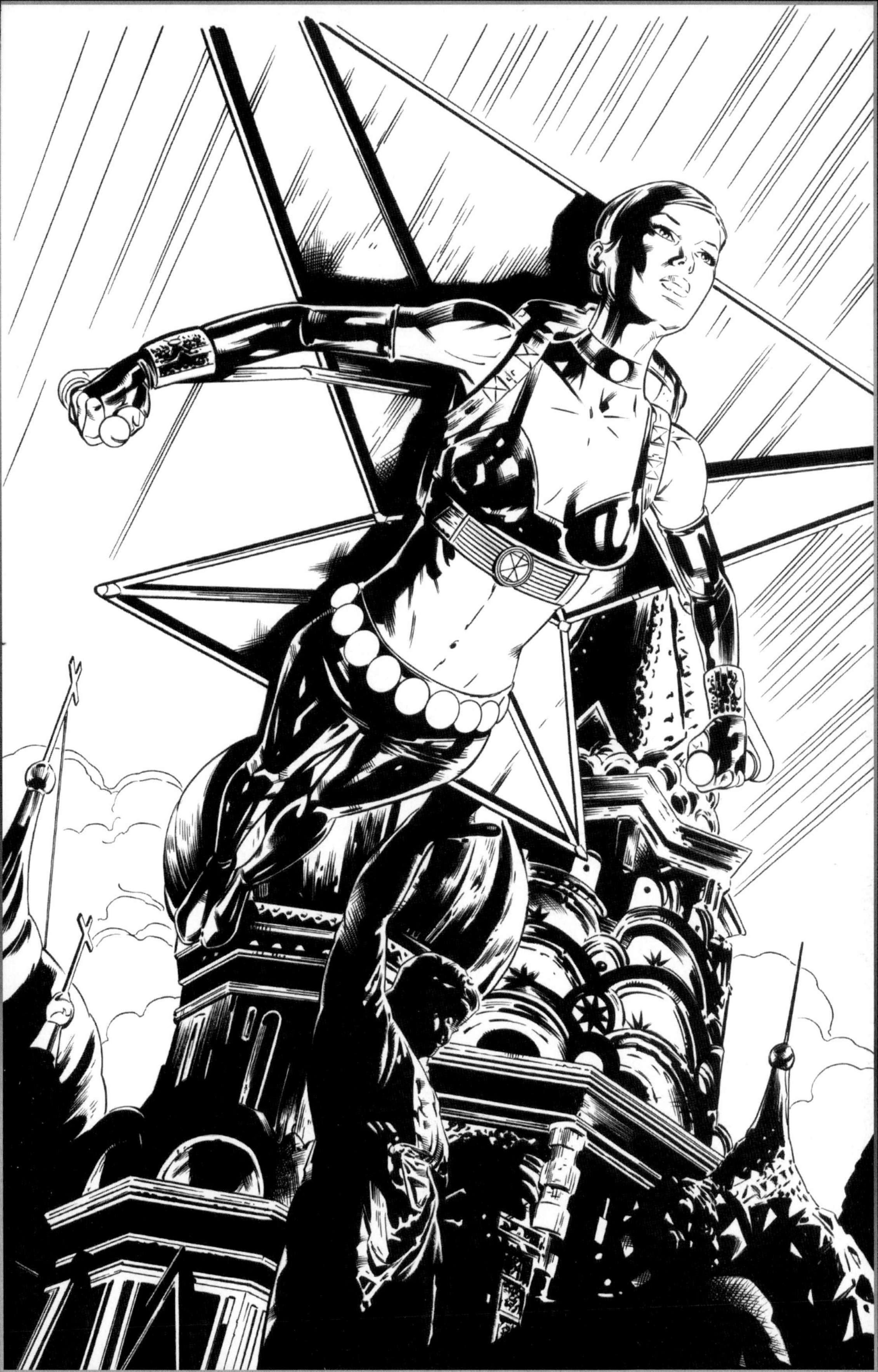

INKS BY **RICK MAGYAR**

CHAPTER 2 PAGES 3-6

PENCILS BY **STEVE KURTH**

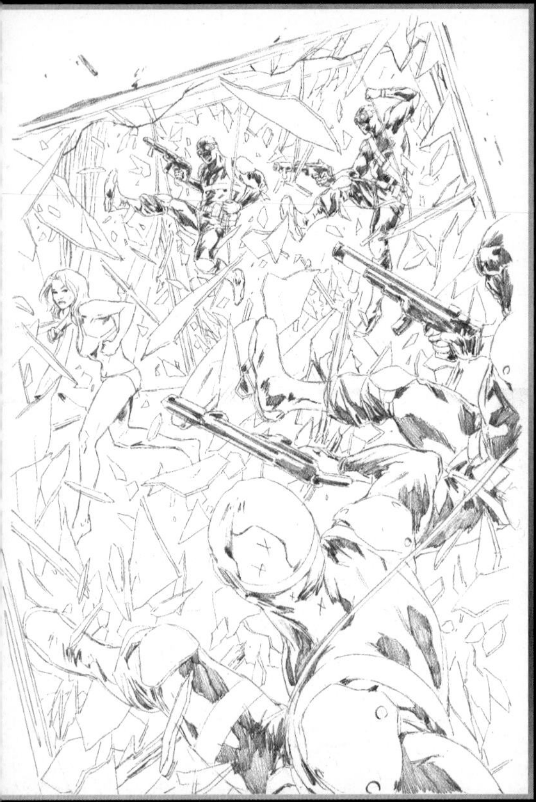

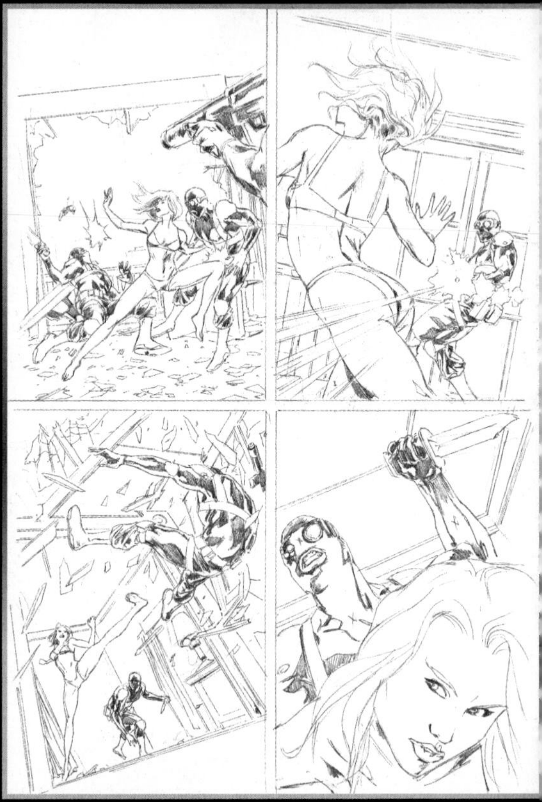

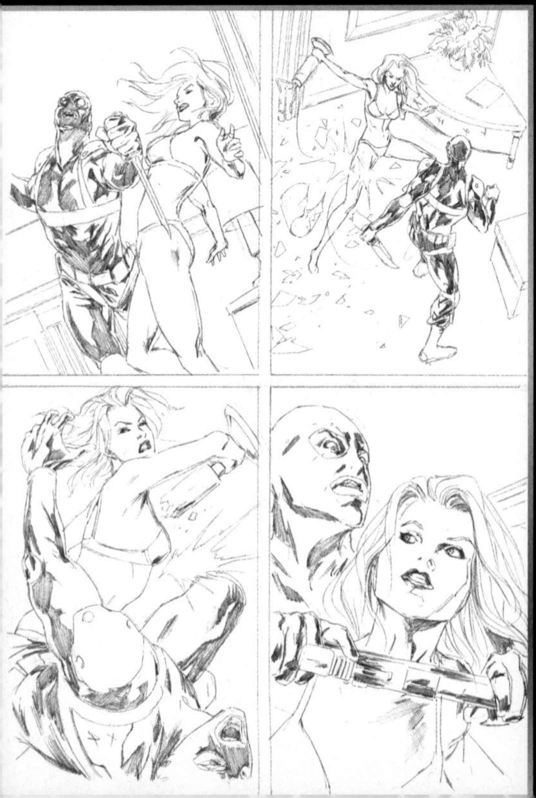

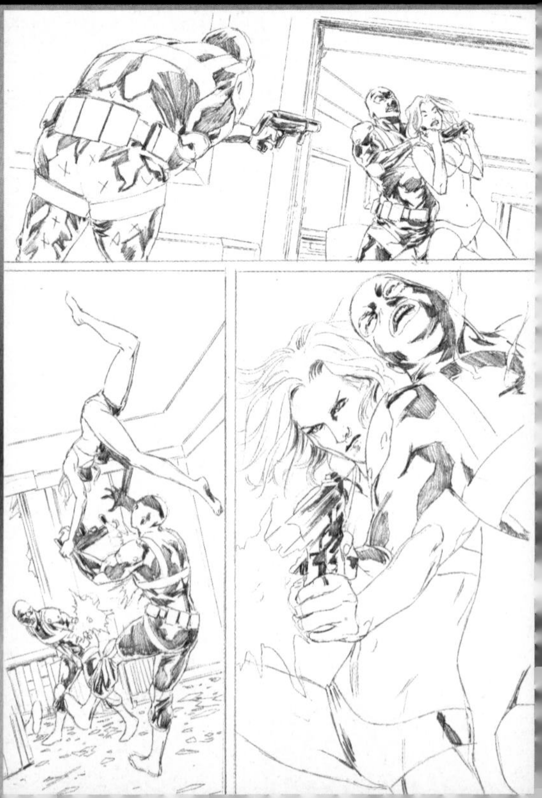

CHAPTER 3 PAGES 1-4

PENCILS BY **RON LIM**

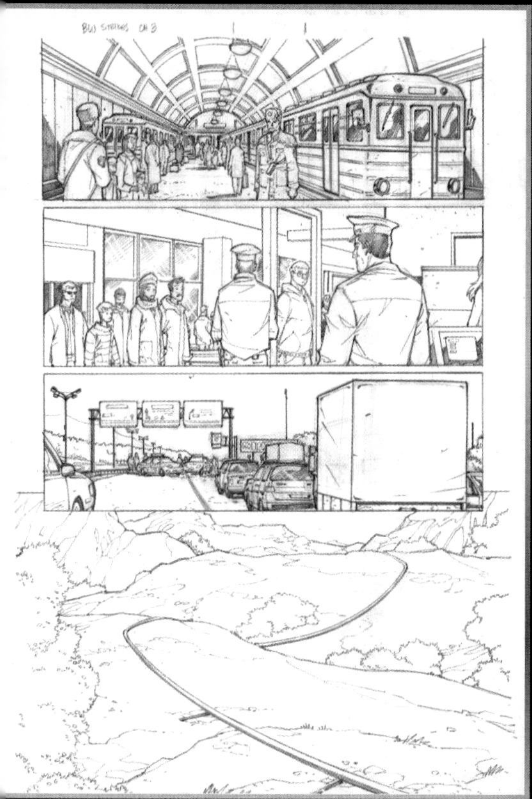
BW STRIKES CH 3 1 1

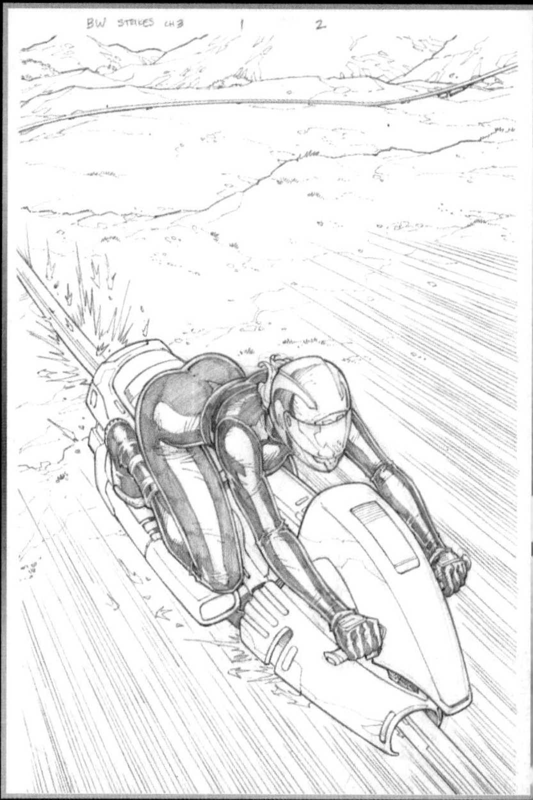
BW STRIKES CH 3 1 2

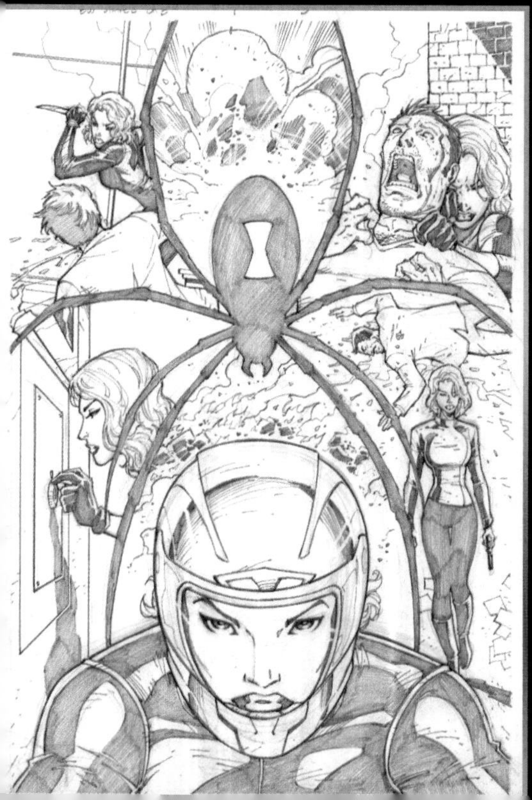

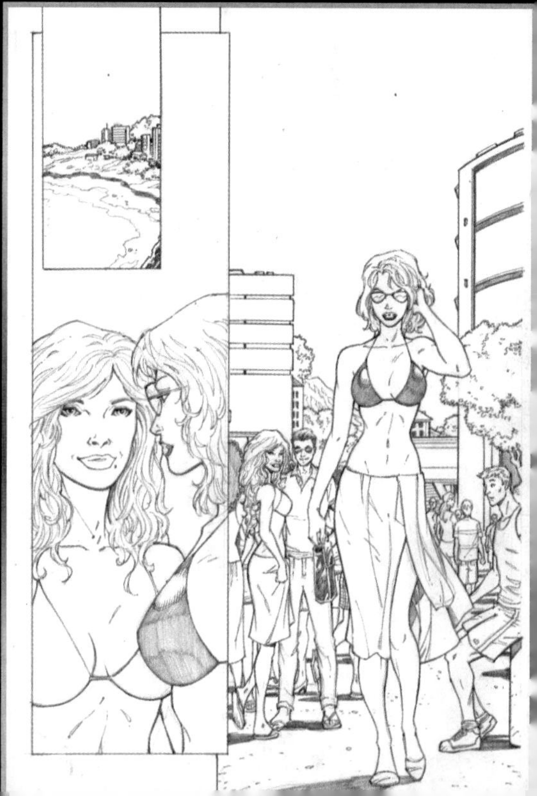

CHAPTER 4 PAGES 7–10

PENCILS BY **AGUSTIN PADILLA**

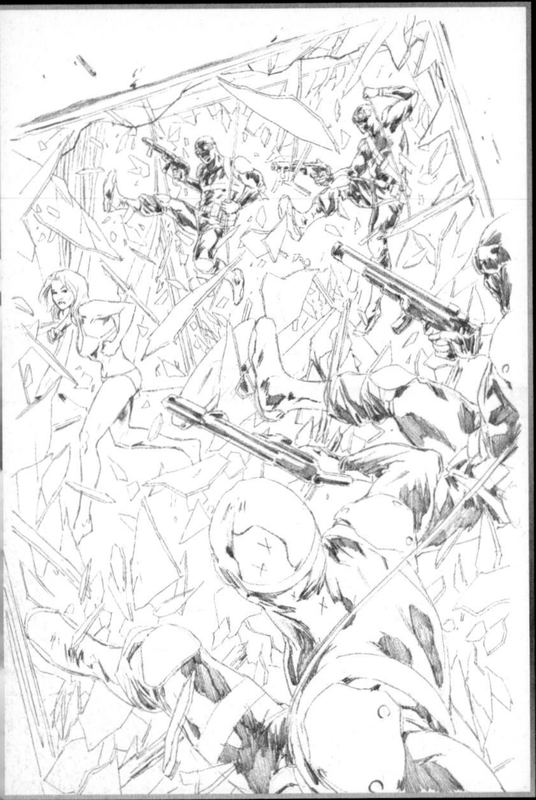

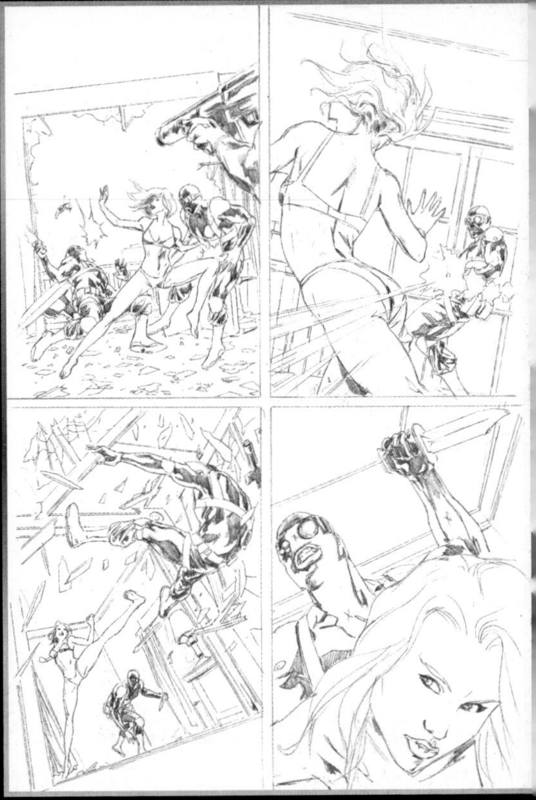

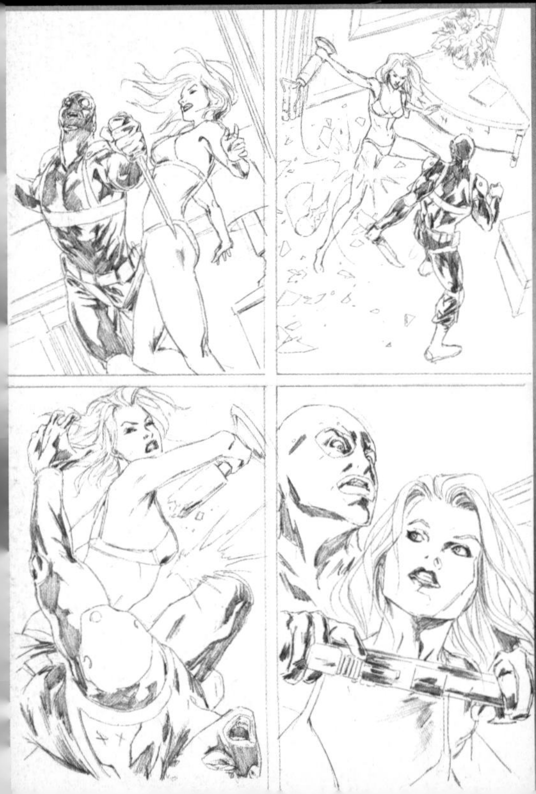

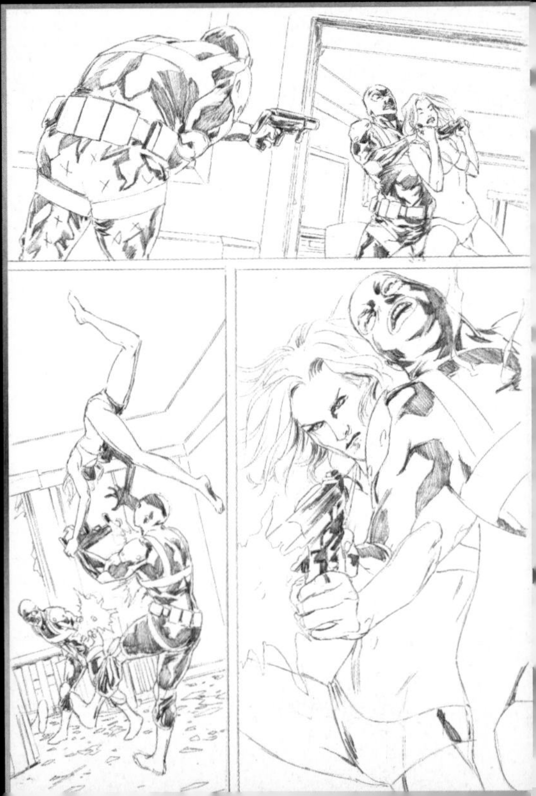

CHAPTER 5 PAGE 2 PROCESS

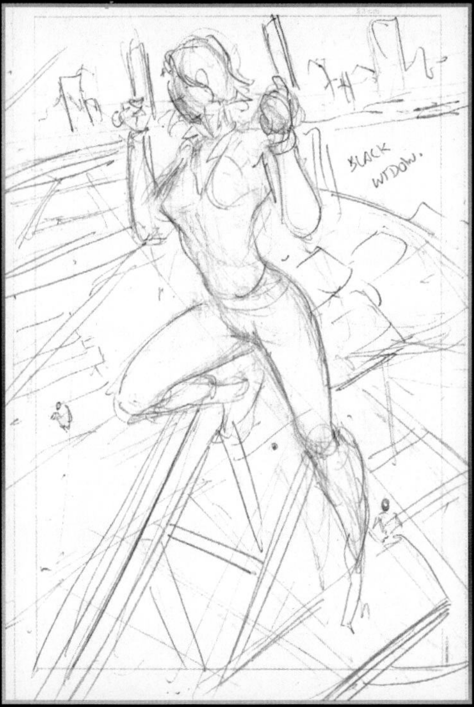
BLACK WIDOW.

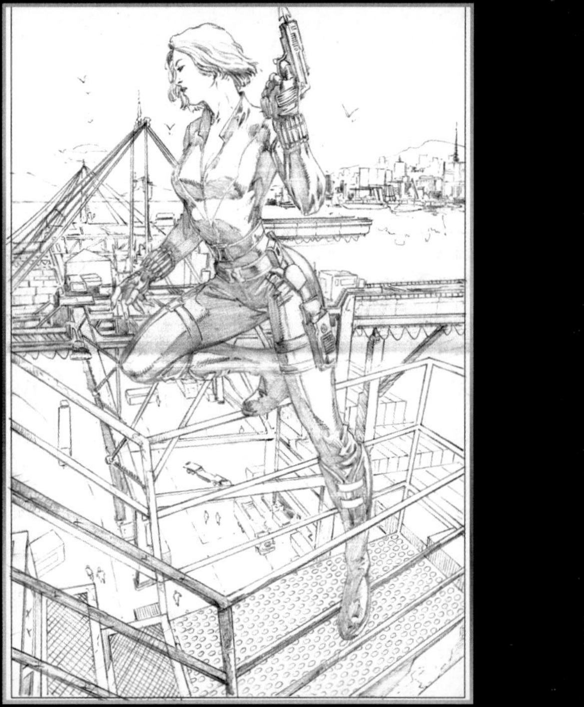

LAYOUTS & PENCILS BY **WELLINTON ALVES**

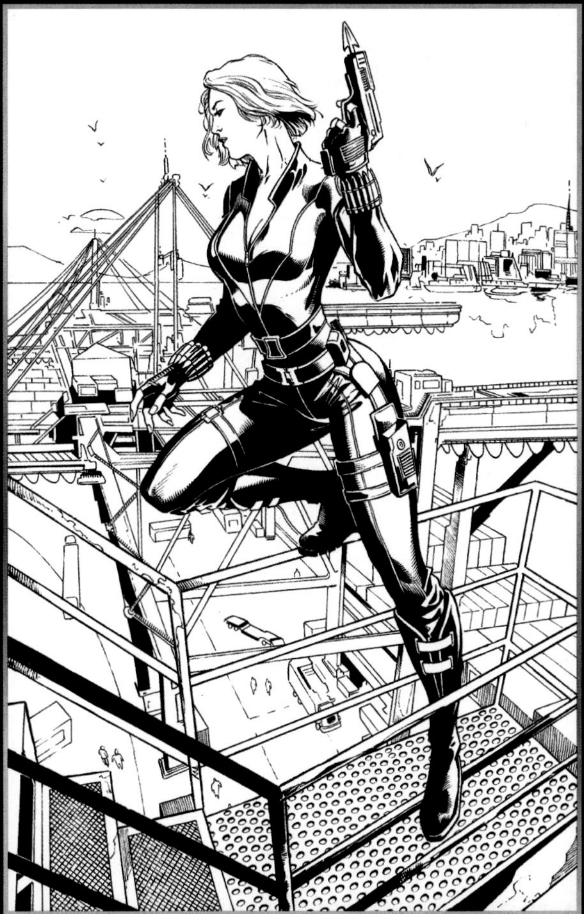

CHAPTER 5 PAGE 10 PROCESS

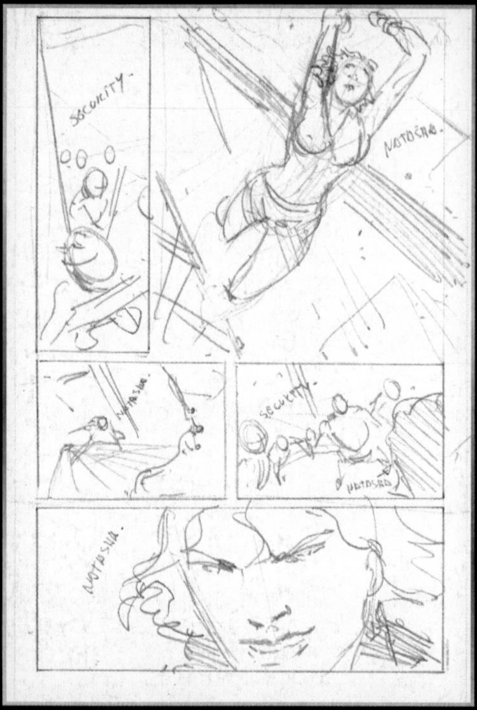

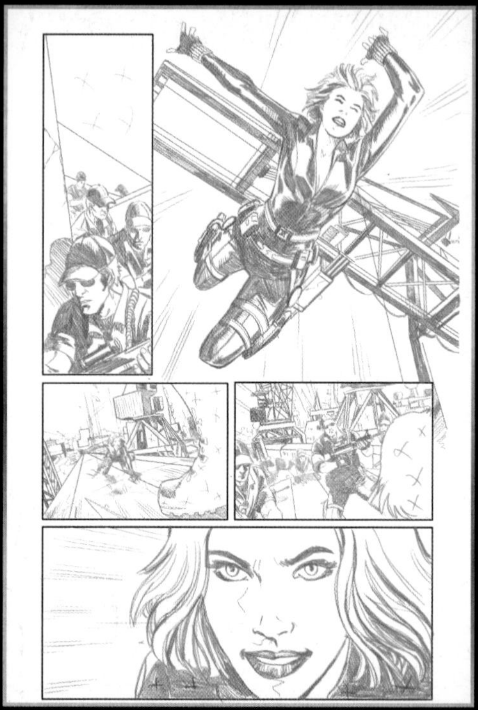

LAYOUTS & PENCILS BY **WELLINTON ALVES**

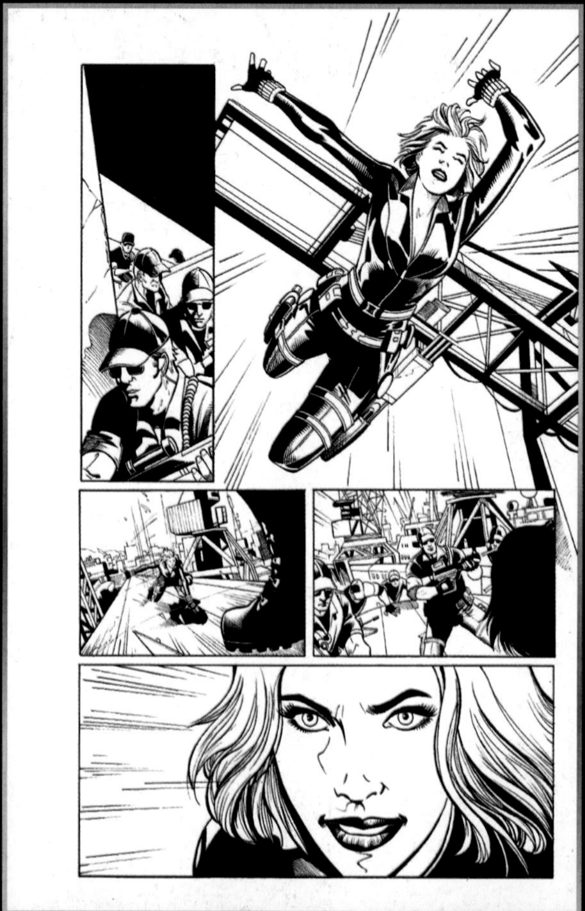

INKS BY **NELSON PEREIRA**

CHAPTER 6 PAGES 3-6

ART BY **RENATO ARLEM**

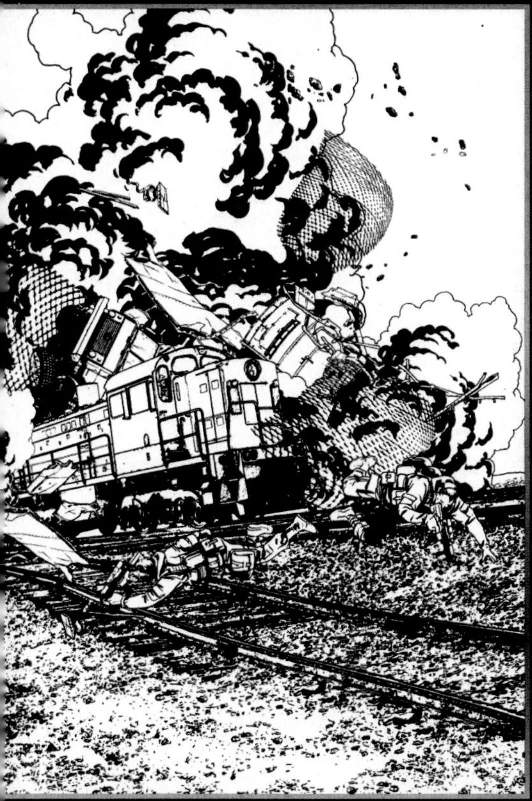

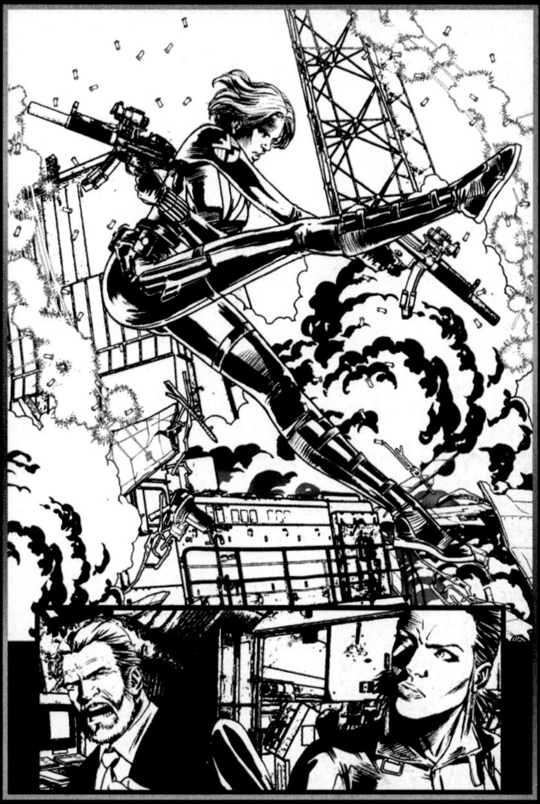

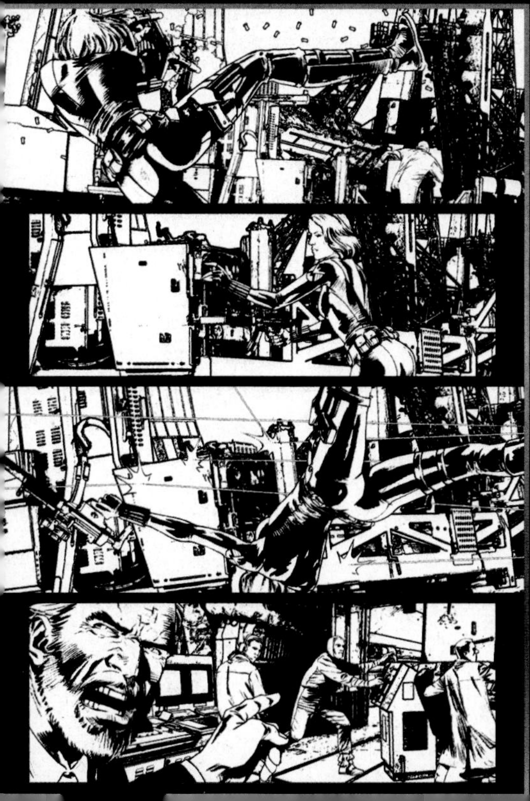

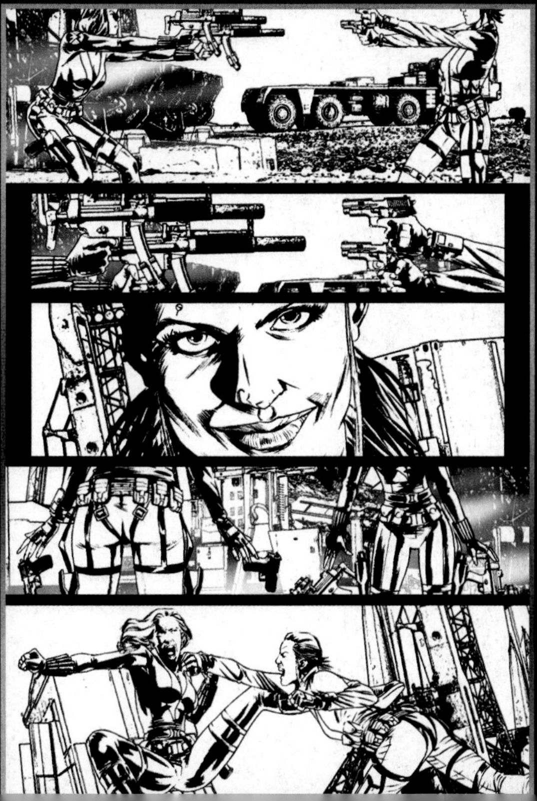